Reinhold Friedl, Thomas Grill, Nikolaus Urbanek, Michelle Ziegler (eds.)
Xenakis – Back to the Roots

Reinhold Friedl studied piano, composition, musicology and mathematics. He received his PhD at Goldsmiths University London and is guest professor at the Katarina Gurska Institute in Madrid. He directs the avantgarde ensemble *zeitkratzer* and released over a hundred CDs and LPs as a composer and performer. He received numerous prizes and fellowships as well as commissions by the French state, Berliner Festspiele, Wiener Festwochen, and BBC London, among others.

Thomas Grill works as a composer and performer of electroacoustic music, as a media artist, technologist and researcher of sound. He earned a doctorate in composition and music theory at Universität für Musik und darstellende Kunst Graz and researched as a Post-Doc at the Austrian Research Institute for Artificial Intelligence (OFAI) in the domain of machine listening and learning. He is currently heading the certificate program in electroacoustic and experimental music and co-heading the Artistic Research Center at Universität für Musik und darstellende Kunst Wien.

Nikolaus Urbanek is professor for musicology and currently serves as Dean of Research Studies at mdw – Universität für Musik und darstellende Kunst Wien. His research focuses on philosophy of music, music historiography, and theory of musical writing.

Michelle Ziegler is Deputy Director of the Seewen Museum of Music Automatons and a lecturer in Basel, Bern and Vienna. Previously, she worked as a postdoc at the chair of history of technology at ETH Zürich and the Paul Sacher Stiftung Basel. Her research areas include music of the 20th and 21st centuries, music and technology, archival practices and digital historiography.

Reinhold Friedl, Thomas Grill, Nikolaus Urbanek,
Michelle Ziegler (eds.)

Xenakis – Back to the Roots

Philological Approaches to Electroacoustic Music

[transcript]

The authors acknowledge the financial support by the Open Access Fund of the mdw – University of Music and Performing Arts Vienna.

Bibliographic information published by the Deutsche Nationalbibliothek
The Deutsche Nationalbibliothek lists this publication in the Deutsche Nationalbibliografie

First published in 2025 by mdwPress, Vienna and Bielefeld
© Reinhold Friedl, Thomas Grill, Nikolaus Urbanek, Michelle Ziegler (eds.)

transcript Verlag | Hermannstraße 26 | D-33602 Bielefeld | live@transcript-verlag.de

Cover layout: bueronardin/mdwPress
Cover illustration: Iannnis Xenakis, Indiana University, 1972. *Collection Famille Xenakis DR.*
Copy-editing: Johannes Fiebich
Proofread: Kimi Lum

https://doi.org/10.14361/9783839474297
Print-ISBN: 978-3-8376-7429-3 | PDF-ISBN: 978-3-8394-7429-7
EPUB-ISBN: 978-3-7328-7429-3

Contents

Introduction
Reinhold Friedl, Thomas Grill, Nikolaus Urbanek and Michelle Ziegler 7

Writing Electroacoustic Music
Xenakis's Œuvre as a Theoretical Challenge
Nikolaus Urbanek 11

Archives, Sources, Persons and Personae in the Art of Electronic Sounds
Laura Zattra 37

Sketching on Paper and Tape
Creative Practices of Early Tape Music
Michelle Ziegler 59

Synchronising Different Temporalities
A Challenge of Writing in *Musique Mixte* from 1958 to 1960
Elena Minetti 79

Common Sonic Entities in the Electroacoustic and Orchestral Music of Iannis Xenakis
James Harley 101

Spatial Treatment of Sound in the *Polytope de Cluny*
Pierre Carré and François Delécluse 107

Orchestrating Noise
Traces of *Mycènes alpha* in *Anémoessa*
Marko Slavíček 129

Sonic Otherness. Traces of Traditional Musics in Xenakis's
Electroacoustic Œuvre
Reinhold Friedl.. 145

The Voice of the UPIC: Technology as Utterance
Peter Nelson... 169

La légende de Xenakis
Curtis Roads... 183

Why Did I Decide to Erase all Production Tapes of my Musique Concrète
Except for the Final Compositions?
A Clarification
Michel Chion 197

Xenakis: Back to the Roots
A Conversation with Nikolaus Urbanek and Michelle Ziegler
*Jan Brocza, Reinhold Friedl, Thomas Grill, Katharina Klement, Christian Tschinkel
and Anatol Wetzer*... 203

About mdwPress.. 225

Introduction

Reinhold Friedl, Thomas Grill, Nikolaus Urbanek and Michelle Ziegler

This volume is the result of a symposium at the University of Music and Performing Arts Vienna (mdw) in May 2022 on the occasion of the 100th anniversary of the birth of Iannis Xenakis. It focuses on the electroacoustic work of the Greek-French composer. Taking advantage of the possibilities at mdw, the symposium approached Xenakis's electroacoustic works from two perspectives – through theoretical reflection on the one hand and through the performance of all of Xenakis's electroacoustic works on the other. The performances at mdw's Klangtheater offered a unique opportunity to directly perceive continuities and discontinuities in his electroacoustic œuvre, giving audiences the chance to expand their experience by listening to both the composer's aesthetic development and the technological changes taking place from the mid-1950s to the mid-1990s.

The electroacoustic work of Iannis Xenakis can be differentiated into individual phases, each of which is related to different aesthetic, technical and historical contexts.[1] An early first phase in the late 1950s and early 1960s is marked by his experiences in Le Corbusier's architectural studio, his contact with Pierre Schaeffer and his work at GRMC (Groupe de recherches de musique concrète). Inspired by *musique concrète*, Xenakis used pre-recorded acoustic material in his electroacoustic works, which could range from crackling and hissing like burning charcoal to noises sounding like jet engines or the processed recordings of bells. This phase comprises the following tape works: *Diamorphoses* (1957), *Concret PH* (1958) for the Philips Pavilion of the Brussels World's Fair, *Analogique B* (1959), *Orient-Occident* (1960) and finally the scandalous *Bohor* (1962) – the two withdrawn film soundtracks *Vasarely* (1960) and

---

1   The years of composition given in this book are based on the Xenakis catalog of works by Durand-Salabert-Eschig (https://www.durand-salabert-eschig.co m/en-GB/Composers/X/Xenakis-Iannis.aspx) and the website of "Les amies de Xenakis" (https://www.iannis-xenakis.org/en/category/works/). In cases of doubt, the information follows the premiere dates and not the composition dates, as in the case of *La Légende d'Eer*, for example.

Formes rouges (1961) should also be mentioned in this context. The second phase is marked by the composition of the first 'polytope', *Polytope de Montréal* (1967) for the French Pavilion at the World's Fair in Montréal, the ballet *Kraanerg* (1969) combining instrumental and tape music and the 12-channel work *Hibiki Hana Ma* (1970) for the World's Fair in Osaka. The transition to what James Harley calls the third phase of large multimedia spectacles is rather smooth: *Persepolis* (1971), *Polytope de Cluny* (1972), *La Légende d'Eer* (1978) – the latter for the inauguration of the Centre Pompidou in Paris. Central to this phase of his electroacoustic composing is the inclusion of space against the background of the specific local and architectural conditions as well as the coordination of the specific multimediality of light, movement and music – which required not least the technically demanding synchronisation of sound spatialisation, lights, lasers and music. The fourth phase is marked by the development of the computer-based sound synthesis system UPIC (Unité Polyagogique Informatique de Centre d'Études de Mathématique et Automatique Musicales/CEMAMu), which allows the user to directly transform graphic structures – realised with the help of an electromagnetic pen on a large electromagnetic drawing board – into musical ones. The sonic results of this phase are *Mycènes alpha* (1978), the radiophonic work with texts by Françoise Xenakis *Pour la paix* (1981), *Taurhiphanie* (1987), *Voyage absolu des Unari vers Andromède* (1989) and the withdrawn work *Erod* (1997). The fifth and final phase in the early 1990s comprises only two computer-generated works: GENDY 301/GENDY 3 (1991) and S.709 (1994). Harley calls it the 'phase of stochastic synthesis'.

This richness of different approaches as well as Xenakis's ambition to configure his electroacoustic material on his own using sophisticated processes (multiplicative tape techniques, stochastic synthesis, granulation, to name just a few) gave rise to an extensive body of sources. This allows glimpses into his compositional process but also vividly demonstrates the experimental and at times almost contradictory ways in which he proceeded. Against this backdrop, a philological study of this heterogenous material is not only essential but also promises to be fruitful for future research of other electroacoustic musical works and source studies. The questions to be addressed are quite fundamental and include the following: In what sense can electroacoustic recordings be regarded as text? What do words like "original" and "authenticity" mean, and what are the consequences for electroacoustic music's performance and interpretation? Furthermore, due to the specific material situation of the sources of electroacoustic music, basic philological research is urgently needed: tapes are increasingly falling victim to physical decay, unsystematic digitisation is obscuring musical evidence, and some machines used for the reproduction of electroacoustic music have long since been discarded and disappeared. What's more, and not insignificantly, there exists an urgent need to preserve knowl-edge of how to use these machines and read the various carrying media. Against this background, a philological approach that interprets historical documents not only as textual sources but also as cultural sources could provide valuable insights.

That is why the contributions in this volume are particularly dedicated to a philological approach under the title 'Back to the Roots'. The perspective taken by the collected contributions is twofold: On the one hand, the volume is primar-ily dedicated to specific philological case studies of Xenakis's electroacoustic work and thereby contributes to Xenakis research, which has received rather little attention to date (section "Philological Practice"). On the other hand, the special characteristics of Xenakis's compositions allow essential insights into basic philological research in the field of electroacoustic music (section "Philo-logical Context").

Philological Context: Based on musical-philological considerations, Niko-laus **Urbanek** discusses the question of how Xenakis's electroacoustic œuvre represents a particular challenge for the development of a theory of musical writing, with a view to current approaches in transdisciplinary writing research. Laura **Zattra** reflects on the personal archives of different composers of elec-troacoustic music as a whole body of sources and a mirror of the collector's personality, incorporating mixed methods of philology, archaeology, oral his-tory and ethnography. In the case of early tape music, Michelle **Ziegler** argues that a comprehensive evaluation of compositional practices needs to consider sketches on paper in connection with sketches on tape, as they both reveal inte-gral parts of the creative process. Elena **Minetti** explores the writing strategies of different composers to achieve a specific function in *musique mixte*: the syn-chronisation of musical events between recorded sounds and live instruments or voices.

Philological Practice – Xenakis's Challenge: As a vantage point for the subse-quent philological studies of Iannis Xenakis's works, James **Harley** anchors the electroacoustic music of the composer in his orchestral œuvre by demonstrat-ing common sonic entities in both. Two case studies then evaluate expansive archival sources: Pierre **Carré**/François **Delécluse** demonstrate that the recent discovery of a digital command tape for the *Polytope de Cluny* not only allowed different re-enactments of the multimedia show in 2022, but in combination with an examination of other archival documentation gives an insight into Xe-nakis's thinking on sound and space. Based on a close study of the sources for the electronic piece *Mycènes alpha* and the instrumental piece *Anémoessa* (1979) for choir and orchestra, Marko **Slavíček** argues that for Xenakis self-borrowing was a means of exploring instances of sonic material in diverse contexts, relying on drawing as a compositional tool. Reinhold **Friedl** digs for hidden sources and shows that Xenakis was not only inspired by traditional musics but also borrowed their sounds extensively in his electroacoustic work. Peter **Nelson** breaks with the notion of the legendary intransigence of Xenakis's computer instrument UPIC by reimagining it as the re-intonation of ancient voices, thereby envisioning "technology as utterance".

Back to the Roots: The third and final section of the book reveals the liveliness of an encounter with Xenakis's person and music with the accounts of two of Xenakis's companions and with a round table on the performance practice of his electroacoustic works. Curtis **Roads** describes how his encounters with Xenakis provided a clear direction for starting his own composition algorithms and in general fostered an understanding of composing as a contribution to humanity. Michel **Chion** explains the decision to dispose of the production tapes for his *musique concrète* from a composer's perspective in order to avoid the undocumented publication of single elements and to prevent the work from being misunderstood as a "succession of pretty sounds" that might be abused as such in other music. In the concluding roundtable, Jan **Brozca**, Reinhold **Friedl**, Thomas **Grill**, Katharina **Klement**, Christian **Tschinkel** and Anatol **Wetzer** give insight into their decisions in the preparation of the performances in 2022 and thereby reveal the variety and vitality of approaches that consider the roots of the past and result in a lively actualisation of Xenakis's electroacoustic work.

The editors are deeply indebted to Max Bergmann and the mdwPress Board of Trustees for including this volume in the mdwPress publishing programme. We would also like to thank the anonymous reviewers whose peer reviews provided important information. Many thanks also go to Kimi Lum for her fantastic foreign language editing and to Johannes Fiebich for his help in finalising the manuscript. Last but not least, many thanks to the authors for their wonderful co-operation.

Basel – Berlin – Vienna, summer 2024
Reinhold Friedl, Thomas Grill, Nikolaus Urbanek and Michelle Ziegler

Writing Electroacoustic Music
Xenakis's Œuvre as a Theoretical Challenge

Nikolaus Urbanek

Even though the catalogue of electroacoustic works represents only a small part of Xenakis's extensive œuvre, it is nonetheless a very central group of works, to which eminent music-historical significance must be attributed in various respects.[1] As he was not bound by instrumental limitations and traditional performance conventions, Xenakis had the opportunity to develop creative ideas and musical concepts with great radicalism. Not least against this background, the discussion of Xenakis's electroacoustic works remains an extremely productive challenge in several respects. On the one hand, the electroacoustic works of Xenakis reflect in their chronological progression central situations of a history of electroacoustic music that essentially also refers to developments in the field of (studio) technology. On the other hand, the musical, medial and material heterogeneity – ranging from tape compositions with the inclusion of pre-existing acoustic and musical material, to works of '*musique mixte*' (a combination of tape music with instrumental music), to the great multimedia ' spectacles' that allow space, light and music to interact, to graphically conceived computer music – leads to considerable differences in the given compositional practices – to which the surviving sources, at least, bear eloquent witness.

---

1   As James Harley elaborates: "Those works, however, are influential beyond their number. Any history of electronic music must place Xenakis as a central figure, both for his innovations and for the impact his music has had on successive generations. His involvement in the creation of multimedia 'spectacles' brought him wide exposure, although his uncompromising aesthetic vision precluded fame and fortune on a popular scale" (Harley 2002: 33).

Back to the Roots?
Towards a Philology of Electroacoustic Music

But what do we actually hear when listening to the electroacoustic music of Iannis Xenakis? This challenging question marks the starting point of Reinhold Friedl's dissertation *Towards a Philology of Electroacoustic Music – Xenakis's Tape Music as Paradigm* (cf. Friedl 2019). It is not meant to be a rhetorical question but deals, rather, with a remarkably delicate issue in a very concrete sense: As Friedl has extensively shown, commercially available versions of some works and even official performance versions contain major faults. These faults include the use of incorrect sample rates in the transfer of individual versions, fundamental errors in digitisation (for example, the performance version of *La Légende d'Eer* was digitised backwards) or the absence of individual tracks or entire passages, etc. (cf. Friedl 2012, 2015, 2019). Friedl develops his diagnosis starting from the obvious irritation of basic observations (e.g., different lengths of different versions) and continues this in the analysis and comparison of diverse sources such as master tapes, official rental material for performance as well as commercially available versions on CD. Finally, the reflections gained from the acoustic sources are discussed on the basis of further workshop materials (sketches, notes on technical conditions, scores, but also letters and ego documents among others), so that Friedl plausibly explains the process of creation of selected works on the basis of the workshop materials and in locating the individual (textual) sources stemmatologically within this. On the basis of his comprehensive research, Friedl succeeds in making clear how profitable it can be to go back to the sources when researching electroacoustic music; this is indispensable in order to be able to secure the foundations, to develop an understanding that there may be not only one *original* but *multiple manifestations* of a single work, to identify and eliminate existing errors – ultimately with a view to publishing a critical edition of the works.[2]

But when do we know that something is an error at all? Symptomatic in this context is Gérard Pape's response to Friedl's error diagnoses with regard to the transferring of *La Légende d'Eer*:

> Why does Friedl call it a 'fault' that the test tones were left in? (Here I mean in the new master tape that Salabert has published, not in the Mode recording, which does not include these tones.) If they were included on the master tape, Xenakis must have put them there for a reason. In any case, it was

---

2   See (and/or listen) for an attempt at a critical edition of the electroacoustic works of Iannis Xenakis: http://www.karlrecords.net/iannis-xenakis-100th-anniversary-box-sets (accessed September 10, 2023).

quite typical to include such tones for performance reasons at the time (1970s). Anyone that knows Xenakis' music, even a little, wouldn't make the mistake to think the test tones are part of his music. (Pape 2015: 123)

Regardless of how the question regarding the error is ultimately to be decided, the strategy of Pape's argumentation is of considerable interest at this point: It makes clear that the diagnosis of what can be regarded as an error at all can only be made plausible on the basis of intensive philological research, which also refers to theoretical, historical, aesthetic and compositional contexts. Pape's argumentation is by no means based exclusively on source findings, but also on the intentions (of the composer or the publisher) and the customary practices of the respective environment at the time of the composition. This shows that the first thing to be clarified is whether a certain moment that is assumed to be defective is to be evaluated in the context of "common language usage", as a remarkable "compositional audacity" or simply as a "textual error" in need of correction (Urbanek 2013: 160f.). The answer to the question of musical error therefore does not result solely from the comparison and analysis of preserved sources[3] – the recourse to the preserved sources is a necessary condition, but by no means already a sufficient one. At this point, musical philology comes into play as the scientific discipline that deals with the issue of the error in a methodologically assured manner and develops criteria for higher textual criticism, which ultimately presupposes an interpretation of the sources on the basis of the inclusion of the respective context (cf. Feder 1987; Urbanek 2013; Appel and Emans 2017).

However, it must be noted that a philology of electroacoustic music has not yet been developed to the extent that can be claimed for the general philology of music. Since fundamental questions present themselves differently with regard to electroacoustic music, this also applies to terminological issues and the relation to established musical philology. The endeavour of developing a philology of electroacoustic music can and must take its starting point in the specificity

---

3   "The question of what constitutes an error is ultimately left to interpretation: Is a technical error to be considered a musical error? Is a release with the wrong sample rate wrong and should accordingly be withdrawn? Or is it simply a matter of transposition, which no one cares about in Schubert songs?" "Die Frage aber, was ein Fehler ist, bleibt schließlich der Interpretation überlassen: Ist ein technischer Fehler als musikalischer Fehler zu werten? Ist eine Veröffentlichung mit falscher Samplerate falsch und sollte demnach zurückgezogen werden? Oder handelt es dabei schlicht um eine Transposition, wie sie bei Schubertliedern niemanden kümmert?" (Friedl 2012: 39) Unless otherwise stated, all translations by the author.

of the sources (but should go beyond that): An essential point in which a specific philology of electroacoustic music will complement the general debates of musical philology concerns the status, function and relevance of the significant sources within the creative processes. Against this backdrop Zattra elaborates

> that sources, or 'texts' as philologists call them, have a fundamental role for the study of computer music. This type of research already shows an important background of studies, that is the textual criticism, or the philology of music. Musicological investigation of electroacoustic music should start from that and rethink philological methodologies in the light of what an electroacoustic music source could be. (Zattra 2006: 1)

In his discussion of the source situation of La Légende d'Eer, Friedl refers to the specific heterogeneity of sources that must necessarily be included in the analysis of the creative process: "Texts, graphic drafts, scores, realisation sketches from the studio, et cetera, must be taken into account just as much as material tapes, multitrack versions, stereo reductions for CD release, et cetera"[4] (Friedl 2012: 33). This is what Zattra systematises in her discussion of the concept of musical sources in the field of creative processes of electroacoustic music:

> Nevertheless the text within electroacoustic music is not necessarily a visible or symbolic trace. In the computer music[5] field a *witness* can indifferently be: 1) the audio source, that is the tape where the computation is analogically converted, or the CD, the mini disc, the memory of the computer; 2) the data storage device containing the digital data and algorithms for any process of synthesis, transformation, spatialization, automatic composition; 3) printed digital scores; 4) traditional scores in the case of mixed music; 5) different sketches by the author; 6) articles dedicated to the piece; 7) mental texts. (Zattra 2006: 2)

Considering the special status of musical sources in the field of electroacoustic music this systematisation is an important starting point. However, the effort to establish a philology of electroacoustic music cannot stop here. In her contribution to this volume, Michelle Ziegler points out a fundamental difference between sources on paper and sources on tape, which is also eminently significant for the development of a philology of electroacoustic music and has to be

---

4   "Texte, graphische Entwürfe, Partituren, Realisationsskizzen aus dem Studio et cetera müssen genauso berücksichtigt werden wie Materialtonbänder, Mehrspurversionen, Stereo-Reduktionen zur CD-Veröffentlichung, et cetera." (Friedl 2012: 33)

5   Under the term 'computer music', Zattra understands a historical phase of development from the late 1950s to the 1990s, subsequently replaced by the phase of "digital music" (cf. Zattra 2006: 2).

taken into account: Unlike notations on paper, both production and reception of sonic recordings always require a "technical mediator". Against this background, Ziegler argues that due to the "challenges of mixed media sources in sketch studies" the philology of electroacoustic music "requires mixed methods and an expansion of traditional sketch studies" (cf. the contribution by Michelle Ziegler in this volume).

With regard to the specific situation of electroacoustic music, the mediality and materiality of the technical equipment of the studios is therefore of particular importance. The necessary inclusion of technical development, i.e., the special consideration of media history, leads to further points worth considering, as Friedl points out:

> It is necessary to try to set up a genesis of the production process in respect of the media history, including the distinction between technical and musical signals, considering also text sources and oral history, and last but not least the visualization of the sound files. Also the role of the edition houses is much more important than for example in literature, because of the different legal situation, the access to the archives and the economic difference, a smaller market and a more expensive production. The media history has to be considered especially as regards the media compatibilities, technical conventions such as colours indicating the velocity a tape has to be played at, etc. (Friedl 2015: 122)

The analysis and critique of the preserved sources, which must necessarily be extended to develop a philology of electroacoustic music, raise fundamental questions that touch on far-reaching theoretical and methodological issues:

- *Writing Practices*: What is the specific role of the different practices of sketching, drawing, recording, electronic editing, manipulation, and programming in the creative processes of electroacoustic composing? In what sense can we speak of practices of 'writing' here in an emphatic sense?
- *Writing Systems*: What changes with the use of recording or writing systems that allow the direct fixation and manipulation of sound on tapes or other media? What are the theoretical consequences of machines ('technical mediators') being significantly involved in production and reproduction processes?
- *Writing Spaces*: To what extent does the space of composing – for example the electronic studio – play an essential role in the creative process?
- *Performances*: In what sense can we speak of a 'score', 'script' or 'text' in regard to electroacoustic works? To phrase this question slightly differently: Is there a text that is read in order to be sonically realised in a performance? What are the consequences for the performance of electroacoustic music?

Scenes of Musical Writing

The fact that 'writing' electroacoustic music posed a new challenge for composers in the middle of the last century is due not least to the fundamental developments in the technical and media fields, which provide new possibilities and evoke new practices of composing. Elena Minetti describes this in her dissertation *Schrift als Werkzeug. Schriftbildliche Operativität in Kompositionsprozessen früher* musique mixte (1949–1959) as a change in 'scenes of musical writing' (cf. Minetti 2023; for a theorisation of the term 'writing scene' cf. Campe 1991 and, regarding the field of music, more recently also Celestini and Lutz 2023). As already noted above, the changes in the writing scene of electroacoustic music touch on fundamental issues. First of all, it should be noted that the writing scene of composing electroacoustic music takes place in other spaces: The usual composer's workshop (be it the usual study room or a 'Komponierhäuschen' as Gustav Mahler had during his summer vacations) is joined by the electronic studio as an important place for creative work. Usually, this studio is not situated in the realm of the private but in public spaces such as radio stations or universities. In addition, the practices of composing are also changing significantly. Not only does the use of other tools (tapes, microphones, computers) lead to collaborative forms of composing in the electronic studio, in which sound engineers, for example, can play an eminent role, but it also leads to changes in the actions and practices relevant for composing. Thus, the question arises whether one can or should speak of writing in the sense of 'inscribing' (in a way that sufficiently stable material traces are made by writing instruments on a writing media) with regard to the work with sound recordings. Furthermore, a fundamental change can be observed in relation to the material 'products' of the compositional creative process: The 'musical text' of electroacoustic music does not exist primarily in the form of scores *written* on paper but in recordings of the sound itself. This has implication for the status of the text, since the question of original and copy arises in a different way when one thinks about versions and multiple sonic formats (4-channel, 8-channel, stereo, etc.), as they were often produced for specific spaces and performances settings. All in all, fundamental questions concerning the relationship between text, recording and performance are at stake.

In numerous conversations and interviews Xenakis addresses fundamental questions of notating, writing and fixing music. Thus, he answers Bálint Andras Varga's question as to how he arrives at melodic figures with a view to the inadequacies of traditional notation:

The drawing and thinking of the sound-image go hand in hand, the two can't be separated. It would be silly to leave out of account, when drawing, what will sound in reality. We have also to be able to find on paper the visual equivalent of the musical idea. Any changes and modifications can then be carried out on the drawing itself. This feedback has to operate all the time. What advantage do arborescence have over traditional notation? If I use traditional notation I lose the continuity. Let us say that I have a bush of three lines that stem from the same root. If I map it in the Cartesian system of coordinates I have before my eyes the picture of what it sounds like. If I were to write the same on staves I would have to break it down into many staves and continuity would be lost. The whole thing would be much more complicated. [...] While I am composing the rotation has to be quick and easy. After that we can decide on the most practical solution using traditional notation. To help planning I developed with my friends a graphic electromagnetic system at CEMAMu with which we can draw any shape and obtain the corresponding music with the help of a computer. (Varga 1996: 90)

It becomes clear that writing as the visual elaboration of musical thoughts is of considerable relevance for Xenakis, also with regard to the electroacoustic works concerning pictorial or diagrammatic aspects or the specific mediality and materiality between sound recordings and notations. Against this backdrop, it should be called to mind that the 1950s and early 1960s – the phase in which Xenakis enters the stage of music history and also composes his first electroacoustic works – were marked by fundamental debates about musical notation. They were based on the diverse developments in compositional technique and aesthetics that were of central importance in this phase of composing. This holds not only for electronic and electroacoustic music but also for the further development of serial techniques, the inclusion of chance operations, the field of instrumental theatre and (free) improvisation (cf. Borio and Danuser 1997). In addition, there were experiments with notating music in the field of so-called graphic scores (in-depth discussion of recent research into writing, for example concerning Anestis Logothetis and Roman Haubenstock-Ramati: Finke 2019, 2023 and, referring to Sylvano Bussotti: Freund 2022). The (new) notation possibilities were problematised to initiate further debates and documented as a future reference: The annual congress at the Darmstadt Summer Courses in 1964, for example, was dedicated to fundamental questions of musical notation; Earle Brown, György Ligeti, Mauricio Kagel, and Roman Haubenstock-Ramati, important protagonists of the international composer scene, gave lectures (cf. Thomas 1965; Weigel 2023: 12ff.). Haubenstock-Ramati organised an exhibition in Donaueschingen in 1959 with numerous examples of new forms of notation (cf. Zimmermann 2023), and Erhard Karkoschka and John Cage published 'inventories' of new forms of musical notation (Karkoschka 1966; Cage

1969). Against this background, it is not surprising that this neuralgic point in the history of musical notation has received particular attention from music-related writing research in recent years (to name a few further research contributions: Czolbe 2014; Czolbe and Magnus 2015; Grüny 2020; Magnus 2016; Schmidt 2020; Zimmermann 2009).

Towards a Theory of Writing Music[6]

The fundamental questions raised with regard to practices, places, and sources of writing electroacoustic music presuppose, that we take a closer look at the issue of writing music in general. Surprisingly, in the relevant musicological encyclopaedias and lexicons there is no dedicated lemma on the topic of 'writing music' (cf. Minetti 2023: 11). This lack of a separate, consistent theorisation in the field of musical writing is quite significant – perhaps one is so sure of the self-evident, that no further explanation is needed. We finally find what we are looking for under the term 'notation' – as defined in the *New Grove Dictionary of Music and Musicians*: Notation is

> a visual analogue of musical sound, either as a record of sound heard or imagined [...] Broadly speaking, there are two motivations behind the use of notation: the need for a memory aid and the need to communicate. (Bent 2001)

Even if 'notation' and 'writing' are by no means congruent terms, the reference to their functions as memory aid and communication tool addresses two essential elements that can help us in our thinking about musical writing: Music is a temporary, fleeting, ephemeral phenomenon – as soon as it is heard, it is already gone. The written fixation, on the other hand, enables the archiving, distribution and representation of the ephemeral sound phenomenon; music thus gains an independent presence in its written 'fixation' and 'reification'. With the

---

6   The following preliminary considerations on a theory of musical writing are based on two lectures I gave in Cologne and Frankfurt am Main in autumn 2019. They find their theoretical framing in the introduction to this field of research co-authored by Simon Obert, Federico Celestini and Matteo Nanni (cf. Celestini et al. 2020: 1–50) and take figures of thought from the work of the international research project *Writing Music. Iconic, performative, operative, and material aspects in musical notation(s)*, which – funded by the Austrian Science Fund (FWF), the German Research Foundation (DFG) and the Swiss National Science Foundation (SNF) – was carried out at four locations (Giessen, Basel, Innsbruck and Vienna) from 2018 to 2021.

written capturing of music, cultural techniques have developed in quite different forms, enabling a switch of media from the auditory to the visual realm, thus the transformation from a transient to a permanent phenomenon. In this way, music can be saved in memory and reproduced and played back independently of its immediate context of origin. The written capturing overcomes the ephemeral nature of sound, so to speak; it is written in order to fix, to remember, to archive, to communicate, to transmit.

But is that all that must be taken into account when we discuss writing music? Let's take a step back and try to look at the obvious: First of all, we should remember that we usually *perceive* written sources *visually*. As we can *see* and *read* music in its written state, we speak of *visual objects*. With regard to the ontological status of the 'text' of electroacoustic music, which exists for example in the form of tapes, the question of visibility would have to be extended in the direction of (machine) readability. I will return to this central problem in the course of my reflections. Secondly, it is immediately obvious that what is written is always materialised in some way, whether it is written down in pencil on sketch paper, carved in stone with a chisel or fixed within the framework of other writing systems – we therefore always and necessarily speak of *material objects* when we refer to writing. Beyond that, a fundamental fascination of writing music lies in the fact that not only what is already mentally present is *written down*, but that through writing, a space of reality that was not there before is *created*. Loosely formulated, we could perhaps call this process 'composing'.

Even if we take this into account, we would have to emphatically question once again whether the lexical definition quoted above is sufficient. Is not musical writing, understood as the 'visual analogue of musical sound', essentially *underdetermined*? Do other moments play a role that cannot be considered 'visual analogues of sound'? A change of perspective in order to expand the observation space and consider hitherto neglected aspects of musical writing is necessary.

A Change of Perspective – Towards a Broader Understanding of Writing

Writing and writtenness have always been the subject of many reflections, especially in the humanities, arts and cultural studies; as a transdisciplinary object of research, this topic is not particularly new or original. In a certain sense, this debate is also a footnote for Plato, since the discussion of writing inherits from him a formative figure of thought: the idea of the subordination of writing to the spoken word (see Plato 1922: St. 274ff.). This very idea has been authoritative in various forms over a long period of time; for example, in Ferdinand de Saussure's fundamental reflections on linguistics in general, one can read: "Spoken and written language are two different systems of signs; the latter exists only for the purpose of representing the former"[7] (de Saussure 2001: 28).

In this powerful tradition of thought, writing is first and foremost *written language*. As musicians and musicologists, we are by no means unfamiliar with this figure of thought; it not only underpins the definition from the *New Grove Dictionary* quoted above but is also decisive for the development of musical sketch research and large parts of music philology. According to a traditional understanding, musical writing is considered to be – almost parallel to the definition of writing as written language – *written sound*. If I were to exaggerate, I might outline the underlying model as follows: The composer has a vivid and complete idea of sound in her or his creative head and puts it down on paper in an ecstatic act of transcription without any loss or alteration. In this interpretation, the media shift from the world of compositional thought to paper is achieved without any difficulties. This perspective can be emblematically illustrated by the traditional description of Wolfgang Amadeus Mozart's creative process: In great contrast to the 'titan' Ludwig van Beethoven, who struggled to write down his works with a pencil and many sketchbooks,[8] Mozart was long regarded as a pure 'brain worker', whose musical thoughts found their way through the pen into the immediately completely fixed score almost as if by themselves, without any effort of written drafting, sketching, checking, discarding and correcting. The fact that Mozart himself had also worked intensively on paper, as Ulrich Konrad was able to prove in a detailed study of Mozart's sketches (Konrad 1992), was shocking news for music historiographers. The assumption that musical writing primarily represents 'written sound' shows not only a questionable pre-understanding of musical creative processes but also of the traditional idea of the relationship between notation and sounding interpretation: In, or better, through her or his performance, the interpreter reawakens the sound imaginations that have withered in writing to sonic life. (The strange

---

7   "Sprache und Schrift sind zwei verschiedene System von Zeichen; das letztere besteht nur zu dem Zweck, um das erstere darzustellen." (de Saussure 2001: 28)
8   Against this background, it is quite understandable that musical sketch research has in principle established itself as a sub-field of Beethoven research and continues to receive the essential theoretical and methodological impulses from there, cf. in this context the extensive and standard-setting project *Beethovens Werkstatt – Genetische Textkritik und digitale Musikedition*: https://beethoven s-werkstatt.de (accessed August 14, 2023).

metaphor of a 'living interpretation' in contrast to an 'inanimate writing' is all too common here and points to the precarious relationship between musical writing and performance.) To cut a long story short: In this scenario, writing is regarded as a sign *for* something else – musical writing is exclusively an indication of the musical sound. In this traditional interpretation, writing would then be a completely transparent medium that neutrally serves the sole purpose of archiving and communicating pre-existent sound or pre-existent ideas about sound.

In recent years and decades, there have been various changes in thinking about writing, which, for all their differences, do coincide in one aspect:[9] It is increasingly being questioned whether writing should really be committed solely to representing signs for *something else*, or whether it might not be more adequate to think of writing as a medium *in its own right* (see, e.g., Grube et al. 2005). In order to do justice to the phenomenon of writing as a fundamental *cultural technique* in its entire breadth, we must take into account that "writings open up possibilities for action that are denied to their oral form"[10] (Krämer 2011: 1). Against this theoretical background, special attention to fundamental aspects of writing-specific materiality, the focus on the discussion of the visual perceptibility of musical writing, the consideration of phenomena of performativity inscribed in musical writing systems as well as the analysis of operative moments in the act of writing itself promise particular gain. These four aspects represent constitutive and inescapable moments of musical writing and, moreover, are to be understood to a considerable extent as genuinely writing-bound aspects in which what one might call the *inherent capacity of writing* manifests itself in a paradigmatic way. These are aspects in which it becomes particularly clear that (musical) writing is not limited to being written language or written sound.

The proposed change of perspective does not seek to deny that different musical sign systems have been developed in the course of music history to ensure fixing, archiving and transmitting the ephemeral musical sound through notation, but points out with emphasis, that musical writing is not limited to

---

9   With regard to new impulses in writing research, see, among others, the relevant publications listed in the bibliography, especially: Greber et al. (2002), Grube et al. (2005), Gumbrecht and Pfeiffer (1993), Krämer and Giertler (2011), Krämer and Bredekamp (2003), Krämer et al. (2012), Raible (1999), Strätling and Witte (2006).

10   "An ihrem Anfang stand die Entdeckung, dass Schriften Handlungsmöglichkeiten eröffnen, welche ihrer mündlichen Form versagt bleiben". (Krämer 2011: 1)

the mere "referentiality" of a pure system of communication – musical writing is always *more* than written sound.

Materiality – Operativity – Iconicity – Performativity

Of course, these four aspects are not symmetrical to each other but intertwined in many ways. I would like to comment on them briefly, in some places referring to specific moments of Iannis Xenakis's creative processes. By referencing the four aspects of materiality, operativity, performativity and iconicity, I am referring to the aforementioned theoretical approach that has been developed in the *Writing Music* research project in recent years (cf. Celestini et al. 2020 for further theoretical context). My point in making this reference is twofold: Firstly, the theoretical framework developed here seems to me to offer some productive considerations for approaching the situation of Xenakis's electroacoustic composing. Secondly, the electroacoustic work of Xenakis seems to me to pose a veritable challenge to a theory of musical writing and in this sense serves as a kind of stress test for the theoretical approach.

Materiality

An indispensable prerequisite without which there can be no writing is the existence of writing materials: Materially available things with which something can be recorded in writing are always needed (for a discussion in the context of general writing research see, e.g, Greber et al. 2002). In this context we differentiate materials that are used for writing and materials upon which writing is done. Writing is bound to the writing materials used in each case: "Writing is done in accordance with the material, i.e., the material is used according to its properties – one does not chisel in paper or dip a pencil into the inkwell"[11] (Celestini et al 2020: 15). Writing is dependent on a materially existing flatness, a physical surface. This results in a special spatiality of two-dimensionality, which leads to the temporally ordered succession of sonic events being transformed into a spatially ordered arrangement of written characters on a vertical and horizontal plane. This, of course, also has consequences for electroacoustic composing.

Asked what he had on the table in front of him when he started to write a score, Xenakis replied:

---

[11]   "Schreiben geschieht materialgerecht, d.h. das Material wird entsprechend seiner Eigenschaften verwendet – in Papier wird nicht gemeißelt und der Bleistift nicht ins Tintenfass getaucht." (Celestini et al 2020: 15)

The notes of a scale, for instance. Or a sieve[12]. Or other notations about the synthesis with cellular automata, or pages with staves so that I can start writing, combining the various materials. [...] Everything could be useful at any one time. (Varga 1996: 184, 188)

If "everything" can be of use in due course – what does this mean for the musical creative process? What is it that constitutes a source within the framework of a creative process? These first preliminary considerations already suggest that, especially regarding the electroacoustic work of Xenakis, it might be extremely worthwhile to ask to what extent and in what way the materials and tools of writing influence the writing itself, since in this context *everything* that serves as a tool for composers must be taken into account – therefore, we have to broaden the analytical horizon with respect to the 'writing' situation of electroacoustic music: the studio or the software, etc.

Operativity

The concept of 'operativity' was coined in the context of current debates on writing and literacy, especially by the philosopher Sybille Krämer, and in its theoretical anchoring it represents a strong argument for the necessary expansion of the understanding of writing in the direction of a non-phonographic concept of writing, because here it can be made clear that in the aspect of operativity a salient feature emerges "where writing *transcends* language"[13] (Krämer 2005: 24): "Writings [...] do not only represent something, but also open up spaces for handling, observing and exploring what is represented"[14] (Krämer 2009: 104). Writing, including musical writing, serves here as a tool to produce something new; musical writing, *as a tool for composing*, opens up new spaces for thinking.

In the sense of a 'diagrammatic operativity', Xenakis refers to the importance of 'explorative-epistemic' writing (cf. Ratzinger 2023; Celestini et al. 2020: 24), for example, with regard to *Pithoprakta*:

---

12   Cf. on the concept of 'sieve': "Why no new theories? I don't know. Perhaps because I concentrated on constructing pieces which should be architecturally more ... I don't know how to put it. In all these years I've been working on the theoretical construction of sieves – that is, of scales, with the help also of the computer." (Varga 1996: 199).

13   "Worin die Schrift die Sprache *überschreitet*: Dies ein Stück weit auszuloten, ist Motiv und Antrieb der folgenden Überlegungen". (Krämer 2005: 24)

14   "Schriften [...] stellen nicht nur etwas dar, sondern eröffnen damit Räume, um das Dargestellte auch zu handhaben, zu beobachten, zu explorieren". (Krämer 2009: 104)

> As far as rhythms are concerned, there's no trace of the golden section; I applied probability theory almost exclusively. I spent many months studying and experimenting in order to be able to keep all that in hand and head. I wrote down parts separately, made diagrams to find the suitable parameters of the formulas. The fact that we know a formula doesn't on its own ensure that it will achieve our aim. We have to work keeping an eye on the end result. In other words: I had to imagine how all that would sound. And that took a long time. (Varga 1996: 75f.)

In order to clarify this fact, which remains largely unquestioned in its obviousness, from a scriptural-theoretical point of view: Musical writing serves not only the transcriptive *representation of* already existing sonic imaginations but also the creative *production of musical* sound events and (sound) phenomena. The neuralgic point of an analysis of the category of operativity within the framework of a theory of musical writing now lies in the fact that moments play a role here that have no direct "equivalent on the sound level" (Raible 1997: 29, quoted in Krämer 2003: 160) or at least on the level of sonic instantiation: What is written – as what is to be read – is available in a completely different way than sound: it can be discarded, deleted, modified, varied, improved, continued, glossed, commented on, etc. These are genuinely script-based moments in which the – ultimately also practical – potential of writings proves itself in a paradigmatic way. A spoken word, a sung sound, cannot be undone – in the realm of writing, however, there is the possibility of deleting, erasing, correcting. Ephemeral sound events, to generalise, become *manageable, reflectable* and *manipulable* in their written reification. At this neuralgic point, the study of Xenakis's (electroacoustic) work (cf. on this issue fundamentally Xenakis 1992) provokes the question of how the theoretical framework expands when, against the background of algorithmic composing, aspects of the (auto)operativity of machine writing are also to be included (cf. with a view to a theory of writing Krämer 2005: 45f.; Grube 2005).

Iconicity

If we assume that notations are *visually perceptible objects*, it makes sense to also question them with regard to their own pictoriality, their own visual logic (cf. Nanni 2013: 407ff; id. 2015; Nanni and Henkel 2020). What the written actually looks like is thus part of the writing process and not merely an ingredient – the discourse on *notational iconicity* also opens up a variety of possibilities for connection with regard to the thematisation of musical notations (Krämer and Giertler 2011); writing is characterised by its hybrid character – writing is always a discursive and iconic medium at the same time (cf. especially Krämer

2003, 2006, 2009). The question of iconicity or of visual logic, was traditionally not considered a central aspect of musical notation – epistemic attention was paid not to the *how* but to the *what* of what was written.

The field of iconicity seems to be particularly relevant for the discussion of Iannis Xenakis's composing: In her article "From hand to ear (or seeing is hearing)", which deals with the 'visualization of Xenakis's creative process', Sharon Kanach describes Xenakis's creative process as follows:

> Graphic, non-musical representation offers Xenakis the immediacy of visual observation of his own creative process, and therefore makes 'what lies beneath' conscious and thus analysable. Although Xenakis almost systematically makes use of accurately recorded scores *before* transcribing them into classical notation, he sometimes delves into the reverse process, that is, transcribing an existing musical work into a graphic representation. His search for universality in the arts, and in music in particular, is thus verified not only by the ear but also by the eye.[15] (Kanach 2009a: 212)

This perspective on the relevance of the visual finds support in various interviews and conversations in which Xenakis emphasises the special relevance of the visual for his composing in general.[16] Xenakis's experiences as an architect play a major role in this context – an explanatory pattern that Xenakis research also likes to use (cf. also Kanach and Lovelace 2010):

> Graphics are indispensable; there are things that can be more easily manipulated through drawing. I acquired this experience during the twelve years I dealt with architecture with Le Corbusier. (Xenakis 1986, quoted in Kanach 2009b: 90, see also Kanach 2009a: 212)

---

15 "Graphische, nicht-musikalische Repräsentation bietet Xenakis die Unmittelbarkeit der visuellen Beobachtung seines eigenen kreativen Prozesses und macht daher das, 'was darunterliegt', bewusst und damit analysierbar. Obwohl sich Xenakis fast systematisch genau aufgezeichneter Partituren bedient, *bevor* er sie in klassische Notenschrift transkribiert, vertieft er sich mitunter auch in den umgekehrten Prozess, das heißt, er transkribiert ein vorhandenes musikalisches Werk in eine graphische Darstellung. Seine Suche nach Universalität in den Künsten und insbesondere in der Musik wird so nicht nur vom Ohr, sondern auch vom Auge überprüft." (Kanach 2009a: 212).

16 "The constraints and spatiality of graphic design seem to be a constant in Xenakis' creative process. From the steel-reinforcement inspired glissandos in *Metastaseis*, through the symbolic manipulation of 'screens of grains' in *Analogique A/B* to later works like *Evryali*, with their less formalized arborescent structures, drawing is a key tool in his compositional process. The graphic possibilities of the UPIC encapsulated this, while at the same time attempting to improve the efficiency of the work-flow." (Nelson 2010: 376).

For the discussion of the significance of the aspect of the iconic in the context of musical writing, Xenakis's creative processes accordingly present themselves as particularly valuable challenges: In her contribution "Spuren, Linien, Klänge und die graphische Notation als Grenzfall", which opens the latest volume of the book series on a *Theory of Musical Writing* (cf. Celestini and Lutz 2023), Sigrid Weigel also points to the special significance of the pictorial, the iconic within the creative process of Iannis Xenakis:

> An outstanding, very special example of this are the countless drawings by Iannis Xenakis, in which his music and sound installations first took shape before compositions were generated from them and transferred into the form of a musical notation. Xenakis, whose experience with graphic designs came from architecture during his many years of collaboration with Le Corbusier, saw these drawings as designs and models. In doing so, the composer, who renewed composing on the threshold of electronic music, resorted to mathematical, stochastic models [...] to combine definiteness and indeterminacy, timelessness with movement, 'often by drawing freehand the shape or texture of the sound he was looking for, and then casting about for the mathematical tool that would allow him to fix this shape precisely.'[17] (Weigel 2023: 18)

Referring to Xenakis's ground-breaking '*glissando* composition' *Metastaseis* (1953–54) for 61 instrumentalists, Weigel makes the analysis of the creative process of Iannis Xenakis fruitful as an "outstanding, very special example" in order to raise the question as to "the How of *Writing Music*" in general:

> A classic example of this is the composition *Metastaseis* (1953/54), which caused a sensation in Donaueschingen in 1955: "He began by sketching arcing shapes – ruled parabolas. In this pleasingly mindblending form, lines at right angles drawn at regular intervals produce a graceful curve at their points of intersection. In this composition he assigned each of forty-six

---

17 "Ein herausragendes, sehr spezielles Beispiel dafür sind die zahllosen Zeichnungen von Iannis Xenakis, in denen seine Musik und seine Klanginstallationen zuerst Gestalt gewonnen haben, bevor daraus Kompositionen generiert und in die Form einer musikalischen Notation übertragen wurden. Xenakis, dessen Erfahrungen mit graphischen Entwürfen aus der Architektur während seiner langjährigen Zusammenarbeit mit Le Corbusier stammen, verstand diese Zeichnungen als Entwürfe und Modelle. Dabei griff der Komponist, der das Komponieren an der Schwelle zur elektronischen Musik erneuerte, auf mathematische, stochastische Modelle [...] zurück, um Bestimmtheit und Unbestimmtheit, Zeitlosigkeit mit Bewegung zu verbinden, 'often by drawing freehand the shape or texture of the sound he was looking for, and then casting about for the mathematical tool that would allow him to fix this shape precisely." (Weigel 2023: 18; quotation in citation: Hewett 2010: 29).

ruled lines to separate string instruments – violin, viola, and so on. [...] Every detail was carefully plotted out". [...] The draft character of Xenakis's drawings as a first musical writing in material form, which precedes both the methodical, as it were, technical composition work and the notation intended for the performing musicians, points once more to the fundamental question of the role of writing in the process of generating music, to the How of *Writing Music*.[18] (Weigel 2023: 18f.)

However, we cannot stop here with regard to an approximation to the electroacoustic work of Xenakis. Significant in this context is the anecdote told by Gérard Marino that links the emergence of the UPIC system with the difficulties of notating *Metastaseis*:

> Writing the glissandi in sixty-one different orchestra parts by hand was quite arduous [...]. Xenakis had to transcribe the graphic notation into traditional notation so that the music could be played by the orchestra. At this time, he came up with the idea of a computer system that would allow the composer to draw music. Indeed, graphic representation has the advantage of giving a simple description of complex phenomena like glissandi or arbitrary curves. Furthermore, it frees the composer from traditional notation that is not general enough for representing a great variety of sound phenomena. In addition, if such a system could play the score by itself, the obstacle of finding a conductor and performers who want to play unusual and 'avant-garde' music would be avoided. (Marino et al. 1993: 259f.; see also Nelson 2010: 374)

Although something can be seen in the creative process of UPIC in the truest sense of the word, (it should be noted that Xenakis himself published images of the 'score pages' of *Mycènes alpha* as visual material, cf. Xenakis 1978), the actual process of reading – in the sense of a 'trans-lation' from the visual to the acoustic – is left to the machine. The readability does not aim at a reading interpretation process by a human being, but at a machine readability; a 'visual logic' (cf. Celestini et al. 2020: 25ff.) only plays an indirect, mediated role here. This points to the fact that in the field of electroacoustic music, materials that are visible or on which something is visible are by no means the only ones that

---

18   "Klassisches Beispiel hierfür ist die Komposition *Metastaseis* (1953–54), die in Donaueschingen 1955 Furore machte. [...] Der Entwurfs-Charakter von Xenakis Zeichnungen als einer ersten musikalischen Schrift in materieller Gestalt, die sowohl der methodischen, gleichsam technischen Kompositionsarbeit als auch der für die ausführenden Musiker bestimmten Notation vorausgeht, verweist einmal mehr auf die prinzipielle Frage nach der Rolle der Schrift im Prozess der Generierung von Musik, nach dem Wie von *Writing Music*" (Weigel 2023: 18f.; quotation in citation: Lovelace 2010: 40).

are relevant, here let us call to mind the specific situation of audio tapes and other electronic or digital storage media. Against this background, the aspect of iconicity thus requires an essential theoretical expansion.

Performativity

Performativity as a specific aspect is of great interest for a theory of musical writing in at least two respects: On the one hand, musical writing is characterised precisely by the fact that it is related to a performative event – in this it differs significantly from non-musical writings; the connection to a performative situation is, in a sense, the *differentia specifica* of musical notations (cf. Celestini et al. 2020: 37). In this regard, David Magnus plausibly speaks of an 'aural latency' of musical writing:

> What one looks at are thus *aural latencies*, optically perceptible figures that, due to their ambiguous visual nature and intended musicality, constantly challenge the gaze anew and demand a performative execution. [...] The view of the pictorial score thus resembles an 'oscillating seeing' that prepares a tonal realisation between the shape and arrangement of the pictorial elements.[19] (Magnus 2015: 127)

Against this backdrop, Xenakis's electroacoustic work rattles the foundations of traditional performance theories. One does not have to go as far as Gérard Pape implies in regard to performing *La Légende d'Eer*:

> The question of performance model is crucial here. The role of the tape projectionist is much closer to that of a conductor than to a pop music DJ. Here 'remixing' the piece is not a question of electronically transforming the 8 tracks into a new entity, but rather trying to bring out the underlying formal structure of the work in a way that is fluid and unique to each musical performance, to each musical space where it is to be performed. (Pape 2010: 369)

But, nevertheless, it should be noted, that a comprehensive explanation of an 'ontology of the musical text' of electroacoustic music is needed in order to

---

19   "Worauf man blickt, sind also *aurale Latenzen*, optisch wahrnehmbare Gestalten, die aufgrund ihrer mehrdeutigen visuellen Beschaffenheit und intendierter Musikalität den Blick stets aufs Neue herausfordern und einen performativen Vollzug verlangen. [...] Der Blick auf die bildliche Partitur gleicht somit einem 'oszillierenden Sehen', das zwischen Gestalt und Anordnung der bildlichen Elemente eine klangliche Realisierung herauspräpariert." (Magnus 2015: 127, cf. also id. 2016).

explain the precarious relationship between recording, written capturing, performance and interpretation in the electroacoustic music of Xenakis; here, the development of the aspect of performativity within the framework of a theory of musical writing could provide essential impulses.

On the other hand, one could speak of a sort of performativity which is *embedded* in musical notations themselves. As Federico Celestini further explains, musical writing is characterised by a dual character of 'inscribed corporeality' and 'transcribed performance' (cf. Celestini et al. 2020: 33ff.). As the concept of 'transcribed performance'[20] provides figures of thought that could, for example, give new impulses to a discussion of Xenakis's UPIC-system, the concept of 'inscribed corporeality' could be traced very well in regard of some workshop materials by Xenakis, when – in the context of the interrelation of music and architecture often mentioned in research – the aspect of 'gesture' in a visual, musical and corporal sense is made productive:

> Compared to phonetic writing, musical writing offers the possibility of graphically representing the course of movement of a gesture through its more pronounced analogue components. If musical writing combines the visual and the acoustic, space and time, the iconic and the syntagmatic, the phenomenon of musical gesture adds the body.[21] (Celestini et al. 2020: 33)

Writing Electroacoustic Music

To summarize with a perspective on Xenakis's creative process what has been developed so far: It becomes clear that the four aspects of musical writing discussed above – materiality, operativity, iconicity, and performativity – play an essential role and can contribute to understanding some moments of Xenakis's

---

20 "Musical writing not only brings together different modes of the medial, but also connects the fields of activity of composition and improvisation. Moments of performative practice find their way directly into the 'happening' of musical writing." "Die musikalische Schrift führt nicht nur unterschiedliche Modi des Medialen zusammen, sondern verbindet auch die Betätigungsfelder der Komposition und Improvisation zusammen. Momente der performativen Praxis finden unmittelbar Eingang in das 'Geschehen' der musikalischen Schrift." (Celestini et al. 2020: 34)

21 "Im Vergleich zur phonetischen Schrift bietet die musikalische Schrift durch ihre stärker ausgeprägten analogen Komponenten die Möglichkeit, den Bewegungsverlauf einer Geste graphisch darzustellen. Wenn die musikalische Schrift Visuelles und Akustisches, Raum und Zeit, Ikonisches und Syntagmatisches verbindet, kommt im Phänomen der musikalischen Geste der Körper hinzu." (Celestini et al. 2020: 33).

creative process. However, it has also become clear that all aspects as theoretical categories reach their limits when we take into account the specifics of Iannis Xenakis's creative processes. The sources and compositional tools that witness the 'writing' process of Xenakis's electroacoustic works range from pencil and paper to the computer system UPIC – this raises the question of their specific materiality. It is obvious that questions of performativity are becoming virulent. In addition to what has already been discussed above, I would also like to mention the aspect of notation of space that is known to represent a central issue of numerous (electroacoustic) works by Xenakis. The connection of the aspects of iconicity and operativity seems particularly fascinating: Sharon Kanach has discussed the importance of writing, drawing and sketching in the creative process of Iannis Xenakis as the operative tool (cf. Kanach 2002). In this context she quotes Xenakis himself, who refers to the significance of this visual operativity – it becomes clear that iconic and operative aspects are closely intertwined within his creative process.

> In retrospect, I think it was more natural for me to draw. Sometimes, I would draw, and my drawings represented musical symbols. I knew traditional solfège, but a certain freedom of thought could not occur that way. I was convinced that one could invent another way of writing music. I started imaging sound phenomena with the help of drawings: spirals, intersecting planes, etc. (Xenakis 1979 quoted in Kanach 2009b: 90, see also Kanach 2009a: 212)

Although it becomes clear that it might well be quite productive to analyse Xenakis's composition of electroacoustic music from the perspective of the four aspects mentioned, it also becomes clear that an expansion of the theoretical framework is necessary when we speak about *writing electroacoustic music* in connection with the œuvre of Xenakis. Thus, on the one hand, it has become obvious that the four aspects are intertwined to a considerably greater degree in the field of electroacoustic music; on the other hand, with regard to the individual aspects, it is necessary to consider further moments: In this sense, a changed status in the field of materiality must be taken into account when – for example, with regard to electronic media and digital data (cf. Münnich 2019) – 'writing materials' are used that resist a simple differentiation into materials that are used for writing and materials upon which writing is done and for which fundamental parameters such as a basic two-dimensional flatness are barely relevant. Regarding the aspect of performativity, the status of the 'text' of electroacoustic music in particular leads to a fundamental reassessment of the relationship between text and performance. Just as the field of operativity requires a fundamental expansion to include the aspect of machine writing, which also takes into account questions of auto-operativity, the field of iconicity proves the necessity of an expansion to include questions of (machine) readability.

Considering all these very fundamental issues, the question of musical writing is raised with some vigour: It can be assumed that the electroacoustic work of Iannis Xenakis might provide manifold challenges and thus serve as a kind of 'stress test' for all considerations towards a theory of writing music. It is the aim of this volume to take up this challenge and to link questions of a philology of electroacoustic music, questions of a theorisation of the foundations of musical writing, and the analysis and historical-technical-medial contextualisation of Iannis Xenakis's electroacoustic work.

Bibliography

Appel, Bernhard, and Emans, Reinmar, eds. (2017) *Musikphilologie. Grundlagen – Methoden – Praxis*, Laaber: Laaber-Verlag (Kompendien Musik 3).

Bent, Ian (2001) "Notation", in *The New Grove Dictionary of Music and Musicians*, ed. by Stanley Sadie, Macmillan Publishers; https://doi.org/10.1093/gmo/9781561592630.article.20114 (accessed August 17, 2023).

Borio, Gianmario, and Danuser, Hermann, eds. (1997) *Im Zenit der Moderne. Die Internationalen Ferienkurse für neue Musik Darmstadt 1946–1966. Geschichte und Dokumentation*, Freiburg im Breisgau: Rombach.

Cage, John (1969) *Notations*, New York: something else press.

Campe, Rüdiger (1991) "Die Schreibszene. Schreiben", in *Paradoxien, Dissonanzen, Zusammenbrüche. Situationen offener Epistemologie*, ed. by Hans Ulrich Gumbrecht and K. Ludwig Pfeiffer, Frankfurt am Main: Suhrkamp, 759–772.

Celestini, Federico, and Lutz, Sarah, eds. (2023) *Musikalische Schreibszenen | Scenes of Musical Writing*, Paderborn: Brill (Theorie der musikalischen Schrift 4).

Celestini, Federico, Nanni, Matteo, Obert, Simon, and Urbanek, Nikolaus (2020) "Zu einer Theorie der musikalischen Schrift. Materiale, operative, ikonische und performative Aspekte musikalischer Notationen", in *Musik und Schrift: interdisziplinäre Perspektiven auf musikalische Notationen*, ed. by Carolin Ratzinger, Nikolaus Urbanek, and Sophie Zehetmayer, Paderborn: Fink (Theorie der musikalischen Schrift 1), 1–50.

Czolbe, Fabian (2014) *Schriftbildliche Skizzenforschung zu Musik. Ein Methodendiskurs anhand Henri Pousseurs Système des paraboles*, Berlin: Mensch und Buch Verlag.

Czolbe, Fabian, and Magnus, David, eds. (2015) *Notationen in kreativen Prozessen*, Würzburg: Königshausen & Neumann.

de Saussure, Ferdinand (2001) *Grundlagen der allgemeinen Sprachwissenschaft*, ed. by Charles Bally and Albert Sechehaye, 3rd edition, Berlin/New York: de Gruyter.

Feder, Georg (1987) *Musikphilologie. Eine Einführung in die musikalische Textkritik, Hermeneutik und Editionskritik*, Darmstadt: Wissenschaftliche Buchgesellschaft.

Finke, Gesa (2019) "Partituren zum Lesen und Schauen. Bildlichkeit als Merkmal graphischer Notationen", in *Zeitschrift der Gesellschaft für Musiktheorie* 16/1, 21–39; https://doi.org/10.31751/1001 (accessed August 17, 2023).

Finke, Gesa (2023) "Das Verhältnis der graphischen Notation zur abstrakten Malerei am Beispiel von Roman Haubenstock-Ramati und Anestis Logothetis", in *Musikalische Schreibszenen / Scenes of Musical Writing*, ed. by Federico Celestini and Sarah Lutz, Paderborn: Brill (Theorie der musikalischen Schrift 4), 415–434.

Freund, Julia (2022) "Bild und Zeichen in der musikalischen Schrift. Überlegungen zur Interpretation der frühen graphischen Partituren Bussottis im Lichte von Adornos Reproduktionstheorie", in *Dialektik der Schrift. Zu Adornos Theorie der musikalischen Reproduktion*, ed. by Julia Freund, Matteo Nanni, Jakob M. Schermann, and Nikolaus Urbanek, Paderborn: Brill (Theorie der musikalischen Schrift 3), 147–189.

Friedl, Reinhold (2012) "Was ist ein Fehler? – Xenakis' La Légende d'Eer: Versuch einer kritischen Edition elektroakustischer Musik", in *MusikTexte* 135, 33–39.

Friedl, Reinhold (2015) "Iannis Xenakis' La Légende d'Eer: Towards a Critical Edition of Electroacoustic Music", in *Iannis Xenakis – The electroacoustic music*, ed. by Makis Solomos, Paris: L'Harmattan, 109–122.

Friedl, Reinhold (2019) *Towards a Philology of Electroacoustic Music – Xenakis's Tape Music as Paràdigm*, PhD thesis, Goldsmiths, University of London.

Greber, Erika, Ehlich, Konrad, and Müller, Jan-Dirk, eds. (2002) *Materialität und Medialität von Schrift*, Bielefeld: Aisthesis (Schrift und Bild in Bewegung 1).

Grube, Gernot (2005) "Autooperative Schrift – und eine Kritik der Hypertexttheorie", in *Schrift. Kulturtechnik zwischen Auge, Hand und Maschine*, ed. by Gernot Grube and Werner Kogge, Munich: Fink, 87–114.

Grube, Gernot, and Kogge, Werner, eds. (2005) *Schrift. Kulturtechnik zwischen Auge, Hand und Maschine*, Munich: Fink.

Grüny, Christian (2020) "Scores: Notation zwischen Aufbruch und Normalisierung", in *Musik und Schrift: interdisziplinäre Perspektiven auf musikalische Notationen*, ed. by Carolin Ratzinger, Nikolaus Urbanek, and Sophie Zehetmayer, Paderborn: Fink (Theorie der musikalischen Schrift 1), 135–158.

Gumbrecht, Hans Ulrich, and Pfeiffer, K. Ludwig, eds. (1993) *Schrift*, München: Fink (Materialität der Zeichen 12).

Harley, James (2002) "The Electroacoustic Music of Iannis Xenakis", in *Computer Music Journal* 26/1 (*In memoriam Iannis Xenakis*), Cambridge: MIT, 33–57.

Harley, James (2004) *Xenakis: His Life in Music*, New York: Routledge.

[Haubenstock-Ramati, Roman (1959)] *musikalische grafik* [exhibition catalogue, Universal Edition in Donaueschingen], n.p.

Hewett, Ivan (2010) "A Music Beyond Time", in *Iannis Xenakis: Architect, Composer, Visionary*, ed. by Sharon Kanach and Carey Lovelace, New York: The Drawing Center (Drawing Papers 88), 17–33.

Kanach, Sharon (2002) "Xenakis's hand, or the visualization of the creative process", in *Perspectives of New Music* 40/1, 190–197.

Kanach, Sharon (2009a) "Sichtbare Musik. Notationsübertragung im Œuvre von Iannis Xenakis", in *Notationen. Kalkül und Form in den Künsten*, ed. by Hubertus von Amelunxen, Dieter Appelt, and Peter Weibel, Berlin/Karlsruhe: Akademie der Künste, 212–215.

Kanach, Sharon (2009b) "From hand to ear (or seeing is hearing) Visualization of Xenakis's creative process: methods and results", in *Iannis Xenakis – Das elektroakustische Werk*, ed. by Ralph Paland and Christoph von Blumröder, Cologne: Verlag Der Apfel (signale aus köln | musik der zeit), 83–98.

Kanach, Sharon, and Lovelace, Carey, eds. (2010) *Iannis Xenakis: Architect, Composer, Visionary*, New York: The Drawing Center (Drawing Papers 88).

Kanach, Sharon, ed. (2010) *Performing Xenakis*, translated, compiled and edited by Sharon Kanach, Hillsdale/New York: Pendragon (The Iannis Xenakis Series 2).

Karkoschka, Erhard (1966) *Das Schriftbild der Neuen Musik. Bestandsaufnahme neuer Notationssymbole. Anleitung zu deren Deutung, Realisation und Kritik*, Celle: Moeck.

Konrad, Ulrich (1992) *Mozarts Schaffensweise: Studien zu den Werkautographen, Skizzen und Entwürfen*, Göttingen: Vandenhoeck & Ruprecht (Abhandlungen der Akademie der Wissenschaften in Göttingen, Philologisch-Historische Klasse 3/201).

Krämer, Sybille (2003) "'Schriftbildlichkeit' oder: Über eine (fast) vergessene Dimension der Schrift", in *Bild, Schrift, Zahl*, ed. by Sybille Krämer and Horst Bredekamp, Munich: Fink, 157–176.

Krämer, Sybille (2005) "'Operationsraum Schrift'. Über einen Perspektivenwechsel in der Betrachtung der Schrift", in *Schrift. Kulturtechnik zwischen Auge, Hand und Maschine*, ed. by Gernot Grube, Werner Kogge, and Sybille Krämer, Munich: Fink, 23–57.

Krämer, Sybille (2006) "Zur Sichtbarkeit der Schrift oder: Die Visualisierung des Unsichtbaren in der operativen Schrift. Zehn Thesen", in *Die Sichtbarkeit der Schrift*, ed. by Susanne Strätling and Georg Witte, Munich: Fink, 75–84.

Krämer, Sybille (2009) "Operative Bildlichkeit. Von der 'Grammatologie' zur 'Diagrammatologie'? Reflexionen über erkennendes 'Sehen'", in *Logik des Bildlichen. Zur Kritik der ikonischen Vernunft*, ed. by Martina Heßler and Dieter Mersch, Bielefeld: transcript, 94–122.

Krämer, Sybille (2011) "Editorial. Vom Nutzen der Schriftbildlichkeit", in *Sprache und Literatur* 42, ed. by Sybille Krämer and Mareike Giertler, Paderborn: Fink, 1–5.

Krämer, Sybille, and Bredekamp, Horst, eds. (2003) *Bild, Schrift, Zahl*, Munich: Fink.

Krämer, Sybille, and Giertler, Mareike, eds. (2011) *Sprache und Literatur* 42, Paderborn: Fink.

Krämer, Sybille, Cancic-Kirschbaum, Eva, and Totzke, Rainer, eds. (2012) *Schriftbildlichkeit. Wahrnehmbarkeit, Materialität und Operativität von Notationen*, Berlin: Akademie.

Lovelace, Carey (2010) "How Do you Draw a Sound?", in *Iannis Xenakis: Architect, Composer, Visionary*, ed. by Sharon Kanach and Carey Lovelace, New York: The Drawing Center (Drawing Papers 88), 35–84.

Magnus, David (2015) "Aurale Latenzen. Über Gestalt und Operativität in der bildlichen Notation", in *Die Schrift des Ephemeren. Konzepte musikalischer Notationen*, ed. by Matteo Nanni, Basel: Schwabe (Resonanzen 2), 111–128.

Magnus, David (2016) *Aurale Latenz. Wahrnehmbarkeit und Operativität in der bildlichen Notationsästhetik von Earle Brown*, Berlin: Kadmos.

Marino, Gérard, Serra, Marie-Hélène, and Raczinski, Jean-Michel (1993) "The UPIC System: Origins and Innovations", in *Perspectives of New Music* 31/1, 258–269.

Minetti, Elena (2023) *Schrift als Werkzeug. Schriftbildliche Operativität in Kompositionsprozessen früher* musique mixte (1949–1959), PhD thesis, mdw – University of Music and Performing Arts Vienna.

Münnich, Stefan (2019) *Musikalische Schrift und ihre Codes. Studien zur Genese, Theorie und Digitalität einer Wechselbeziehung*, PhD thesis, University of Basel (print in preparation).

Nanni, Matteo (2013) "Das Bildliche der Musik. Gedanken zum *iconic turn*", in *Historische Musikwissenschaft, Grundlagen und Perspektiven*, ed. by Michele Calella and Nikolaus Urbanek, Stuttgart: Metzler, 402–428.

Nanni, Matteo (2015) "Quia scribi non possunt. Gedanken zur Schrift des Ephemeren", in *Die Schrift des Ephemeren. Konzepte musikalischer Notationen*, ed. by Matteo Nanni, Basel: Schwabe (Resonanzen 2), 7–14.

Nanni, Matteo, and Henkel, Kira (2020) *Von der Oralität zum SchriftBild. Visuelle Kultur und musikalische Notation (9.–13. Jahrhundert)*, Paderborn: Brill | Fink (Theorie der musikalischen Schrift 2).

Nelson, Peter (2010) "Performing the UPIC system of Iannis Xenakis", in *Performing Xenakis*, ed. by Sharon Kanach, Hillsdale: Pendragon, 373–390.

Pape, Gérard (2010) "Interpretating Xenakis' Electro-Acoustic Musik: *La Légende d'Eer*", in *Performing Xenakis*, ed. by Sharon Kanach, Hillsdale: Pendragon, 369–372.

Pape, Gérard (2015) "Questions and Remarks on *La Légende d'Eer*'s versions", in *Iannis Xenakis – The electroacoustic music*, ed. by Makis Solomos, Paris: L'Harmattan, 123–124.

Plato (1922) *Phaidros*, translated, annotated and furnished with a comprehensive index by Constantin Ritter, second revised edition, Leipzig: Meiner.

Raible, Wolfgang (1997) "Von der Textgestalt zur Texttheorie. Beobachtungen zur Entwicklung des Text-Layouts und ihren Folgen", in *Schrift, Medien, Kognition. Über die Exteriorität des Geistes*, ed. by Peter Koch and Sybille Krämer, Tübingen: Stauffenburg, 29–41.

Raible, Wolfgang (1999) *Kognitive Aspekte des Schreibens*, Heidelberg: Universitätsverlag Winter (Schriften der Philosophisch-historischen Klasse der Heidelberger Akademie der Wissenschaften 14).

Ratzinger, Carolin (2023) "Complex Relations. Reflections on the operativity of writing music", in *Musikalische Schreibszenen / Scenes of Musical Writing*, ed. by Federico Celestini and Sarah Lutz, Paderborn: Brill (Theorie der musikalischen Schrift 4), 231–249.

Ratzinger, Carolin, Urbanek, Nikolaus, and Zehetmayer, Sophie, eds. (2020) *Musik und Schrift: interdisziplinäre Perspektiven auf musikalische Notationen*, Paderborn: Fink (Theorie der musikalischen Schrift 1).

Schmidt, Dörte (2020) "Schrift. Werk. Performance. Neue Musik", in *Musik und Schrift: interdisziplinäre Perspektiven auf musikalische Notationen*, ed. by Carolin Ratzinger, Nikolaus Urbanek, and Sophie Zehetmayer, Paderborn: Fink (Theorie der musikalischen Schrift 1), 275–300.

Strätling, Susanne, and Witte, Georg, eds. (2006) *Die Sichtbarkeit der Schrift*, Munich: Fink.

Thomas, Ernst, ed. (1965) *Notation Neuer Musik*, Mainz: Schott (Darmstädter Beiträge zur Neuen Musik 9).

Ungeheuer, Elena, ed. (2002) *Elektroakustische Musik*, Laaber: Laaber-Verlag (Handbuch der Musik im 20. Jahrhundert 5).

Urbanek, Nikolaus (2013) "Was ist eine musikphilologische Frage?", in *Historische Musikwissenschaft, Grundlagen und Perspektiven*, ed. by Michele Calella and Nikolaus Urbanek, Stuttgart: Metzler, 147–183.

Varga, Bálint András (1996) *Conversations with Iannis Xenakis*, London: Faber and Faber.

Weigel, Sigrid (2023) "Spuren, Linien, Klänge und die graphische Notation als Grenzfall. Theoretische Überlegungen zur musikalischen Schrift im Anschluss an Derrida", in *Musikalische Schreibszenen / Scenes of Musical Writing*, ed. by Federico Celestini and Sarah Lutz, Paderborn: Brill (Theorie der musikalischen Schrift 4), 3–37.

Xenakis, Iannis (1978) "Mycenae – Alpha 1978", in *Perspectives of New Music* vol. 25, No. 1/2, 12–15.

Xenakis, Iannis (1979) interview: Rey, Anne, and Dusabin, Pascal: "Si Dieu existait, il serait bricoleur", in *Le monde de la musique* 11, 92–97.

Xenakis, Iannis (1986) interview: Clare Rémy: "Sons, probabilités, graphismes. Le mélange étonnant de Xenakis", in *Micro-systèmes* 65, 78–82.

Xenakis, Iannis (1992) *Formalized Music: Thought and Mathematics in Music*, rev. ed., compiled and ed. by Sharon Kanach, Hillsdale: Pendragon.

Zattra, Laura (2006) *The critical editing of computer music*, EMS: Electroacoustic Music Studies Network, Beijing; http://www.ems-network.org/IMG/EMS2006-LZattra.pdf (accessed August 5, 2023).

Zimmermann, Heidy (2009) "Notationen Neuer Musik zwischen Funktionalität und Ästhetik", in *Notationen. Kalkül und Form in den Künsten*, ed. by Hubertus von Amelunxen, Dieter Appelt, and Peter Weibel, Berlin/Karlsruhe: Akademie der Künste, 198–211.

Zimmermann, Heidy (2023) "Mise en page. Roman Haubenstock-Ramati als Initiator editorischer Neuerungen bei der Universal Edition", in *Musikalische Schreibszenen / Scenes of Musical Writing*, ed. by Federico Celestini and Sarah Lutz, Paderborn: Brill (Theorie der musikalischen Schrift 4), 181–208.

Archives, Sources, Persons and Personae in the Art of Electronic Sounds

Laura Zattra

Introduction

What can we deduce from the composers' personal archives? What do archives tell us about the person who has collected and organised (or disorganised) them over the years, about their own creative process, about their 'workshop'?

I have 'used' personal and institutional archives for 20 years for the purpose of constructing histories of authors, works, centres and collaborations, and incorporating philology, oral history, ethnography with an emphasis on sound technology and society studies. In each of my specific research projects, the individual sources served me in view of the single purpose of a project: analysing a musical work, reconstructing the creative process, reconstructing a biography or the history of an electronic music centre. In the past, I was less interested in reflecting on what a whole body of sources can reveal to us. But lately, the very organisation of these places (physical or virtual) has led me to think about what the sources can tell us about a musician's way of approaching his or her work. In this paper I consider the very close relationship between the process of accumulating documents and the person who carries out this operation.

These thoughts arose almost by themselves from the method of study I have developed over the years, a method that combines philology, archaeology, oral history and ethnography with an emphasis on science, technology, social studies, and creative process studies. In my mixed approach, I always try to consider all available sources (paper, audio, video, computer, etc.), including non-textual sources and (written or oral) 'memorial sources' (sources containing stories with a memorial character or ethnographic documents). I believe that one of the most interesting recent musicological approaches is the one that reconstructs *la fabrique des œuvres*, the compositional 'workshop' of one composer. With this method, initiated in 2008, Nicolas Donin and Jacques Theureau studied the physical, technical and mental environment of some composers (Donin and Theureau 2008a). They also give an overview of the writings that deal with the terms of 'art cabinet', logbook, analysis or self-analysis of a creative activity in music (id. 2008b). The cognitive ergonomics of the compositional activity they propose sees the atelier-workshop as "the environment which provides [the creative process] with the conditions of possibility (material, tools, archives) and the set of technical problems, stylistic options, anticipations and memorisation of the elements of the work to come" (ibid.: 8).

Over the years, my mixed method of research enabled me to determine the interaction between agents and operations in the creative process, but also to reconstruct lost sources (Zattra 2007). Finally, on an even deeper level, it often allowed me to discover hidden figures who were indispensable to the creative process (e.g., computer music designers and sound designers).

Texts and Sources

Electroacoustic music is characterised by a rich heterogeneity of sources (see Figure 2.1). Researchers who study them and deal with archives need to develop varied and specialised skills and to correspondingly establish new analytical tools. In fact, the texts (contents) and sources (media devices, instruments) may document different phases of creation, alteration, deletion, rewriting, interpretation and, due to their heterogeneity, are to be considered witnesses in the broadest sense. Sources can indeed be classified according to their form: digital, on paper or audio-video, and texts, according to their information content and the 'code' used to convey this information.

Such a typology cannot therefore be presented as a simple extension of, or equivalent to, the typologies specific to the study of literary texts or the art of the past. Indeed, it introduces new concepts and makes it necessary to expand the notion of 'text', to carefully examine the nature of information content and to take into account the multiplicity of documents that shape the production of a work. It may also be worthwhile to briefly recall the main difference between the notion of 'source' and that of 'text': A source is generally a physical testimony, a material unit, while a text is its information content (I have discussed the taxonomy of sources and texts in Zattra 2011, 2015).

Figure 2.1 exemplifies the heterogeneous nature of sources. In the case of electroacoustic and computer music, we find among them a list of digital data for synthesis; sketches of a piece (e.g., Olivier Messiaen's sketch of *Timbre-durées*, a tape music piece; Battier 2010).

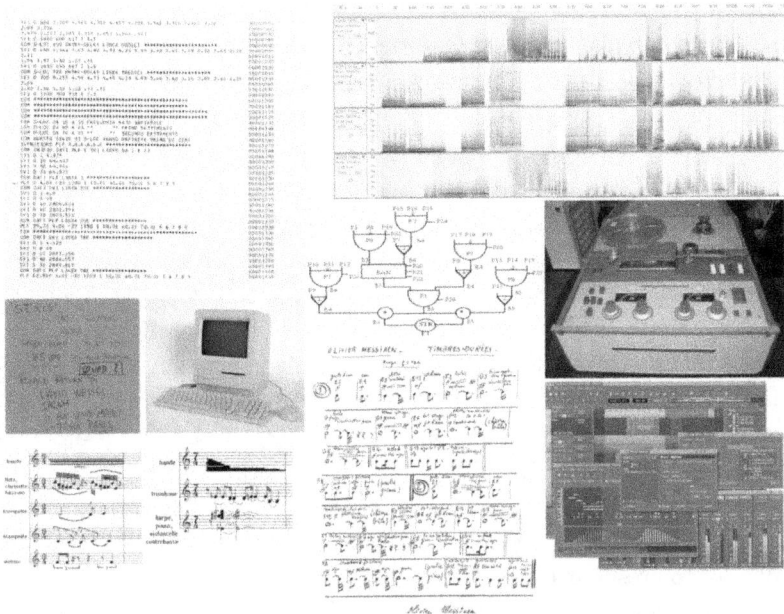

Figure 2.1: *Fausto Razzi,* Progetto secondo, Music5 *score, p. 3, personal archive Alvise Vidolin; Spectrogram of Teresa Rampazzi,* Taras su tre dimensioni, *personal archive Laura Zattra; Sony tape recorder 777 owned by Teresa Rampazzi and Ennio Chiggio, personal archive Ennio Chiggio; Rui Nuno Capela, Qtractor-Screenshot, Digital audio workstation, https://commons.wikimedia.org/w/i ndex.php?curid=45607792 (accessed November 1, 2024), Public Domain; Handwritten sketch of Olivier Messiaen,* Timbres-durées, *(Battier 2010: 2); Laura Zattra, transcription of parts of York Höller,* Résonance *from the Breitkopf & Härtel score; Red box containing the audio tape of John Chowning,* Stria, *IRCAM archives; Macintosh Classic XO computer, https://commons.wikimedia.o rg/w/index.php?curid=10101 (accessed November 1, 2024), Photo by Alexander Schaelss; Laura Zattra, Block diagram of Instrument 1, Wolfgang Motz,* Sotto Pressione, *personal archive Laura Zattra.*

Moreover, there are also boxes, e.g., the red box containing the audio tape of *Stria* (1977) by John Chowning. Sources also include a spectrogram representation of a computer music piece, a computer itself, a tape machine, etc. Each of these sources has its unique material specificity, its own content, and requires its own 'reading code' to access the 'text'.

The philological method helps to illuminate the comprehension of these texts. The technique is based on observation and the accurate description of sources related to a piece of music. They always tell something interesting about the genetic process, possible variants or versions of the music piece, etc. Philological investigations differ from musicological analyses. An analyst employs the sources in a less systematic approach, he uses them as a way to demonstrate his hypothesis and feels free to choose the more useful sources for his own purposes; he considers sources according to their content. The philologist, on the contrary, tries to consider the whole spectrum of the sources and considers both the aspects of the content and their material appearance.

If we analyse the storage medium, we can distinguish four main types of media in electroacoustic music: paper, audio, video (analogue or digital), digital (computer data, bits, codes). Paper can be used to store all sorts of written information content: composition sketches (e.g., work diagrams, notes, drafts of traditional score parts in the case of mixed music, pre-calculation materials), paper output of digital data of any kind printed for checking by the composer or compiler or to preserve a stage of creation, paper sheet music printed in conventional notation in the case of mixed music. The format designates not only the dimensions of the sheet of paper, but also the way in which it was folded or collected (e.g., punched cards were writing media at a certain era of computer music).

The audio medium has been only recently considered by traditional philology, which normally focuses on music texts existing in paper form (one of the first scholars was Angela Ida De Benedictis 2004, 2009). Many electroacoustic music pieces exist only in audio format: Analogue tapes are sources *per se*, as are CDs, MiniDiscs, digital audio files, etc. Unlike paper – a medium whose content seems immediately readable to us (assuming that we master that code, e.g., music notation, the alphabet, or a specific language) – audio and digital media always present the need for an intermediate 'reading' phase. In other words, a clear distinction should be made between the existence and the accessibility of such sources: That is to say, a document of this type does not exist if it is not reproducible and accessible. For example, accessing a digital audio source – and being able to qualify the degree of elaboration of its content – generally involves playing it and viewing it, by means of a graphical environment, in the form of a sonogram. Or, the technical 'reading' stage will make it possible to identify the cuts in a magnetic tape, to understand the characteristics of the different tracks, to make assumptions about the formal assembly; at a more local level, it makes it possible to advance in the knowledge of the types of sounds used (spectral properties, distinction between sounds of acoustic origin and of electronic origin, etc.).

'Codicology' in electroacoustic music is the study of audio media as physical objects. In fact, many problems are related to the preservation and restoration of the audio storage medium, for example, deteriorating tapes or CDs containing computer music data that are no longer readable. This discipline is very specialised and often benefits from collaboration between musicologists and sound engineers (see Orcalli 2006; Orcalli bases his theorisation on the writings of Storm 1980; Schüller 2001).

In musicology, the audio-visual medium, which was considered a fundamental source for the first time in 2008 by musicologist Bruno Bossis, is undoubtedly an exegetical document (although as a compositional strategy it was adopted well before, in audio-visual composition). With the project FIELD (FIlm on ELectroacoustics Database) Bossis studied this type of source, which he calls 'film trace', from 2008 on, identifying the descriptive categories and the keywords that characterise it in order to create databases (Bossis 2009a, 2009b). These documents include documentaries (sometimes unpublished), recordings of studio work sessions, recordings of rehearsals and concerts, a collection of reactions from the public, interviews, etc.

Another type of storage medium is the digital data storage device. Computers as such pose a much more dizzying series of questions than magnetic tapes, digital discs or external memories. Indeed, the computer is both an instrument and a medium. It is used for creation (composition and musical writing), for production (data management, calculations, conversions, etc.), for performance and reproduction (it reads and rereads, it calculates and recalculates, etc.) and music data storage. It can be the support of elementary or very complex contents, calculations or sound events, basic processes or high-level processes (specialised languages like Fortran, Pascal, C, just to mention a few, up to higher level programs such as Max, Pure Data, Steinberg Cubase, Csound, Audacity, Ableton Live, the infinite series of digital audio workstation software). Digital sources should include the Internet as a complex system of software, a network that connects and transforms information, an archive of primary and secondary sources (audio, video or textual) and an instrument of creation.

Finally, among the audio and audio-visual sources, interviews with the actors of the creative process are crucial. These interviews, whether produced within the framework of an ethnographic survey or in other contexts, are necessary for the reconstruction of a music whose essential 'know-how' is based on oral tradition (transmission of composition techniques, collaboration between the various contributors to the creative process). These oral sources are valuable for safeguarding the finer (often private) details of the creative process. The memory of the protagonists conveys knowledge that other sources cannot reveal. Compared to the material fixity of the other sources, these carry a high degree of instability. Oral documents are important for computer music research when the protagonists are still active and can therefore contribute to the knowledge of the creative process. As a result, computer music and electroacoustic music scholars often finds themselves at the crossroads of musicology and socio-ethnography (see Zattra 2021).

Archives, Persons and Personae

Archives are containers for these heterogeneous sources. Archives assemble documents of the past and the present (ongoing projects). They hold records deemed important enough to be maintained, which of course means that other materials may have been considered superfluous by their creators and thrown away. Archives can also change in nature over time: Previously they were only physical sites; now they are also virtual (online archives or computer memory). The instability of archives and the secrets they can hide in their structure have led me to consider what they can reveal to us beyond the single sources preserved in them.

This difference in storage has led me to identify two meanings of the concept of the archive (these thoughts are connected to the different *nuances* of meaning that Michel Foucault adopts in his theories, although my ongoing thinking touches on more practical and basic implications). In a sense, the archive can be considered a place (virtual or material) as an emanation of the artist, almost a mirror. Through their own archives, artists communicate with and talk to themselves. Hence, how they organise their materials shows how they perceive themselves and their work. Filing, rearranging, storing, etc., the present or the past, can help them understand a process, a phase, a development. It may correspond to the practice of metacognition, the self-awareness of the thought processes and the understanding of the patterns behind them.

On the other hand, the archive (virtual or material) is something that may be specifically created for others, for all those who come afterwards, who can decide to study those materials, be they musicologists or performers, etc. In that sense, the archive can be considered an entry point for us for reconstructing a history, a history of ideas and therefore, to borrow Foucault's theory, an *episteme* or a 'discursive formation', an underlying system of thought, and the "conditions of possibility of all knowledge, whether expressed in a theory or silently invested in a practice" (Foucault 1970: 168). My attempt at theorising these concepts is based on the elementary and yet complex difference between the concepts of life and form: 'life' means what we are (our *person*, human beings), 'form' signifies what we seem to be (our *persona*, our role, our character, the aspect we present to others or what is perceived by others). Related to that is the concept of the 'mask'. In fact, the etymology of the term 'persona' derives from the Latin *'persōna'*, a term probably of Etruscan origin, which meant 'theatrical mask'.

In building an archive (this could also be the mere memory of a computer), artists externalise their persons. If they do this just for themselves, there is a close connection between person and persona. But through documents, they are also giving voice to their personas. Thus, scholars or performers who access those archives will first of all access the persona and only through this, the person as well. I will give some examples – the first two are from my experience with personal archives (the ones of Teresa Rampazzi and John Chowning), then I will describe my involvement with an institutional archive (the Studio di Fonologia di Milano now kept at the NoMus Association in Milan) and finally my experience with personal archives donated to a foundation (Camillo Togni's and Fausto Romitelli's collections at the Fondazione Cini in Venice).

Teresa Rampazzi

I became aware of the importance of Teresa Rossi Rampazzi (1914–2001) in 1999, when I was writing my master's thesis (see Zattra 2020). At that time Rampazzi was 85 years old and living in a nursing home (see Zattra 2016a and my ongoing web project dedicated to Teresa Rampazzi[1]). The same year, Rampazzi's children had donated their mother's archive to the University of Padua (see Figure 2.2). Rampazzi was in a precarious state of health and had withdrawn from her music composition activity. The collection consists of approximately 50 audio tapes with her music (including final versions and production tapes), plus about 150 tapes with music she received from colleagues and friends and music she recorded from the Radio 3 Programme of the RAI, the national public broadcasting company of Italy. The physical items include letters (e.g., one from fellow composer Pietro Grossi, another one from her written to one of her students, the composer and teacher Mauro Graziani), a binder holding working notes, texts describing the pieces she wrote and a printed digital 'score' made using a computer program named ICMS. Today, 20 years later, these documents still have neither been inventoried nor made accessible to the public.

---

1   http://www.teresarampazzi.it (accessed April 5, 2023).

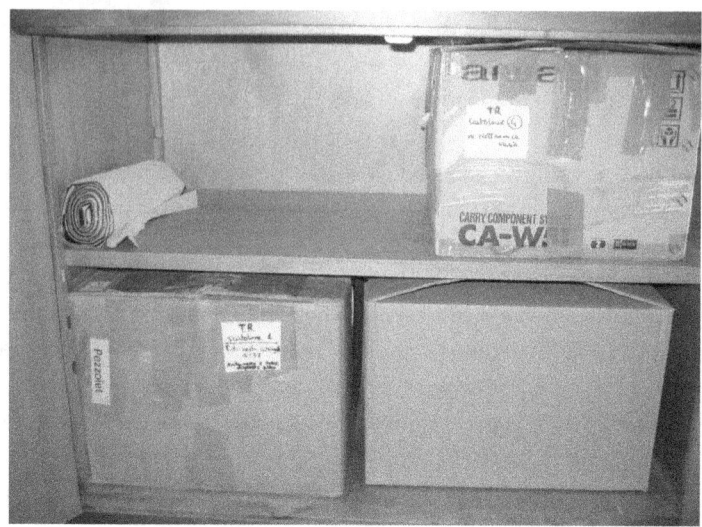

Figure 2.2: *Collection Teresa Rampazzi, Department of Cultural Heritage, University of Padua. Photo by Laura Zattra.*

It was difficult to listen to her music, as a digitisation of the tapes was only made later in 2005. It also soon became clear that this collection of the composer, pedagogue and pioneer of electronic music in Italy was incomplete. This is due to two reasons: The composer had donated her writings to friends, collaborators and relatives (books, texts, correspondences); furthermore, she was reluctant to leave written traces of her activity. As a consequence, Teresa Rampazzi's archive is not located in a single place. For example, most of her books had been donated to the Conservatory of Music in Padua at various times from 1984 on. So, her personal library is mostly kept there.[2]

Some of her analogue electronic instruments (her synthesisers) can be found in the electronic music studio within the same conservatory: She left them there when she retired from teaching (in 1972, she founded one of the first electronic music courses in Italy and donated her instruments to the institution). As mentioned, other people in Italy and abroad own letters from her, tapes, books or other writings. Research had to include interviews with these people who had known and collaborated with her.

---

2   Rampazzi's daughter donated a few remaining books and catalogues to me a few years ago, among them the original edition of Pierre Schaeffer's *Traité des objets musicaux* of 1966, with Schaeffer's dedication to Rampazzi.

The nature of her dispersed archive reflects Rampazzi's personality. She was forward-looking and modern (she loved, for instance, contemporary architecture and contemporary interior design). She was interested in new developments, ahead of her time and ingenious in her ability to see how music was supposed to evolve. She duly discharged everything that could remind her of the past, including letters and photographs (she didn't like being photographed). She was interested in the future. Unfortunately, as a result Rampazzi's last creative period in particular was forgotten, a fate she shares with other women composers who are "either ignored or thought to be marginal", such as Delia Derbyshire or Constança Capdeville (Morgan 2017: 238; Magalhães 2022). In recent years, however, many studies (and archives) have flourished and are finally filling these voids. In the case of Teresa Rampazzi, I have developed a website (teresarampazzi.it), written several articles and analyses, participated in conferences and meetings, and established a project with the record label "Die Schachtel" (started in 2008) to salvage and release Teresa Rampazzi's music, most of which had still been previously unpublished.

John Chowning

There are numerous sources related to Chowning's research and music production – e.g., the famous papers about frequency modulation and spatialisation (Chowning 1971, 1973) and his many interviews and lectures – but so far, no comprehensive story of his research and production has been published nor the situation of his archives discussed. For this, I have, with François-Xavier Féron, not only led research in different archival funds but, above all, I have collected 27 hours of interviews with the composer/researcher in nine different sessions, within the framework of the RAMHO project (Musical Research and Acoustics: an Oral History) (IRCAM/Centre Pompidou 2021: 19).

Chowning's 'archive' is a miscellany of different supports and contents stored in different places. His published works and his scores and computer data have been archived by himself in digital form on his computer. Since 2007, copies of the majority of these sources can also be found in the Stanford University Archives (CCRMA SAILDART Archive). These sources are mostly scans of paper printouts of digital data, and various other documents, some handwritten notes, used for research, synthesis, calculation, etc. These materials have been used to reconstruct the story of *Stria*, Chowning's best-known piece (see Zattra 2007, 2016b; Baudouin 2007; Dahan 2007; Meneghini 2007). The SAILDART Archive holds a lot of historic sources concerning the CCRMA and John

Chowning.[3] Bruce Baumgart created the facility to provide online access to the almost one million files from the 1970s and 1980s stored in the archive of the Stanford Artificial Intelligence Lab. SAILDART includes messages written in the internal messenger service. For my particular research on Chowning, I could find documents written by him which contained programming instructions (related to compositions and software), as well as other texts including letters that he sent to colleagues around the world and simple messages between them. This turned out to be a true gold mine of information that sheds light on the everyday life of this researcher and composer, including the atmosphere in the laboratory.

However, Chowning told us that some documents and photos are still in his garage (he showed us some of them during the interviews). This part of his private archive has neither been organised nor published to date. The interviews with Chowning conducted by François-Xavier Féron and me are crucial to understanding (and presenting to readers, possibly in the future) his reactions to the heterogeneous sources we presented to him in chronological order. This research teaches us countless issues on a methodological level, including how to handle a mixture of methodologies such as history, philology, archival research and oral history.

A small example demonstrates how a private source can bring forward the musicological analysis of the compositional process, the study of working conditions and workflow, and finally the analysis of the person: In May 2005, John Chowning found a meaningful handwritten document (undated, see Figure 2.3) showing a plan of *Stria* with more sections than the final version of the piece (e.g., T163 between T0 and T286). According to other sources, T163 would have slightly overlapped, beginning at second 163 (Zattra 2007). This *Stria* version has seven sections: T0, T163, T286, T466, T610, T754F, and END. Also, the F at the end of T754 occurs only here; another important detail shown here is the overall duration: 987″ =16′27″, a duration longer than both final versions.

This source from Chowing's private archive was unpublished until 2007. In that year we decided to release it on the DVD that was part of *Computer Music Journal* 31:4, which was dedicated to *Stria*. This DVD included all sources used for the analysis and reconstruction of the piece (the sketch appears among the 'Unpublished sources', folder 7, John Chowning Manuscripts). *Computer Music Journal* 31:3 and the DVD (*Computer Music Journal* 31:4) constitute the first 'critical editions' of a computer music composition in history.

---

3   The list of these sources can be found here: https://www.saildart.org (accessed April 5, 2023; see also Nelson 2015).

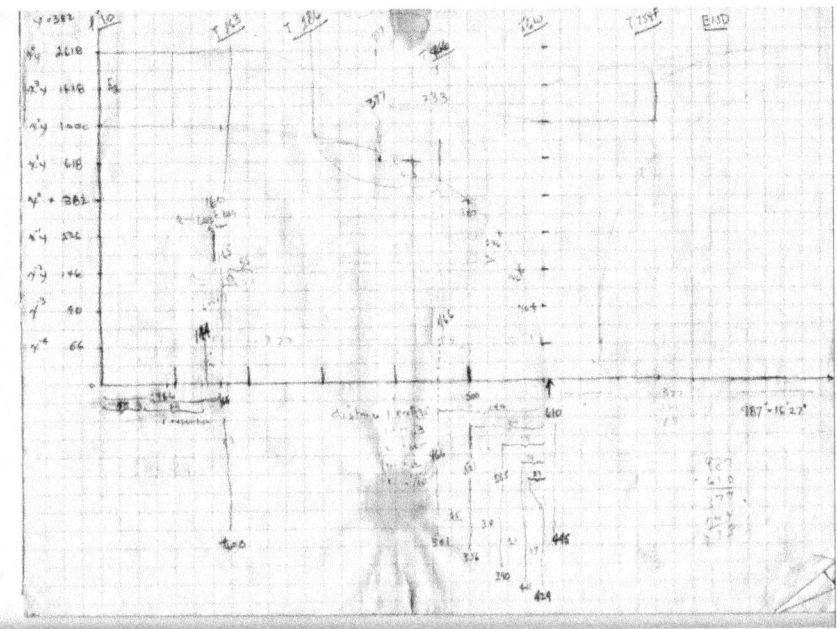

Figure 2.3: *John Chowning,* Stria, *plan, personal archive John Chowning. Also published in Zattra 2007: 55.*

The abovementioned source also helps us discover some background on the typical working conditions at the CCRMA. There is a coffee stain on the paper. Chowning told us, this might be a hint that the draft was made in an all-night working session. The plan of *Stria* is therefore important for many reasons: it is handwritten, therefore it shows the hand of the composer; it demonstrates an initial phase of the composition, which later evolved through the removal of some sections; and finally, it also shows some aspects relating to the composer's lifestyle.

The NoMus Archive (Milan) and the Studio di Fonologia Musicale di Milano della RAI

The NoMus Association in Milan was founded in 2013 on the initiative of Maria Maddalena Novati. She had worked at RAI since 1979 during the last years of activity of Marino Zuccheri, who was a technician and music assistant of the Studio di Fonologia della RAI (national public broadcasting company of Italy) in Milan (see Figure 2.4) and retired in 1983.

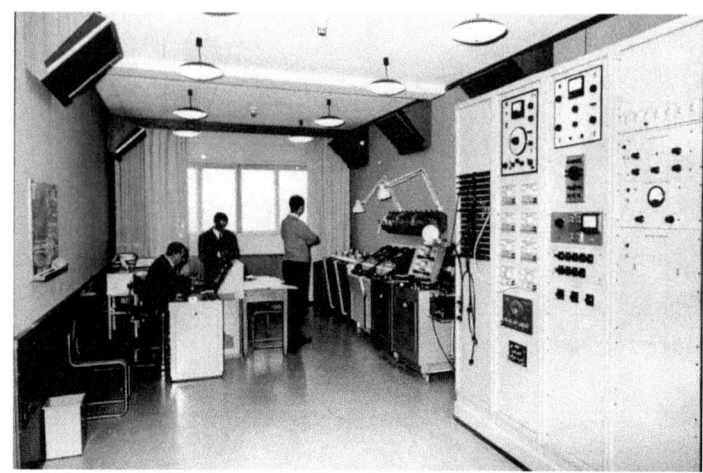

Figure 2.4: *Studio di Fonologia at RAI in Milano, Italy, 1968. From left: Marino Zuccheri, Angelo Paccagnini, Luigi Nono, NoMus Archive, Collection Angelo Paccagnini.*

Novati literally saved the instruments, tapes, correspondence and much more from the Studio di Fonologia.

> One day I found all the tapes in the corridor [of the RAI]: they were being thrown away, because apparently the closet where they were stored was needed. So I rushed to the new manager to explain what was really in those boxes (excerpted from: Palma 2019, translation by the author).

The materials of the Studio di Fonologia have never been systematically archived, but correspondences, tapes and other material were indeed collected. During the 1990s, Novati archived the remaining materials (with the retirement of Zuccheri the studio was officially closed) by such criteria as nature, topic, author, and support (for a better explanation, see Novati 2001). Once she retired in 2013, Novati suggested that these materials be saved once and for all. She rented a space next to her house in Milan and founded the association for the NoMus Archive, which has since become authoritative not only for the history of the Studio di Fonologia, but also for many other topics of historical and cultural interest, including the collections dedicated to Marino Zuccheri, Alfredo Lietti (physicist and technician at the Studio), Angelo Paccagnini (director of the Studio from 1968 to 1970), Gino Marinuzzi Jr., Luigi Russolo, Francesco Balilla Pratella and Sylvano Bussotti.

Figure 2.5: *Maria Maddalena Novati at the RAI studio just before her retirement (Lawendel 2009).*

I visited the Studio for the first time in 2012, a few months before Nova-ti's retirement, in order to conduct research on Angelo Paccagnini (Zattra 2014, 2018). Figure 2.5 shows Mrs. Novati in front of her computer at RAI with the in-house catalogue of the Studio materials. I therefore had the privilege not only of seeing her work at the original site (at that time she was working on the digi-tisation of many reels), but also of seeing the archive moved later in 2013 from its place of origin to the warehouses of the Museum of Musical Instruments at the Castello Sforzesco in Milan, of witnessing a process of digitisation of other tapes, paper materials and the correspondence (the originals are owned by RAI and stored at the Castello Sforzesco) and therefore of seeing the copies 'reas-sembled' at the new location, at NoMus, in an organisation that represents (or mirrors) its creator, Mrs. Novati. In this case, the NoMus Archive reflects the person and persona of Novati, "discreet and indefatigable", who understands the importance of history and preservation, "the one who saved the RAI Pho-nology Studio", a person who after her retirement chose "to sell her house, buy a new one with an adjacent 'store' and found an association with an emblema-tic name, NoMus [Novecento Musica, but also Novati Musica]" (Di Marco 2016, translation by the author).

Camillo Togni

The Italian composer and pianist Camillo Togni (1922–1993) is one of the most important dodecaphonic composers in Italy, even though he is still little known abroad. He participated in the First International Dodecaphonic Congress in Milan in 1949 and attended the Ferienkurse in Darmstadt from 1951 to 1957. One of the most important works from his dodecaphonic period is *Variazioni* for piano and orchestra (1945–46) and major works from his total serialism phase include *Rondeaux per dieci* (1963–64) and a trilogy of operas (*Blaubart* (1972–75) and *Barrabas* (1981–85), the third part, *Maria Magdalena*, has remained unwritten). Togni composed his only tape piece, *Recitativo*, in March 1961 at the Studio di Fonologia della RAI in Milan. The composer stored the archival material relating to this piece in a very organised way (some of the following reflections also appear in Zattra 2021) "with a particular vocation to save any life document from decay or oblivion" (Togni 2001: 2).

The Camillo Togni Collection is kept at the Fondazione Giorgio Cini in Venice. His collection has been "ordered and rearranged following the draft of archiving arranged by the composer himself before his disappearance in 1993" (ibid.). In my research I reconstructed the creative process of *Recitativo* (Zattra forthcoming). The order in which he gathered the materials (sketches, notes, literature he had studied to learn electronic music technology, and materials related to the re-performance of the piece in 1991 in Brescia) shows both the daily organisation in view of those who subsequently study his music and a very ordered creative process. For instance, the choice of frequencies (mostly sinusoidal sounds) can be reconstructed thanks to a very rich handwritten source: A light brown cardboard folder labelled in black marker "Appunti per pezzo elettronico (1961)" (Notes for electronic piece) contains 137 pages with numbers and schemes. Leafing through this manuscript, we can literally see the creative process pass before our eyes page by page from the choice of pitches to the structure of the three definitive sections, including the decision not to add other sections. These 'notes' are compiled by Togni in this cardboard folder, closed by a push button bearing two white adhesive labels, on the front and on the spine, indicating: "CAMILLO TOGNI/RECITATIVO/PEZZO ELETTRONICO/1961". In this cardboard folder is also a book he used to study acoustics and psychoacoustics (Righini [1960]).[4] In it we find annotations in Togni's very precise and

---

4   The book by Pietro Righini contains 136 typewritten pages, including printouts of some sonograms on photographic paper. This volume was a cornerstone publication in Italy during the early electronic music era for those learning the new sound world. Since it was written at RAI during the same period Togni worked

neat handwriting with passages occasionally underlined with a ruler in graphite or blue/red pencil.

Fausto Romitelli

Fausto Romitelli's (1963–2004) collection is housed at the Fondazione Giorgio Cini in Venice (Romitelli's personal archive was donated to the Foundation by his family in 2016). Among the sources, I was able to see the complete list of computer files (patches, programmes) printed as screenshots and on paper as well as Romitelli's computer of the 1990s. It is a Macintosh Classic personal computer designed, manufactured and sold by Apple Computer in 1991 (see Figure 2.6).

Figure 2.6: Macintosh Classic, *https://commons.wikime dia.org/w/index.php?curid=10101 (accessed November 1, 2024). Photo by Alexander Schaelss.*

It is very likely that this was the computer he bought when he began studying new technologies at the *Cursus d'informatique musicale* at the IRCAM (Institut de recherche et coordination acoustique/musique) in Paris and which he continued to use afterwards until his death. The computer itself is an object to

at the Studio di Fonologia Musicale, it is most likely that someone donated it to him so that he could learn the basics of acoustics, psychoacoustics and timbre.

study in its own right. In fact, it offers many more questions than other elec-troacoustic music sources, since it is both an instrument for composition and a medium.

Romitelli's computer provides an opportunity to present some issues scho-lars must consider when studying computers as a source and as a text (or a se-ries of texts), such as the dating of the machine and its files, the internal organi-sation of the files and what their content can tell us. These provide researchers with an inside view into the composer's atelier. As a material object, Romitelli's computer reveals historical/biographical details.

Musicologist Alessandro Olto carried out the first review of the materials and made paper printouts of some of the documents: The first large printout was entitled *Istituto per la Musica/Fondo Fausto Romitelli – Patchwork Files + Codice Lisp* by Francisco Rocca and contains Patchwork patches and Lisp codes; the second bears the title *Fausto Romitelli/Documentation of new Patchwork Modules* and contains Patchwork modules with a short description.[5] When one consults the archives today, one only has access to the paper printouts.

Studying this documentation, I could show that Romitelli's computer contains some standard system folders (system folder, games, RagTime Disk, Word 5.00) and a folder titled 'Fausto3', where he stored documents and works at irregular intervals. The same irregularity is shown by Romitelli's paper sources in the collection, revealing the frenetic activity of a young compo-ser. However, after a deeper analysis, this apparent haphazardness seems to correspond to his compositional strategy: He did not organise the computer documents by musical pieces or by effects, because the computer 'tools' he used (particularly the Patchwork patches he developed with the help of com-puter music designer Laurent Pottier) formed an 'orchestra' of instruments and effects that he built over time and used in various pieces during the 1990s.

These files are the result of Pottier's collaboration with Romitelli. The first evident aspect is the dating of the files. The dates range from April 1993 to May 1996; only five files are dated much later, 13 July 2001.[6] However, some files are dated 27 August 1956. This is obviously surprising, but it can be explained by a dating error caused by a problem with the lithium battery of the computer (when the battery fails, most Macintosh computers reset to the birth date of one of the designers, Ray Montagne).

---

5   Alessandro Olto studied Patchwork and Lisp codes for the analysis of *EnTrance* realised by Romitelli at the IRCAM in Paris in 1995 with the assistance of the computer music designer Laurent Pottier (Olto 2016).

6   Further research will be necessary to contextualise these last files.

Future comparisons between patches, modules and codes – including a re-construction of their chronology of usage – could shed light on the evolution of Romitelli's compositional approach. Laurent Pottier is an important witness, because he assisted Romitelli during the composition of *EnTrance* in 1995, a work that clearly re-uses some computer materials previously created for *Natura morta* (cf. Olto 2017). For example, I have asked Pottier if they used to make digital sketching, or patches, to try effects and to test different soluti-ons.[7] He confirmed that these sketches consisted of a "calculation of harmo-nic structures in [the software] Patchwork, but also pencil and paper sketches, spreadsheet files, patches and music sheets made with Patchwork" (these pa-per and pencil sketches are stored at the Cini Foundation). When discussing the re-use of the patches – which proves the building of a collaboration and an affinity that has increased over the years – Pottier also says, "We had common musical sensitivities. Exchanges had already taken place during my DEA (EHESS 1992) [bachelor's thesis] where I had analysed his composition *Natura morta con fiamme (1992)*". Some patches (e.g., 'blood', 'cupio1', 'cupio2' or 'domeniche') clearly correspond to specific pieces: *Blood on the Floor, Painting 1986* (2000), *Cupio Dissolvi* (1996), and *Domeniche alla periferia dell'impero* (1996–2000), re-spectively. During my interview, when asked if they had "develop[ed] a specific way to communicate? New terms?", Pottier states that they "have developed specific instruments for CAO (computer-assisted composition) in Patchwork and for synthesis (with Csound)". Pottier's personal archive is also important. He has digital and paper documents and copies of scanned documents. He is the founder of several projects for preserving electronic music through technical porting to current software in order to solve the serious problem of obsoles-cence. Among the numerous articles, papers and projects developed during his collaborations, the two projects *Antony* (Pottier et al. 2018) and *Sidney* (Lemou-ton et al. 2018) were developed at the IRCAM and the University VIII Saint Denis in Paris. Hence, to study Romitelli's music, we must consider sources scattered in various places, the archives of Fondazione Cini, Laurent Pottier's personal archive and probably also the IRCAM's archive, not to mention different oral sources as well.

---

7   Laurent Pottier, personal email, September 19, 2022; further quotes from this email follow. The interview with Pottier as well as other investigations on the creative process of Romitelli, Mauro Lanza/Andrea Valle and Clara Iannotta will be discussed in detail in a forthcoming article.

Conclusions

In this article, I have tried to demonstrate that there is a close connection between the importance of the study of sources in electroacoustic music (source criticism, philology and analysis) and the importance of considering the corpus of sources in their entirety (the archive). An archive – whether it is gathered by the artist or by an archivist – is a mirror of the collector's personality. It is closely related to the image that person wants to convey of him- or herself (of one's persona) and an intimate link to one's inner identity (one's 'person', in line with the etymological meaning of this term). The work of musicologists, in addition to being an archive job based on sources and source criticism, also involves ethnographic and anthropological fieldwork. Archives may be living ecosystems continually evolving for reasons such as the obsolescence of technology and tools. They need to be updated not only for re-performances of a musical piece but indeed also as the living artists continue to advance in their musical and artistic visions. More often than not, we are dealing with open archives precisely because artists continue to produce. Alongside their research work grounded on sources, musicologists therefore have an obligation to hear the direct testimony of these people.

Bibliography

Battier, Marc (2010) "Messiaen and his collaborative musique concrète rhythmic study", in *Olivier Messiaen: The Centenary Papers*, ed. by Judith Crispin, Newcastle upon Tyne: Cambridge Scholars Publishing, 1–27.

Baudouin, Olivier (2007) "A Reconstruction of *Stria*", in *Computer Music Journal* ("The Reconstruction of Stria") 31/3, 75–81; https://doi.org/10.1162/comj .2007.31.3.75 (accessed March 27, 2024).

Bossis, Bruno (2009a) "FIELD: A Film and Video Database as a Musicology Source on Electroacoustic Music", in *Proc. of the Electroacoustic Music Studies Conference*, Buenos Aires; http://www.ems-network.org/ems09/papers/bo ssis.pdf (accessed March 27, 2024).

Bossis, Bruno (2009b) "La Perception de l'acte artistique à travers les films sur la création électroacoustique – l'exemple de l'IRCAM", in XII *Jordans de Estética e historia del teatro marplatense y congreso internacional de estética*, Fundacion Destellos, CD ROM.

Chowning, John (1971) "The Simulation of Moving Sound Sources", in *Journal of the Audio Engineering Society* 19/1, 2–6; reprinted in *Computer Music Journal* 1/3, 48–52.

Chowning, John (1973) "The Synthesis of Complex Audio Spectra by Means of Frequency Modulation", in *Journal of the Audio Engineering Society* 21/7, 526–534; reprinted in Weiiand, Frits, ed. (1975) *Musical Aspects of the Electronic Medium, Report on Electronic Music*, Utrecht: Institute of Sonology; reprinted in *Computer Music Journal* 1/2, 1977; reprinted in Roads, Curtis, and Strawn, John (1985), *Foundations of Computer Music*, Cambridge: MIT Press.

Dahan, Kevin (2007) "Surface Tensions: Dynamics of *Stria*", in *Computer Music Journal* ("The Reconstruction of Stria") 31/3, 65–74; https://doi.org/10.116 2/comj.2007.31.3.65 (accessed March 27, 2024).

De Benedictis, Angela Ida (2004) "Scrittura e supporti nel Novecento: alcune riflessioni e un esempio (*Ausstrahlung* di Bruno Maderna)", in *La scrittura come rappresentazione del pensiero musicale*, ed. by Gianmario Borio, Pisa: ETS, 237–291.

De Benedictis, Angela, and Scaldaferri, Nicola (2009) "Le nuove testualità musicali", in *La filologia musicale. Istituzioni, storia, strumenti critici*, ed. by Maria Caraci Vela, vol. II, Lucca: LIM, 71–116.

Di Marco, Francesco (2016) "Maddalena Novati, una vita per la musica contemporanea", in *Cultweek*, 20 January 2016; https://www.cultweek.com/mad dalena-novati/ (accessed March 27, 2024).

Donin, Nicolas, and Theureau, Jacques, eds. (2008a) *La fabrique des oeuvres, Circuit. Musiques Contemporaines* 18/1.

Donin, Nicolas, and Thereau, Jacques (2008b) "Ateliers en mouvement: interroger la composition musicale aujourd'hui", in *La fabrique des oeuvres, Circuit. Musiques Contemporaines* 18/1, 5–14.

Foucault, Michel (1970) *The Order of Things: An Archaeology of the Human Sciences*, New York: Random House.

IRCAM/Centre Pompidou (2021) *Rapport d'activité*, https://www.ircam.fr/me dia/uploads/uploads/Rapports%20activite/rapport-activite-2021-ircam .pdf (accessed March 27, 2024).

Lawendel, Andrea (2009) "Studio di fonologia RAI – intervista a Maddalena Novati", 7 October 2009; http://radiolawendel.blogspot.com/2009/10/stud io-di-fonologia-rai-intervista.html (accessed March 27, 2024).

Lemouton, Serge, Bonardi, Alain, Pottier, Laurent, and Warnier, Jacques (2018) "On the Documentation of Electronic Music", in *Computer Music Journal* 42/4, 41–58; https://doi.org/10.1162/COMJ_a_00486 (accessed March 27, 2024).

Magalhães, Filipa (2022) "Musicological Archaeology and Constança Capdeville", in *TDR: The Drama Review* 66/3, 64–77; https://doi.org/10.1017/S105420 4322000302 (accessed March 27, 2024).

Meneghini, Matteo (2007) "An Analysis of the Compositional Techniques in John Chowning's *Stria*", in *Computer Music Journal* ("The Reconstruction of Stria") 31/3, 26–37; https://doi.org/10.1162/comj.2007.31.3.26 (accessed March 27, 2024).

Morgan, Francis (2017) "Pioneer Spirits: New media representations of women in electronic music history", in *Organised Sound* 22/2, 238–249; https://doi.org/10.1017/S1355771817000140 (accessed March 27, 2024).

Nelson, Andrew J. (2015) *The Sound of Innovation: Stanford and the Computer Music Revolution*, Boston: MIT Press.

Novati, Maddalena (2001) "The Archive of the *Studio di Fonologia di Milano della Rai*", in *Journal of New Music Research* 30/4, 395–402; https://doi.org/10.1076/jnmr.30.4.395.7495 accessed March 27, 2024).

Olto, Alessandro (2016) *EnTrance. Spettralismo e composizione assistita all'elaboratore in Fausto Romitelli*, PhD thesis, Università degli Studi di Udine.

Olto, Alessandro (2017) "Between Spectrum and Musical Discourse. Computer Assisted Composition and New Musical thoughts in *EnTrance* by Fausto Romitelli", in *Sounds, Voices and Codes from the Twentieth Century. The Critical Editing of Music at Mirage*, ed. by Luca Cossettini and Angelo Orcalli, Udine: Mirage, 419–452.

Orcalli, Angelo (2006) "Orientamento ai documenti sonori", in *Ri-mediazione dei documenti sonori*, ed. by Sergio Canazza and Mauro Casadei Turroni, Udine: Forum, 15–94.

Palma, Mattia L. (2019) "Le signore della musica/Maddalena Novati: Io, Berio e Stockhausen", in *CultWeek*, 18 December 2019; https://www.cultweek.com/le-signore-della-musica-maddalena-novati-io-berio-e-maderna/?fbclid=IwAR2baBzsThsHHoKVqu7yDWAi7QuN_QlResufp6PyqzqoZ3elvsHJ-Qj9fx8 (accessed March 27, 2024).

Pottier, Laurent, Bonardi, Alain, Lemouton, Serge, and Warnier, Jacques (2018) "*Antony*: Collaborative preservation system for music with electronics. Towards a digital repository of versioned computer music software environments and the creation of a documentary database", ECLLA; https://musinf.univ-st-etienne.fr/recherches/antony_en.html (accessed March 27, 2024).

Righini, Pietro ([1960]) *Acustica Musicale*, Milano: RAI editions RADIOTELEVISIONE ITALIANA.

Schüller, Dietrich (2001) "Preserving the facts for the future: Principles and practices for the transfer of analog audio documents into the digital domain", in *Journal of Audio Engineering Society* 49/7–8, 618–621.

Storm, William (1980) "The establishment of international re-recording standards", in *Phonographic Bulletin*, vol. 27, 5–12.

Togni, Camillo (2001) *Carteggi e scritti di Camillo Togni sul Novecento Italiano*, Florence: Leo Olschki.

Zattra, Laura (2007) "The Assembling of *Stria* by John Chowning: A Philological Investigation", in *Computer Music Journal* ("The Reconstruction of Stria") 31/3, 38–64; https://doi.org/10.1162/comj.2007.31.3.38 (accessed March 27, 2024).

Zattra, Laura (2011) *Studiare la Computer Music. Definizioni, analisi, fonti*, Padua: Edizioni Webster.

Zattra, Laura (2014) "Angelo Paccagnini", in *Dizionario Biografico degli Italiani – Vol. 80, Enciclopedia Treccani*, Roma/Catanzaro: Abramo Printing & Logistics, 51–54; https://www.treccani.it/enciclopedia/angelo-paccagnini_%28Dizionario-Biografico%29/ (accessed March 27, 2024).

Zattra, Laura (2015) "Génétiques de la computer music", in *Genèses Musicales*, ed. by Nicolas Donin, Almuth Grésillon, and Jean-Louis Lebrave, Paris: Presses universitaires de Paris Sorbonne, 213–238.

Zattra, Laura (2016a) "Teresa Rampazzi", in *Dizionario Biografico degli Italiani – Vol. 86, Enciclopedia Treccani*, Roma/Catanzaro: Abramo Printing & Logistics, 51–54; https://www.treccani.it/enciclopedia/teresa-rampazzi_%28Dizionario-Biografico%29/ (accessed March 27, 2024).

Zattra, Laura (2016b) *John Chowning – Stria* (online multimedia analysis); https://brahms.ircam.fr/fr/analyses/Stria/ (accessed March 27, 2024).

Zattra, Laura (2018) "Angelo Paccagnini: Composer, Director of the Studio di Fonologia di Milano, Teacher, Actor, Conductor, Writer and Musicologist", in *Marino Zuccheri & Friends*, ed. by Maria Maddalena Novati, Laura Pronestì, and Marina Vaccarini, Milan: Die Schachtel, (with CD: DS35/1), 115–123.

Zattra, Laura (2020) „*Taras su tre dimensioni* by Teresa Rampazzi: Documenting the Creative Process", in: *Between the Tracks: Musicians on Selected Electronic Music*, ed. by Miller Puckette and Kerry L. Hagan, Cambridge, MA/London: MIT Press, 2020, 241–265.

Zattra, Laura (2021) "The Electroacoustic Music Archives at the Fondazione Giorgio Cini: A Review of the Camillo Togni, Fausto Romitelli, and Giacomo Manzoni Collections", in Archival Notes 6, 87–99.

Zattra, Laura (forthcoming) "Recitativo for tape (1961) by Camillo Togni. Tracking the creative process for his only work of electronic music", in a forthcoming book dedicated to Camillo Togni, ed. by Angela Carone and Christoph Neidhöfer.

Websites

https://www.saildart.org, accessed April 5, 2023 (CCRMA SAILDART Archive).
http://www.teresarampazzi.it, accessed April 5, 2023 (Teresa Rampazzi's site, created by Laura Zattra).

List of Figures

Figure 2.1: Fausto Razzi, *Progetto secondo*, Music5 score, p. 3, personal archive Alvise Vidolin; Spectrogram of Teresa Rampazzi, *Taras su tre dimensioni*, personal archive Laura Zattra; Sony tape recorder 777 owned by Teresa Rampazzi and Ennio Chiggio, personal archive Ennio Chiggio; Rui Nuno Capela, Qtractor-Screenshot, Digital audio workstation, https://commons.wikimedia.org/w/index.php?curid=45607792 (accessed November 1, 2024), Public Domain); Handwritten sketch of Olivier Messiaen, *Timbres-durées*, (Battier 2010: 2); Laura Zattra, transcription of parts of York Höller, *Résonance* from the Breitkopf & Härtel score; Red box containing the audio tape of John Chowning, *Stria*, IRCAM archives; Macintosh Classic XO computer, https://commons.wikimedia.org/w/index.php?curid=1010 1 (accessed November 1, 2024). Photo by Alexander Schaelss; Laura Zattra, Block diagram of Instrument 1, Wolfgang Motz, *Sotto Pressione*, personal archive Laura Zattra.

Figure 2.2: Collection Teresa Rampazzi, Department of Cultural Heritage, University of Padua. Photo by Laura Zattra.

Figure 2.3: John Chowning, *Stria*, plan, personal archive John Chowning. Also published in Zattra 2007: 55.

Figure 2.4: Studio di Fonologia at RAI in Milano, Italy, 1968. From left: Marino Zuccheri, Angelo Paccagnini, Luigi Nono, NoMus Archive, Collection Angelo Paccagnini.

Figure 2.5: Maria Maddalena Novati at the RAI studio just before her retirement (Lawendel 2009).

Figure 2.6: *Macintosh Classic*, https://commons.wikimedia.org/w/index.php?curid=10101 (accessed November 1, 2024), CC BY-SA 3.0. Photo by Alexander Schaelss.

Sketching on Paper and Tape
Creative Practices of Early Tape Music

Michelle Ziegler

The first issue of the American magazine *Tape & Film Recording* addressed a wide-ranging readership covering both "home" and "professional" sound recording (Mooney 1953). It portrayed the heterogeneous use of tape records in industry and leisure-time activities in 1953. Recording sounds and voices in home, office, plant, school or church served to preserve family memories of children's voices or wedding ceremonies, provide party entertainment, overseas exchanges in "tape clubs" and the documentation of meeting notes in offices. They were also used in highly professional music productions. At the time, different production lines of tape machines – portable or installed, luxurious or functional, with new push buttons, microphones, cords and reels – already catered to the different needs of various individuals using tapes professionally or privately. The size and weight of the portable tape recorders allowed the user to record any kind of sound anywhere. In contrast to the established disc records, the medium of the tape not only simplified recording and playback, but it also made sound manipulation possible during and after the recording process itself by means of cutting, splicing and the use of loops, overdubbing and reverberation. A great variety of practices can also be found in the early artistic use of the tape machine, and it is documented in some of the preserved collections of tape records in composers' archives. In this article I will argue that for a comprehensive evaluation of the compositional processes of early tape music, these sketches on tape have to be considered in connection with sketches on paper: Both reveal integral parts of the creative process.

Sources on Paper and on Tape: Visibility and Audibility

The main difference between music sources on paper and on tape lies in the perceptibility of the inscriptions for the human being: Whereas writing on paper can be perceived visually through reading, the core information of audio recordings is revealed in aural perception through listening.[1] Writing on paper needs specific tools (pen, pencil, eraser, etc.) connected to specific uses in cultural techniques (see Schuiling and Payne 2022); the perception of the written signs and graphics usually does not require a technical mediator (apart from a light source and, if necessary, glasses). The musical realisation of the notation requires voices or instruments and knowledge of turning signs into sounds in the act of performance. Recording on tape however relies on technological equipment both in the process of inscription and playback (in the transformation of magnetic material on a tape by an electric current of an audio signal and in the reverse process of a magnetic imprint inducing voltage changes that are subsequently transformed into sound): The acts of writing and reading are transferred to a machine. The specific affordances of tape include the possibilities of instant playback, erasure and reuse. The procedures of writing on paper and recording on tape share core attributes as reproduction techniques; they can be regarded as an "intermedial field" (Celestini et al. 2020: 30) and a material practice. They entail transformations from one medium to another and capture an ephemeral phenomenon – sound – on a carrier, thereby fixing it in an appearance that is stable (at least for a limited moment in time). Due to their unique medial transductions,[2] they both afford a whole set of unique operative possibilities which make them not only objects of communication, but tools with creative, explorative and cognitive potentials. The operativity of writing and recording has been explored in recent musicological and interdisciplinary research projects, which have revealed specific properties of both procedures as creative practices.

Recent studies have endeavoured to investigate the specific and unique visibility of music writing.[3] References to the theories of notational iconicity (e.g., Krämer 2009) instigated an epistemological shift revealing the explorative and

---

1   This general difference of course does not take into account the fact that writing as a material process entails accompanying aural elements (perceivable for example in the noisy process of the destruction of a draft on paper by crumpling or tearing and musically portrayed in the orchestra piece *Schreiben* (2003–04) by Helmut Lachenmann) and that tapes can be perceived and manipulated visually (for example due to the analogy of tape length and sound length or through the visualisation means of sonograms).

2   For the use of the term 'transduction' for processes of music writing: see Münnich 2019; for the interpretation of the term in Gilbert Simondon's writings: see Assis 2017.

3   See the publication series "Theorie der musikalischen Schrift" of the project *Writing Music. Iconic, performative, operative, and material aspects in musical notation(s)*, e.g., Celestini et al. 2020.

cognitive dimensions of music writing due to its materiality, operativity, performativity and iconicity. The element of operativity in this complex allows us to focus on the specific properties of writing that are connected to its materiality and visibility. Writing as an "explorative, productive, and self-reflexive tool" allows us to arrange, organise, hierarchise, add and delete on a writing surface, where the visual display lets us "evaluate and reflect" upon the notated (Ratzinger 2023: 242). Furthermore, this shift encompasses a great variety of music writing – and especially the heterogenous notations of the 20th and 21st centuries – including not only the various signs, like letters, numbers and other codified shapes of traditional European music notation, but also graphics and drawings. However, the visibility of music notation is a specific one: Writing and reading in the context of music imagination, composition, performance and analysis are always closely connected to thinking, hearing and performing sound. They reveal a unique bond between the visual elements and their aural equivalents: A "tipping" (Krämer 2009: 117) that is unique to music notation. Moreover, music writing as an element of a performative art captures musical gestures of melodies, inscribes the corporality of the performative act and transcribes performance (Celestini et al. 2020: 33f.). Intertwined in specific music practices, writing is determined by the aesthetics, compositional practices, specific historical moment and cultural practices of a given writer. The visibility of music writing is therefore specifically coined due to its proximity to sound and its embeddedness in specific performative, creative and historic practices.

It is evident that the new medium of the tape and its specific characteristics as an audio source gave rise to new compositional practices. The "expansion of organology" has projected writing "beyond its flat graphic dimension" towards new creative outlets that were born "from the relationship with the medium itself" (Cossettini and Orcalli 2017: xii). Two aspects unique to the new medium and echoing in the major shift from "symbolic" to "signal inscription" (Magnusson 2019: 13) are the disconnection of sound from its source and the importance of listening within the process of composition. Whereas in the act of reproduction entailed in writing on paper any given object – be it a sound, an image or another phenomenon – can be conveyed only in processes of translation into language, symbols and graphics; the phonograph and the tape allowed for recorded sounds to be dislocated from their original place and brought into ateliers, living rooms and auditoriums. Instant playback options invigorated creative practices by facilitating aural control. "Discrete histories" of the magnetic tape have recently highlighted such specific affordances and challenged a broader "phonographic regime" (Bohlman and McMurray 2017: 7). However, recording on tape did not only bring novelties into the creative processes. The change from one medium to another in artistic practices has to be understood as a process of mutual contagion; recording on tape protracts previous processes of writing on paper. Some early experiments in the electronic studios reveal an even higher reliance on prescriptive tools in the form of writing on paper compared to non-electronic music (De Benedictis 2004: 250) – a development that is rooted in the serial compositional techniques that were deployed at the time. It underlines the historical dimension of creative practices: In the act of composition, past techniques can be continued or transformed and new orientations can be sought. The artistic engagement implies both looking back and looking forward; in a "web of retention and protention" the "recursive, bidirectional temporal relation" of the act of creation allows routines, but also innovation (Born 2021: 10).

Challenges of Mixed Media Sources in Sketch Studies

To date, relatively little musicological research has been conducted on the magnetic tape as a creative means and analyses of compositional processes of early tape music are still rare – even if the equipment and technological affordances are attracting more and more interest in the field of media archaeology and edition philology (e.g., Cossettini and Orcalli 2017; Pasdzierny 2019). An inquiry into tape editing procedures has additional potential: The practices of montage and sound manipulation and the importance of listening in creative processes are precursors of current practices in electronic music, pop music and the digital arts. Tape manipulations are still not broadly considered an artistic practice because of reductions of historiographic narratives, aesthetic prioritisations and imbalances due to canonisations, social hierarchies and separations between so-called art music and popular music and due to the approach to the sources and their handling. Even if the access to the sources and the analytical tools to investigate them have improved significantly within the last two decades, there are still some challenges for studies of sources on tape (and on paper). One challenge lies in the sources on tape themselves, another one in the method of sketch studies and the imbalanced consideration of written and recorded sketches.

Already in the early 2000s, when the influences of the technological equipment on the creativity of composers of early electronic music started to be studied more widely, the preservation of the sources was considered a big challenge (Manning 2006: 81). The situation has improved noticeably in the meantime, thanks to the digitisation of big corpora of primary sources, the increased processing in archives and the expanded focus on a wider range of actors. However, the archival sources for tape music are still often scant and the preservation of the tapes is challenging. The conservation of analogue tape poses problems due to abrasions, mould and chemical processes that destroy the material. The disintegration of the tapes and the detachment of layers over the years lead to damages such as the vinegar syndrome (due to the breakdown of cellulose acetate in early tapes) and the sticky shed syndrome (due to hydrolysis in polyester-based tapes from the 1960s onwards). The standard procedure in archives is to sort out the damaged tapes immediately after arrival, restore the unharmed ones and digitise them, which creates another challenge. Even when all the tapes of a composer are available, the identification of tapes belonging to one composition can be difficult due to sketchy indications on labels or a lack of inventories. Many production tapes are overlooked, because they are not labelled. The only solution is to listen to all the tapes of a specific collection[4] – and also: to listen to them in full length (because of the practice of reusing tapes, which sometimes leaves fragments of earlier recordings at the end of a superimposed passage). In short, listening becomes an important part of the research process.

In the analysis of the compositional process of tape music, sketches on paper and sketches on tape should be related to each other. This requires mixed methods and an expansion of traditional sketch studies (e.g., Zattra 2011). Since sketch studies have been historically established with written paper sources, the methodological framework subsequently still largely disregards other media. This, of course, is mainly due to the research focus on music of the 18th and 19th centuries (especially Beethoven), when paper was the main carrier medium for reproduction. Even recent approaches of genetic criticism focus on handwritten paper sources (Appel 2016: 1). But there is also a shift from this emphasis due to the change of the notion of a musical text and the improvements of analytical tools. In the process of relinquishing the bias of understanding the "work" of music solely as (written) "text", all music information on traditional and non-traditional support materials such as magnetic tape, LPs, CDs and digital devices are considered a "musical text" (De Benedictis and Scaldaferri 2009: 82f.). Monographic studies of the music of the late 20th and 21st centuries strengthen this perspective by examining other technical means like floppy discs and software. Parallel to this change of the ontological understanding, the analysis of non-written sources has profited from a growing field of performance and popular music studies and from aural analysis in research on instrumental and electroacoustic music (e.g., Couprie 2016; Bonardi et al. 2017; Sudo 2021; Battier 2022). Furthermore, audio-visual documentations are crucial to empirical

---

4   In certain cases, the sources are also accessible for computer analysis, in which the identification is supported through automated processes and search algorithms (see e.g., Grill 2012).

studies of the creative process of both electronic and popular music (Donin 2012; Acquavella-Rauch 2020). All in all, this expansion of the focus concerning the materiality of sources has contributed to a wider understanding of what constitutes a creative process.

Based on this short methodological outline, this article will now explore specific working practices, in which writing on paper and recording on tape play specific roles. Three examples show different relations between sketches on paper and on tape: 1) The separation of the two sketching practices (Bebe Barron and Earle Brown, respectively) 2) The interdependences of paper and tape sketches (Edgard Varèse) 3) Paper sketches supplementing the understanding of tracks on tape (Iannis Xenakis).

Separation of two Sketching Practices: Earle Brown's *Octet* (1952–53)

Earle Brown created the piece *Octet* for 8-track tape in a specific work environment: The so-called *Project for Music for Magnetic Tape* (1951–54) was initiated by John Cage, who had tried for some time to establish a centre for experimental music with infrastructure for experiments with electronic music. In 1951, Cage convinced the architect and arts patron Paul Williams to finance the production of tape music within the project that he was going to conceive and organise together with David Tudor (Austin 2004: 193). Around the same time Cage and Tudor met the couple Bebe and Louis Barron, who had acquired an AEG tape recorder in 1948 and installed a studio in their apartment in Greenwich Village in New York in 1950. In this studio the Barrons would later create the iconic soundtrack for the science-fiction film *Forbidden Planet* (1956). Cage and Tudor approached them to work as sound engineers for the *Project for Music for Magnetic Tape*. They were hired to collect and record a library of six categories of sounds: "city sounds", "country sounds", "electronic sounds", "manually produced sounds", "wind-produced sounds" and "small sounds (requiring amplification)". The Barrons also created their own tape composition *For an Electronic Nervous System No. 1*, which was premiered in March 1953 as part of the Festival for Contemporary Arts at the University of Illinois, Urbana, together with new tape works by Christian Wolff, Cage and Brown (Austin 2004: 193).[5] Conceived initially as a creative partnership, Cage eventually preferred

---

5   The pieces premiered in the concert were *Williams Mix* (1951–53) by John Cage, *For Magnetic Tape* (1952) by Christian Wolff, *Octet* (1952–53) by Earle Brown and *For an Electronic Nervous System No. 1* (1954) by Louis and Bebe Barron. Two further compositions, *Imaginary Landscape No. 5* (1952) by Cage and *Intersection* (1953) by Morton Feldman, were created in the course of the project.

a decentralised model with a clear separation of labour (Iverson 2021). Whilst the Barrons contributed the sounds on tape, Cage, Brown, Feldman and Wolff elaborated scores, which Cage, Tudor and Brown realised later, spending hours cutting and splicing the tapes.

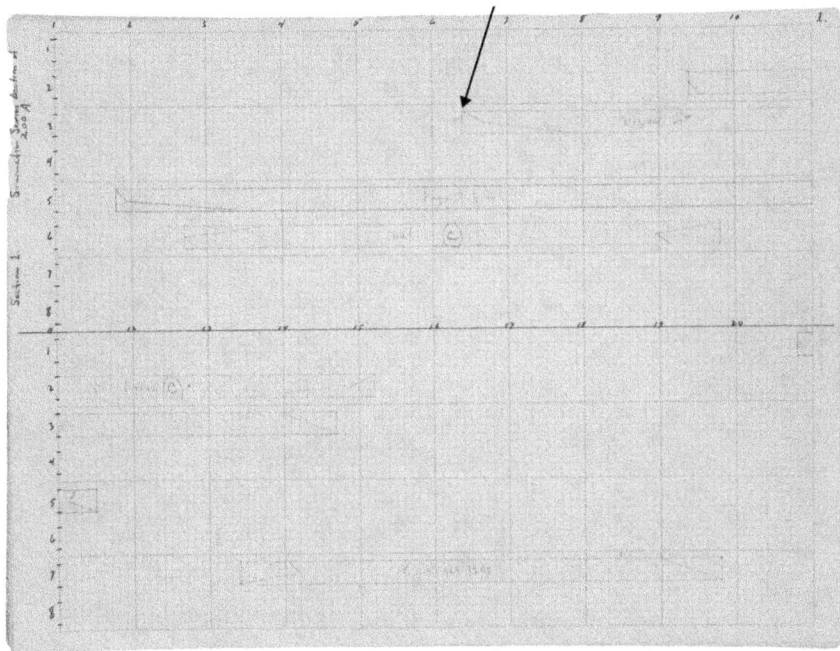

Figure 3.1: *Earle Brown, Octet, score, p. 1, Paul Sacher Stiftung, Earle Brown Collection. Annotation by the author.*

Even if the project was designed as an uneven partnership, both parts of the creative process need to be investigated in order to understand the making of these early tape pieces: the recording and combination of the sounds on tape by the Barrons and the scores and realisation by the four composers. However, the example of Octet by Earle Brown shows that an appropriate study of both processes is nigh on impossible due to an imbalance of documentation. The creative process of the Barrons to date can only be interpreted based on testimonies of the protagonists due to a lack of access to tapes and paper sources,[6]

---

6   This might change in the near future, as the Barron Electronic Music Archive is currently in the process of being digitised and made available for research.

whereas the composition of Brown is documented with a substantial number of sketches on paper preserved in the archive of the Paul Sacher Stiftung in Basel. Both of these processes are worth considering in an analysis of the creative process of the piece.

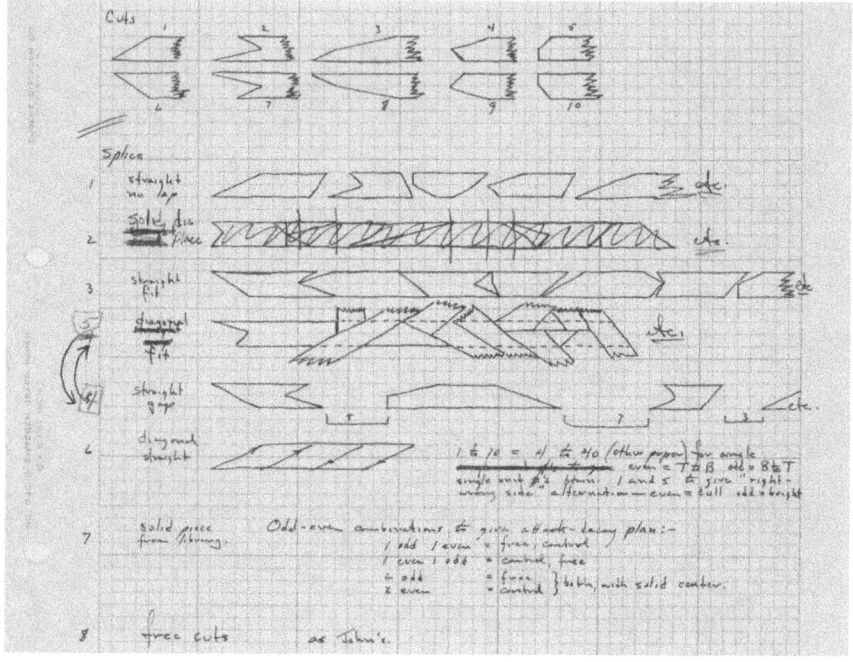

Figure 3.2: *Earle Brown, Octet, detail of "Tape Score 8 Tracks (?)", Paul Sacher Stiftung, Earle Brown Collection.*

The working practices of the Barrons were built on substantial musical and technical experience. Both had a background in music: Bebe had studied piano and composition at Minneapolis University; Louis had been a music student at the University of Chicago. After using their recording equipment to publish audiobooks with "Sound Portraits" of Anaïs Nin, Aldous Huxley and Henry Miller, they soon realised that the tape recorder could be more than a device for recording sound. It could also be a creative tool to obtain unheard sounds by manipulating and reversing tapes and varying the playback speed (Brend 2012: 54). Later on, inspired by Norbert Wiener's cybernetics, Louis built electronic circuits. By deliberately overloading them, the couple created new sounds, thus introducing a random element into their electronic music. Bebe was responsible for the compositional task, she listened to the tapes, then selected and combined the sounds (Eichenberger 2019: 43). For the *Project for Music for Magnetic Tape*, the Barrons created field recordings and collections of sounds according to the specifications of the composers (Straebel 2012: 108). In the process of restoring *Williams Mix*, one of Cage's pieces created during the project, Larry Austin identified the "city sounds" as traffic noise punctuated by car horns, the "country sounds" as recordings of birds, crickets and frogs, the "electronic sounds" as high and low sine and pulse waves, the "manually produced sounds" as jazz piano and the "wind-produced sounds" as human voices (singing as well as spoken words, e.g., from film scenes with Humphrey Bogart). The "small sounds" were the most difficult to identify (Austin 2004: 209).

In contrast to the Barrons' field recordings on tape, Brown's composition was created on paper. In a score of 151 pages he defined the length and position of the sounds and the specific cutting and splicing techniques to be used for each of them (see Figure 3.1). A sketch indicates ten different cuts and eight different splices (see Figure 3.2). For the choice of the tapes from the Barrons' library he essentially followed a recycling procedure; he used the tape scraps left over from the work of the other composers. The sketches and notes stored in the composer's archive at the Paul Sacher Stifting bring to light the use of statistic procedures for defining the points of entrance of the sounds during the total time span of 3,000 seconds (divided into 30 sections of 100 seconds each) and their specific characteristics (length, cuts and splices). Brown stated in a description of the piece that the construction was "based on a 'Table of Random Sampling Numbers'[7] such as those used in experimental scientific work" (quoted after a description of the *Octet* without title in the Earle Brown Collection). The specific sets of numbers determining each individual sound can be found in long lists. For example, the series "1, 3, 6, 5, 4(2), 8, 5, 8, 6" defines a sound on page 1 in track 3 (marked with an arrow in Figure 3.1). After the indication of the page (1) and the track (3), the subsequent numbers specify the starting point (at the fifth tenth of second number 6), the approximate overall duration (4 × 2 seconds), the specific ending point (before the eighth tenth of second number 14), the splice (no. 5 = "diagonal fit", see Figure 3.2), and the cuts for attack and decay (cuts 8 and 6 = broken and straight diagonals, see Figure 3.2). On the basis of this specific cutting and splicing plan, Cage, Tudor and Brown realised the tape composition using what was left over from the tapes

---

7   Brown used Maurice George Kendalls and Babington Smiths *Tables of Random Sampling Numbers* (published by Cambridge University Press in 1951) in the compositional process of *Octet*, *Twenty-Five Pages* (1953) and *Indices* (1954).

that the Barrons had created for the *Project for Music for Magnetic Tape*. Overall, the creative process was divided into sound production (a sound library realised on tape by the Barrons), composition on paper (a precise plan by Brown) and the production of the tapes (the cutting and splicing of tape by Cage, Tudor and Brown). It gave rise to a piece with extreme textural variety and density of sounds, which are perceived as subtle noise changes.

Interdependences of Paper and Tape Sketches: Edgard Varèse's *Déserts* (1952–54)

Figure 3.3: *Edgard Varèse at the Ampex tape recorder, Paul Sacher Stiftung, Edgard Varèse Collection.*

For Edgard Varèse the search for new technologies to create music was a long and arduous path: Already in 1916, he told a journalist that he was looking for "new mechanical mediums which [would] lend themselves to every expression of thought and keep up with thought" (Varèse 1916: 6). Till the mid-century, his search for new sound resources was a long succession of disappointments and failed collaborations. In spring 1953, his situation changed when he got a tape recorder thanks to the support of the painter and doctor Alfred L. Copley (see Meyer 2006: 332). The Ampex 401 was installed in his studio in the spring of 1953 (see Figure 3.3) and Varèse started to record sounds in factories, sawmills, churches and on the street. He used these sounds for the tape interpolations of *Déserts* for winds, piano, percussion and tape (1952–54), but also for two short pieces of music he produced for the film *Around and about Miró* (1955) by Thomas Bouchard and for the *Poème Electronique* (1958). *Déserts* was premiered at the Théâtre des Champs-Elysées in Paris, and the tape interpolations prompted the famous scandal – not least due to the programme placement between Mozart's overture in B-flat and Tchaikovsky's *Symphonie Pathétique* in a regular concert series.

The tape part of *Déserts* has an eventful history: Varèse finished the first interpolation and a part of the second one in New York with the assistance of the sound engineer and composer Ann McMillan. He was then invited by Pierre Schaeffer to work at the GRMC (Groupe de Recherches de Musique Concrète/ Studio d'Essai) in Paris, where he finished the second and created the third interpolation. After the premiere, Varèse altered the interpolations several times, first in Paris at the GRMC just after the premiere, presumably in 1958 in the Philips Studios in Holland while working on the *Poème*, and finally in 1960 at the Columbia-Princeton Electronic Music Center – creating "one of the most complex" corpora of audio sources in the history of electronic music (Cossettini 2017: 112).

The sources of the interpolations of *Déserts* stored in the Paul Sacher Stiftung and the Library of Congress show the interdependences of sketches on different carriers.[8] The steps documented on tape comprehend the collection of sounds, their subsequent manipulation (especially in the third interpolation) and the process of revision. Varèse recorded different categories of sound: instrumental sounds (organ, flute, percussion) and environmental noises (machines in factories or traffic). Some of the remaining production tapes store collections of these sounds: the organ in the Church of Saint Mary the Virgin in New York, a percussion ensemble, noises from factories like Westinghouse, Disston, and Budd Manufacturers (tapes TS 42–44, 46–47, 51, 1001, 1003, 1010, 1016, 1018–19, 1038–39, 5008). Some drafts on paper defining the volume levels of the first and the third interpolation are connected to the sketching process on tape (see Figure 3.4). They indicate not only the variety of sounds used, but also show Varèse's sound descriptions like "wailing" or "stuttering" including

---

8   Considering the high amount of analysis of the piece, it is startling that the sketches on tape have been examined only once in the analysis of the compositional process and only partially (Vernooij 2013: 153–157).

references to the origin of the sounds like "riveting" and "steam hammer". On the first page, for example, the term "swishing" refers to one of the factory noises that is dominant in the first interpolation. These noises are combined with instrumental sounds like percussion (track 1 in blue at the beginning) or flute (track 1 in blue at second 20).

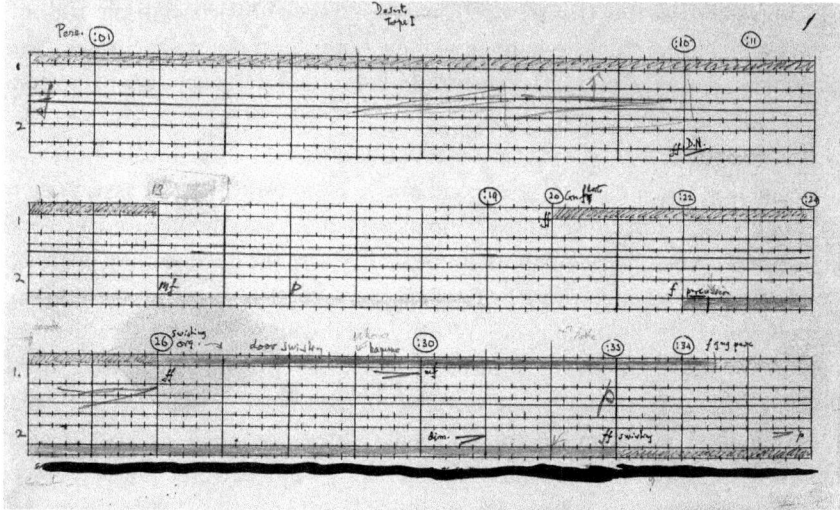

Figure 3.4: *Edgard Varèse,* Déserts, *form plan of the first tape interpolation, Paul Sacher Stiftung, Edgard Varèse Collection.*

The tapes show the composer's special interest in this new medium, but also reveal parallels between the compositional procedures for tape and those for the instrumental parts of *Déserts*. Varèse created motivic connections inside the instrumental part by carefully integrating rhythmic cells of the percussion into the parts for wind instruments (see Ziegler 2022). He also wrote sections for percussion for the interpolations, recorded them and subtly combined them with the tape sounds of different origins. To sum up, the tape and paper sketches document compositional approaches connected to the new medium and show his general artistic concerns at the time: The integration and organic combination of noises and instrumental sounds. Hence, the sketching on tape and paper has to be considered in connection with the general compositional practices, techniques and aesthetics of the composer.

Paper Sketches Supplementing the Tapes:
Iannis Xenakis's *Bohor* (1962)

Iannis Xenakis already had substantial experiences as a composer of electronic music when he composed *Bohor* for 8-track tape in the professional studio of the GRM (Groupe de recherches musicales) in Paris. *Bohor* has been listed as the first 8-track composition of the GRM. However, it was still too early for it to be realised on 8-track tape, as 8-track tape machines were not available yet, so Xenakis used four stereo tape machines and created four stereo tapes. The composition portrays a "single, slowly evolving gesture" (Harley 2002: 39) and the entries of sounds are most likely conceived not by mathematical calculations but through close listening (Gibson 2015: 88). Xenakis's approach shaped the piece's historically novel sound characteristics, and it can be traced back to the sketches on tape and paper.

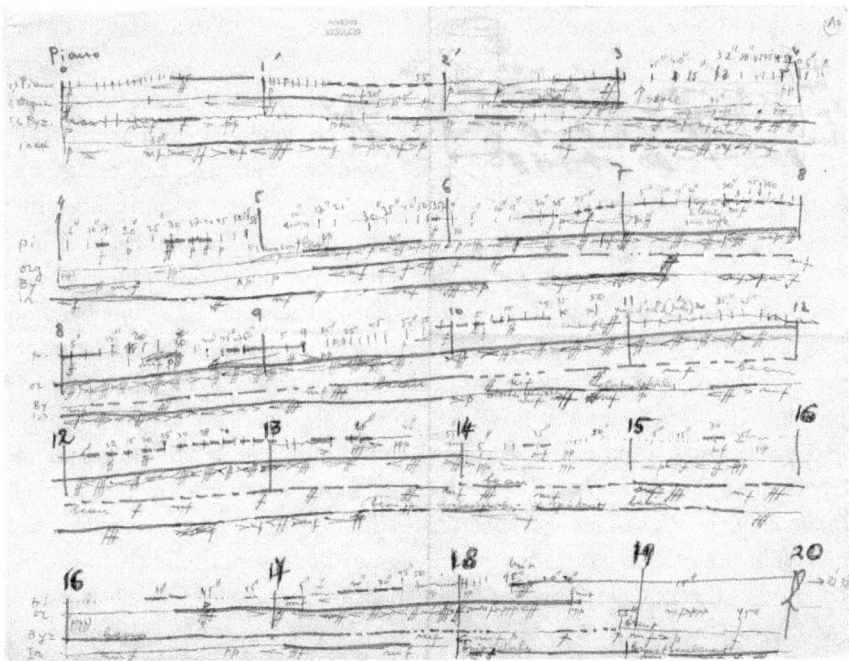

Figure 3.5: *Iannis Xenakis,* Bohor, *scheme, Collection Famille Xenakis DR, OM 33–11, p. 10.*

The sketches on paper in the archives of the Collection Famille Xenakis in Paris show two concerns that support the interpretations of the sources on tape. The first one is the use of recorded sounds of four different origins and the subsequent manipulation of them. Xenakis called the four tracks of the piece "piano", "orgue", "Byzantium" and "Irak" (see Figure 3.5). Reinhold Friedl has revealed that these terms may indicate the source of the sounds, but the piano might be a piano-tige, the organ is certainly not an organ but a Laotian mouth organ, etc. He argued that most likely Xenakis didn't use a piano for the sounds of the first stereo tracks, but a Baschet instrument called piano-tige; those were instruments that were frequently used at the GRM at the time (Friedl 2019: 88). The label "organ" refers to Laotian mouth organ material; "Byzantium" and "Irak", mostly to sounds of jewellery and bracelets from those countries and often bell-like sounds. Xenakis then manipulated the sounds: He transposed them by changing the playback speed of the tape machine, layered them and used echo, reverberation and filters in order to create a dense, constantly shifting sound environment. It allows the listeners to be immersed in sounds. In his scheme we can see the nuances of volume that Xenakis determined for the four tracks (see Figure 3.5).

The second aspect of note is the spatialisation, which was a concern in the whole creative process and led to new adaptations for performances in different concert halls (see Gibson 2015: 95). While working with Le Corbusier to create the pavilion for the 1958 Brussels World's Fair and the "sound routes" that were built for Varèse's *Poème électronique* and Xenakis's *Concret PH* with over 400 loudspeakers, Xenakis had experienced the possibilities of sound spatialisation by electronic means first hand. In *Bohor*, the space as a compositional parameter is already considered in the choice of the aural characterisations of the four stereo tracks. The positions of the loudspeakers and the distribution of the eight tracks in concert halls is then carefully arranged. Although the scheme in the performance material of Éditions Salabert indicates that the stereophonic tracks are to be placed opposite each other, some sketches show that Xenakis made changes for some concerts after the first performance (see Figures 3.6a and 3.6b), adopting a circular or rectangular arrangement of the channels distributed to the loudspeakers. The spatial distribution of the channels is part of the interpretation, it has to be adapted in each performance of the piece according to the shape and the specific acoustics of a concert hall. By providing a range of different possibilities, the sketches of Xenakis's own solutions give insights for the interpretation of the tape sources.

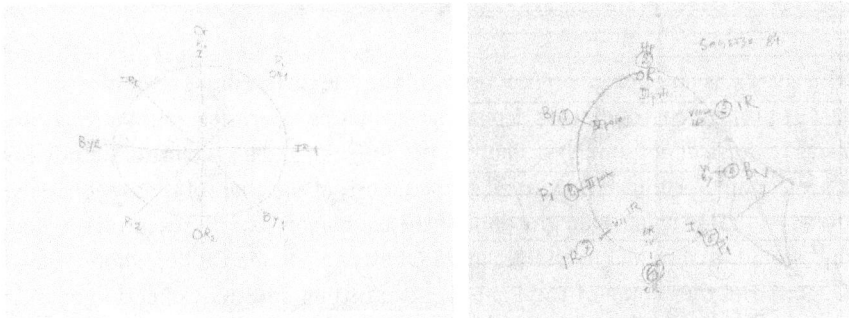

Figures 3.6a and 3.6b: Iannis Xenakis, Bohor, *spatialisation sketches, Collection Famille Xenakis DR, OM 33–11, p. 6v, p. 14.*

Conclusion: Expanded Sketch Studies and the Laboratories of Early Tape Music

The inquiry into the compositional processes of tape music requires an approach that considers sources on tape and on paper. Listening, in this procedure, becomes a more important part of the analytical toolbox and complements the traditional reading of written sources. The sources then have to be interpreted in the context of the compositional practices of the composer at a certain time, which reveals, for example in the case of Varèse and Xenakis, new procedures due to the new medium of the tape, but also their general interests and habits both for instrumental and for electronic music at a certain time. Finally, this again has to be put into perspective by considering the specific projects or studios in their "manifold networks" (Goldman, Gribenski and Romão 2020: 641). The example of Brown shows that the composers had to adapt to the working procedures and the specific equipment; they aligned their own ideas with the given aesthetic, technical and structural setting of certain work environments. By opening the perspective from the sources to individual creative actors and to networks of actors, we get a glimpse of the full scope of the new artistic processes based on the technical reproduction of sound on tape. The proposition for expanded sketch studies, therefore, aims at an integrated approach to sketches on different carriers. It enquires into the studio as a working environment and into collective working practices. The goal is to understand the creation of early tape music as a heterogenous activity in a network of actors: a dynamic laboratory of sound.

* * *

This article is an outcome of my research on the materiality of notation in the DACH project *Writing Music. Iconic, performative, operative, and material aspects in musical notation(s)* at Paul Sacher Stiftung and a preparatory study for a project on tape music continued subsequently at the chair of History of Technology at ETH Zurich. I am grateful for the exchanges in both research projects and would further like to thank Simon Obert, Angela Ida De Benedictis, David Gugerli and the teams of the Paul Sacher Stiftung and the Collection Famille Xenakis for their support.

Bibliography

Acquavella-Rauch, Stefanie (2020) "Musikalische Schaffensprozesse 2.0 – Inkorporation audiovisueller Medien der populären Musik in Methoden der digitalen Edition", in *Brückenschläge zwischen Musikwissenschaft und Informatik. Theoretische und praktische Aspekte der Kooperation*, ed. by Stefanie Acquavella-Rauch, Andreas Münzmay, and Joachim Veit (Musikwissenschaft: Aktuelle Perspektiven. Bericht über die Jahrestagung der Gesellschaft für Musikforschung 2019 in Paderborn und Detmold 3), 115–122; https://doi.org/10.25366/2020.101 (accessed December 11, 2022).

Appel, Bernhard R. (2017) "Beethovens Werkstatt. Genetische Textkritik und Digitale Musikedition", in *Wege der Musikwissenschaft. Beiträge zum Internationalen Kongress der Gesellschaft für Musikforschung 2016*, ed. by Gabriele Buschmeier and Klaus Pietschmann, Mainz: Schott Campus; https://schott-campus.com/beethovens_werkstatt (accessed December 11, 2022).

Assis, Paulo de (2017) "Gilbert Simondon's 'Transduction' as Radical Immanence in Performance", in *Performance Philosophy* 3/3, 695–716.

Austin, Larry (2004) "John Cage's Williams Mix (1951-3): the restoration and new realisations of and variations on the first octophonic, surround-sound tape composition", in *A Handbook to Twentieth-Century Musical Sketches*, ed. by Patricia Hall and Friedemann Sallis, Cambridge: Cambridge University Press, 189–213.

Battier, Marc (2022) "Analyzing Electronic Music. Uncovering the Original Conditions of Production", in *Teaching Electronic Music. Cultural, Creative, and Analytical Perspectives*, ed. by Blake Stevens, New York: Routledge, 58–74.

Bohlman Andrea F., and McMurray, Peter (2017) "Tape: Or, Rewinding the Phonographic Regime", in: *Twentieth-Century Music* 14/1, 3–24.

Bonardi, Alain, Bossis, Bruno, Couprie, Pierre, and Tiffon, Vincent (2017) *Analyser la musique mixte*, Sampzon: Éditions Delatour France.

Born, Georgina (2021) "On Genre, History, and Invention in the Analysis of Creative Processes in Music", in *The Oxford Handbook of the Creative Process in Music*, ed. by Nicolas Donin, 1–24; https://doi.org/10.1093/oxfordhb/978 0190636197.013.4, (accessed December 11, 2022).

Brend, Mark (2012) *The Sound of Tomorrow. How Electronic Music was Smuggled into the Mainstream*, New York: Bloomsbury.

Celestini, Federico, Nanni, Matteo, Obert, Simon, and Urbanek, Nikolaus (2020) "Zu einer Theorie der musikalischen Schrift. Materiale, operative, ikonische und performative Aspekte musikalischer Notationen", in *Musik und Schrift. Interdisziplinäre Perspektiven auf musikalische Notationen*, ed. by Carolin Ratzinger, Nikolaus Urbanek, and Sophie Zehetmayer, Paderborn: Wilhelm Fink (Theorie der musikalischen Schrift 1), 1–50.

Cossettini, Luca (2017) "Tracks in the deserts. Studying the electronic music by Edgard Varèse", in *Sounds, Voices and Codes from the Twentieth Century. The critical editing of music at Mirage*, ed. by Luca Cossettini and Angelo Orcalli, Mirage: University of Udine, 109–136.

Cossettini, Luca, and Orcalli, Angelo, eds., (2017) *Sounds, Voices and Codes from the Twentieth Century. The critical editing of music at Mirage*, Mirage: University of Udine.

Couprie, Pierre (2016) "L'analyse de la musique mixte: vers une redéfinition des 'workflows' en musicologie", in *Regards sur les musiques mixtes*, ed. by Marc Battier, Paris: INA (Portraits Polychromes 23), 231–247.

De Benedictis, Angela Ida (2004) "Scrittura e supporti nel novecento. Alcune riflessioni e un esempio ('Ausstrahlung' di Bruno Maderna)", in *La scrittura come rappresentazione del pensiero musicale*, ed. by Gianmario Borio, Pisa: ETS, 237–291.

De Benedictis, Angela Ida, and Scaldaferri, Nicola (2009) "Le nuove testualità musicali", in *La Filologia Musicale: Istituzioni, Storia, Strumenti Critici*, vol. II, ed. by Maria Caraci Vela, Lucca: Libreria Musicale Italiana, 71–116.

Donin Nicolas (2012) "Empirical and Historical Musicologies of Compositional Processes: Towards a Cross-fertilisation", in *The Act of Musical Composition – Studies in the Creative Process*, ed. by Dave Collins, Farnham: Ashgate, 1–26.

Eichenberger Tatiana (2019) "Wie klang die Zukunft? Forbidden Planet und der Einzug elektroakustischer Klänge in den Science-Fiction-Film der 1950er Jahre", in *Lied und populäre Kultur. Jahrbuch des Zentrums für Populäre Kultur und Musik* 64, ed. by Knut Holtsträter, Tarek Krohn, Nina Noeske, and Willem Strank, Münster/New York: Waxmann, 31–48.

Friedl, Reinhold (2019) "Performances in Iannis Xenakis's electroacoustic music", in *Exploring Xenakis. Performance, Practice, Philosophy*, ed. by Alfia Nakipbekova, Delaware: Vernon Press, 69–87.

Gibson, Benoît (2015) "A propos de Bohor (1962) de Iannis Xenakis", in *Iannis Xenakis, La Musique électroacoustique, Proceedings of the International Symposium 23–25 May 2012*, ed. by Makis Solomos, Paris: HAL, 83–96.

Goldman, Jonathan, Gribenski, Fanny, and Romão, João (2020) "A Connected History and Geography of Studios", in *Contemporary Music Review* 39/6, 639–647.

Grill, Thomas, (2012) *Perceptually Informed Organization of Textural Sounds*, PhD thesis, University of Music and Performing Arts Vienna.

Harley, James (2002) "The Electroacoustic Music of Iannis Xenakis", in *Computer Music Journal* 26/1 (In memoriam Iannis Xenakis), Cambridge: MIT, 33–57.

Iverson, Jennifer (2021) "Unstable Modernism in the Barron Studio", in *Modernism/modernity* 6/2; https://doi.org/10.26597/mod.0215 (accessed December 11, 2022).

Krämer, Sybille (2009) "Operative Bildlichkeit. Von der 'Grammatologie' zu einer 'Diagrammatologie'? Reflexionen über erkennendes Sehen", in *Logik des Bildlichen. Zur Kritik der ikonischen Vernunft*, ed. by Martina Hessler and Dieter Mersch, Bielefeld: transcript, 94–123.

Magnusson, Thor (2019) *Sonic Writing. Technologies of Material, Symbolic, and Signal Inscriptions*, London/New York: Bloomsbury Academic.

Manning, Peter (2006) "The significance of techné in understanding the art and practice of electroacoustic composition", in *Organized Sound* 11(1), 81–90.

Meyer, Felix (2006) "Varèse and his tape recorder", in *Edgard Varèse. Composer, Sound Sculptor, Visionary*, ed. by Felix Meyer and Heidy Zimmermann, Woodbridge: Boydell & Brewer, 332.

Mooney, Mark, ed. (1953) *Tape & Film Recording*, 1/1.

Münnich, Stefan (2019) *Musikalische Schrift und ihre Codes. Studien zu Genese, Theorie und Digitalität einer Wechselbeziehung*, PhD thesis, University of Basel.

Pasdzierny, Matthias (2019) "Tonband, Partitur, Aufführung: Medien- und musikphilologische Überlegungen zur Edition von Bernd Alois Zimmermanns Requiem für einen jungen Dichter", in *Aufführung und Edition*, ed. by Thomas Betzwieser and Markus Schneider, Berlin/Boston: De Gruyter, 217–232.

Ratzinger, Carolin (2023) "Complex Relations. Reflections on the operativity of writing music", in *Musikalische Schreibszenen / Scenes of Musical Writing*, ed. by Federico Celestini and Sarah Lutz, Paderborn: Wilhelm Fink (Theorie der musikalischen Schrift 4), 231–248.

Schuiling, Floris, and Payne, Emily, eds. (2022) *Material Cultures of Music Notation. New Perspectives on Musical Inscription*, London/New York: Routledge (Music and Material Culture 1).

Straebel, Volker (2012) "The Studio as a Venue of Production and Performance: Cage's Early Tape Music", in *Cage & Consequences*, ed. by Julia H. Schröder and Volker Straebel, Hofheim: Wolke, 101–109.

Sudo, Marina (2021) *The Nature of Noise. An Aural Analytical Inquiry of Noise in Contemporary Musical Practice: Xenakis, Lachenmann, Ablinger and Merzbow*, PhD thesis, Katholieke Universiteit Leuven.

Varèse, Edgard (1916) interview, "Composer Varèse to Give New York Abundance of Futuristic Music", in *New York Review* (March 11, 1916), 6.

Vernooij, Eveline (2013) *L'organizzazione del suono in Déserts di Edgard Varèse. Implicazioni analitiche di una critica delle fonti*, PhD thesis, Università degli studi di Udine.

Zattra, Laura (2011) *Studiare la computer music: definizioni, analisi, fonti*, Padua: Libreria Universitaria.

Ziegler, Michelle (2022) "Material – Prozess – Werkkontext. Eine Skizze zu Edgard Varèses Déserts", in *Mitteilungen der Paul Sacher Stiftung 35*, 36–41.

List of Figures

Figure 3.1: Earle Brown, Octet, score, p. 1, Paul Sacher Stiftung, Earle Brown Collection. Annotation by the author.

Figure 3.2: Earle Brown, Octet, detail of "Tape Score 8 Tracks (?)", Paul Sacher Stiftung, Earle Brown Collection.

Figure 3.3: Edgard Varèse at the Ampex tape recorder, Paul Sacher Stiftung, Edgard Varèse Collection.

Figure 3.4: Edgard Varèse, Déserts, form plan of the first tape interpolation, Paul Sacher Stiftung, Edgard Varèse Collection.

Figure 3.5: Iannis Xenakis, Bohor, scheme, Collection Famille Xenakis DR, OM 33–11, p.10.

Figures 3.6a and 3.6b: Iannis Xenakis, Bohor, spatialisation sketches, Collection Famille Xenakis DR, OM 33–11, p. 6v, p. 14.

Synchronising Different Temporalities
A Challenge of Writing in *Musique Mixte* from 1958 to 1960

Elena Minetti

"Writing is historically the first technique for manipulating time"[1] (Kittler 1993: 183; English translation in Krämer 2006: 99). With this phrase, Friedrich Kittler considered writing to be the earliest technique for arranging and reversing events happening on the time axis. In this view, writing is a practice that has the potential to (re)order streams of data through spatial coordinates on two-dimensional surfaces. For this theoretical assumption, Kittler gives a practical explanation, drawn precisely from musical writing practice: He quotes the use of a retrograde of the 'Bach motif' – consisting of the notes B flat, A, C, B natural (in German musical nomenclature: B A C H) – which appears in the Fugue BWV 898 as the reversal of the composer's name (H C A B) (Kittler 1993: 185).

Transferring these considerations to a musicological perspective, musical inscriptions constitute lasting manifestations of ephemeral phenomena progressing in time which, by virtue of being written, can be simultaneously visualised, correlated at a glance and also manipulated and rearranged, as in the 'Bach motif' example (see Krämer 2006; Celestini et al. 2020).

Building on these ideas, this essay focuses on a central function of musical notations, which is closely related to writing's capacity to manipulate and visualise time: The synchronisation of musical events – an issue that in standard western notation, for example, has been encoded through the vertical superposition of simultaneous musical voices. More concretely, this study investigates how writing practices aimed at synchronising sounds became particularly complex and challenging for the composers when recorded electroacoustic sounds entered instrumental performance.

Indeed, in the so-called *musique mixte*, whose first experiments can be traced back to the early 1950s, (at least) two different temporalities coexist: on

---

1   "Als historisch erste solcher Zeitmanipulationstechniken hat selbstredend die Schrift figuriert". (Kittler 1993: 183).

the one hand, the temporality of the live concert, on the other hand, the temporality of the previously recorded track resounding through loudspeakers. A definition of *musique mixte* – a term that is quite nebulous and can be misleading (Sallis et al. 2018: 5–7) – is proposed by Vincent Tiffon in his doctoral thesis (Tiffon 1994) and later in numerous articles (id. 2005, 2013):

> [Musique mixte] is concert music that combines instruments of acoustic origin with sounds of electronic origin, the latter produced in real time – during the concert – or fixed on electronic media and projected via loudspeakers at the time of the concert. (Tiffon 2005: 23)

The definition focuses on the combination of acoustic instruments played at the time of the performance and sounds of electronic origin that can be produced live or can be recorded and played back during the concert. *Musique mixte* in its early form, which combines live musicians with pre-recorded electronic parts, confronts the coexistence of a temporality produced in the past and recorded once and for all and a temporality alive and produced during the concert. Certainly, when a pre-recorded music resonates in performance it becomes alive again, yet the productive origin of that part will remain anchored to a past musical phenomenon.

Having in mind the etymological meaning of the verb 'to synchronise' – that is from the Ancient Greek συγχρονίζω, which literally means 'to be contemporary with, to be at the same time of' – the title of this paper might sound oxymoronic. Synchronising indicates indeed that two or more phenomena have to happen together, as the prefix *syn-* specifies, in a single *chronos*, in a unified temporality (see Jordheim 2017: 59). The phrase 'synchronising different temporalities' intends to underscore the challenge of writing to coordinate musical phenomena that are produced at different times and which then, however, coexist in the performance and in the performance score, too.

The synchronisation of the electronic and acoustic dimensions of *musique mixte* is an issue that scholars studying this genre must inevitably address (Cont 2012; Scaldaferri 2002; Blondeau 2017). This essay proposes to identify by comparative analysis some essential features of the composers' writing strategies to accomplish the task of making the synchronisation of musical temporalities visible. This topic will be examined by comparing the published scores of four *musique mixte* works, composed between 1958 and 1960: *Analogique A et B* (1958–59) by Iannis Xenakis, *Rimes* (1958–59) by Henri Pousseur, *Transición II* (1958–59) by Mauricio Kagel, and *Kontakte* (1958–60) by Karlheinz Stockhausen.[2]

---

2   Tiffon identifies three configurations of *musique mixte*: C+: *musique mixte* in the strict sense, i.e., that which combines instrumentalists with parts recorded

The writing strategies adopted in the four scores will be highlighted, taking into consideration the compositional experiences and aesthetic motivations that led to the creation of these works. Some archival materials show how the hybrid configuration of sound production in the *mixte* ensembles had a great impact on the forms of writing used during the compositional process and also during the preparation of the performance, which was sometimes closely followed by the composers themselves. In the final performance scores, composers were faced with the challenge of how to annotate the human interaction with a recorded sound reality, which is (generally) static and only capable of a non-human, machine-like form of interaction.

At the end of the 1950s, there were no standardised rules involved in finding a form of writing for coordinating the live performance with the delayed time of "fixed sounds" – to use the term coined by Michel Chion (Chion 1991) – and/or recordings during the performance, and that left some space for composers' notational and graphical creativity. Among the works considered, some of their performance scores contain minimal synchronisation instructions, while others use various notational forms, including actual transcriptions of recorded events. To macroscopically classify these differences, the concept of density is used as a parameter indicating the amount of information related to the synchronisation of instrumental and electroacoustic parts. Scores such as Xenakis's *Analogique* A et B and Kagel's *Transición II* show how the synchronising function of music writing can be expressed through a few essential notational signs, that is, through a low density of instructions. Instead, the scores by Pousseur for *Rimes* and by Stockhausen for *Kontakte* use more detailed graphic and notational strategies.

---

in advance; C*: *musique mixte* which associates instrumentalists with electronic parts in real time, and finally, C+*: a combination of the previous two types: *musique mixte* in which the instrumentalists are associated with both previously recorded and live electronic parts. In the abbreviations the letter C stands for 'concert', the cross (+) for electronic parts recorded in advance and the asterisk (*) for electronic parts in real time. (Tiffon 2005: 23f.) The compositions by Xenakis, Pousseur and Stockhausen are ascribable to the configuration of *musique mixte* in the strict sense, which combines instrumentalists with parts recorded in advance. Besides live musicians, *Transición II* by Mauricio Kagel includes recordings made in advance and recordings made during the performance.

Synchronising through a Low Density of Notational Inscriptions

Analogique A et B by Xenakis

As the title suggests, *Analogique A et B* is a twofold piece, also in the compositional genesis of its two parts: The instrumental one for nine string instruments, indicated with the title *Analogique A*, was composed in 1958, while the electronic one, *Analogique B* for sinusoidal sounds, was produced one year later, first in a monophonic format during the summer of 1958 at Hermann Scherchen's studio in Gravesano, and then with a stereophonic disposition of loudspeakers at the studio of the GRM (Groupe de Recherches Musicales) in Paris (Harley 2004: 17). *Analogique A et B* results from the superposition of the two compositions and was premiered in this final configuration in June 1960 at the Festival de la Recherche, organised by the RTF (Radiodiffusion-Télévision Française) in Paris. As stated in a review by Edmund J. Pendleton for *The New York Herald Tribune*, the title of the concert in which *Analogique A + B*[3] was premiered without great success was *The Return of the Interpreter*, alluding to the performer's "uselessness during mechanical experimentation" (Pendelton 1960). Instead, it proposed compositions that brought the instrumental performers back on stage, letting them interact with recorded parts.

The only published score related to *Analogique A et B* concerns the instrumental part and was published by Éditions Salabert in 1968 under the title *Analogique A: partition d'orchestre*. Despite the absence of a published score-like document for the electronic part, this *partition d'orchestre* contains significant information regarding the relationship between the instrumental and electronic components of the piece. First of all, it is clearly stated in the introduction to the score that "it is highly desirable that [*Analogique A*] should be performed to the accompaniment of the *Analogique B* complementary sound tape" (Xenakis 1968). In the same text, Xenakis describes how in both parts of the work "sounds were chosen statistically in arbitrary ranges of frequency, intensity and density. These ranges change in accordance with the transitional probabilities which follow a series of consequential events (the Markov series)".

Analogique A et B are indeed applications of the Markovian stochastic theory, which is illustrated in detail in the second chapter of his *Musique formelles*

---

3   In the review by Pendleton, the work is referred to as *Analogique A + B* and not *Analogique A et B*, as it is later indicated in the published score of *Analogique A* (Xenakis 1968).

(Xenakis 1963: 57–131). Already in 1954 Xenakis began to use probability distributions in the orchestra piece *Pithoprakta* (1955) and to experiment with probability calculations for musical composition – which two years later he would call "stochastic music" (Luque 2009). In *Analogique A et B* he added to the stochastic distribution of musical events the Markovian theory, "introducing a memory during the chaining of probabilistic states. [...] [The complex reasoning] develops the notion of 'frames', i.e., temporal units defined by the parameters of pitch, duration, dynamics and density, which follow one another by means of Markov processes." (Solomos 2017). In *Analogique B* Xenakis introduced, along with the Markovian stochastic theory, experimentations of his "hypothesis" of the granularity of sound: "All sound is made up of small bodies. Thus a 'grain' of sound can be defined approximately as a sound sinusoidal form and a given intensity which has a duration of the 'thickness of the present'" (Xenakis 1968).

The juxtaposition of the two works was not decided by Xenakis programmatically at the beginning of the compositional process. It happened later. Although the works were conceived with analogous compositional mechanisms, they were thought of as distinct universes – a palpable consideration already at the first listening.[4] Explaining Xenakis's quite sparse production of *musique mixte* – besides *Analogique A et B* this includes only *Kraanerg* (1969) and *Pour la Paix* (1981) – Makis Solomos explains how Xenakis "postulates the autonomy of the universe of electroacoustic music. In this sense, he considers – following Varèse – that mixity [*mixité*] is a very delicate matter, which should be used with restraint."[5] (Solomos 2017: 163). In *Analogique A et B*, it seems indeed that the events on tape are interpolated with the instrumental parts without developing any real fusion, dialogue or transitions. A synchronisation is almost circumvented, even in the musical notation.

The visual configuration of the score clearly manifests the attempt to distinguish the two sonic layers. As can be seen from the reproductions of the score (Figures 4.1 and 4.2), *Analogique A* is written in standard western notation, while the starting points of the electronic interpolations of *Analogique B*

---

4   Listen to the recording of *Analogique A et B* from the CD Ensemble Resonanz (2005) *Xenakis: Works for Strings*, conducted by Johannes Kalitzke (Mode 152). Available also at this link: https://youtu.be/sOGkhekIGzo (accessed October 31, 2022).

5   "Xenakis fait partie des compositeurs qui postulent l'autonomie de l'univers de la musique électroacoustique. Aussi, il ne choisit pas la voie de nombre de compositeurs qui pratiquent de la musique mixte, notamment à partir des années 1980, dans l'idée que l'univers électronique n'est qu'une extension du monde instrumental. En ce sens, il estime – à la suite d'un Varèse – que la mixité est une affaire très délicate, qu'il convient d'utiliser avec parcimonie." (Solomos 2017: 163).

are indicated by arrows and their durations in seconds, a chronometric style of time notation, mostly accompanied by fermatas of the instruments (see Figure 4.1). In the few instances when there is an overlap of the two parts, no actual electronic part is written, but a line represents its presence (see Figure 4.2).

Figure 4.1: *Iannis Xenakis,* Analogique A, *orchestra score, p. 3, detail, Durand Salabert Eschig.*

Not referring specifically to this composition, Vincent Tiffon argues that the principle of interpolations, already previously used by Bruno Maderna in *Musica su due dimensioni* (1952) and by Edgard Varèse in *Déserts* (1954) allows composers to elegantly circumvent the question of synchronisation (Tiffon 1994: 213). The synchronisation of acoustic and electronic dimensions in the early attempts of this genre indeed presented itself as a challenge, yet Xenakis's choice, as brilliantly explained by Agostino Di Scipio, reveals deeper aesthetic motivations than eluding a musical problem:

> The close encounter of the two sonic worlds allows us to make "a sensorial and structural comparison" (Xenakis 1971: 31) of two non-identical manifestations of the same compositional process. The *same* is presented as *different*, projected on different time-scales. [...] In other words, by preserving the surface difference, Xenakis pointed to the manifestation of a more profound identity. (Di Scipio 2005: section 3.8)

In *Analogique A et B* the temporalities of the two universes converge in the listening experience, through remembering what has just been heard and what is being listened to, perhaps leading to the recognition of the same internal logic (i.e., a Markovian stochastic process) that has generated them.

Figure 4.2: *Iannis Xenakis,* Analogique A, *orchestra score, p. 5, detail, Durand Salabert Eschig.*

A need for synchronisation of the two parts is not at the heart of the compositional idea, though. In a sketch, dated "14. oct 63" (thus subsequent to the premiere) Xenakis gives a compact and schematic overview of the interlocking plan between the two parts.

On a millimetre sheet (see Figure 4.3), in addition to sketching a layout (circled) indicating the spatial distribution of the sound sources in the concert hall, Xenakis writes down three synchronisation diagrams of *Analogique A et B*: The first one is crossed out; the second one, only partially sketched, is struck through with a wavy line, and the last is the definitive one and is re-squared. In this diagram the x-axis, in which each millimetre corresponds to one second, represents time. Xenakis provides chronometric indications: six centimetres equal a minute, seconds are given at the beginning and end of each section. Line segments represent the sections of the instrumental part A (the upper lines) and those of the electronic part B (lower lines), which are specified by Roman numerals (I to VIII).[6] This sketch testifies to how, even after the premiere, the synchronisation of the two parts continued to be a significant issue that had to be established, perhaps for future performances of the work, since the music score had not yet been published by Éditions Salabert.

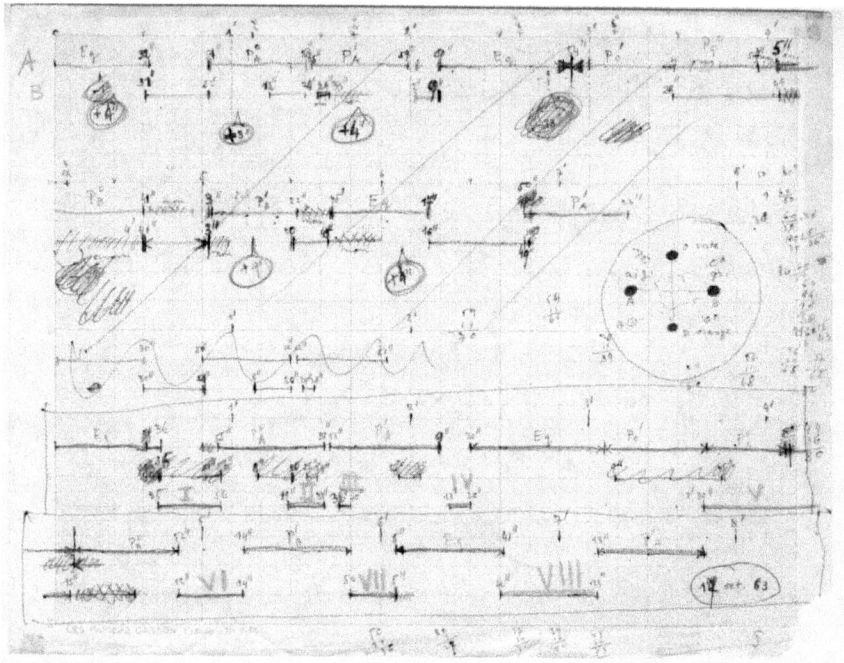

Figure 4.3: *Iannis Xenakis,* Analogique A et B, *sketch, Collection Famille Xenakis DR, OM 5–5, p. 5.*

Transición II by Kagel

Some similarity to *Analogique A et B* concerning the form of writing chosen to fulfil the synchronising function are traced in *Transición II* by Kagel. His encounter with electronic music in autumn of 1957 was for him the introduction to a "new musical time" (Kagel 1962: 15). Working on his first electronic composition *Transición I* for tape, he began "researching some relations between

---

6   As in this sketch, in the score published five years later (1968) the tape sections are indicated by Roman numerals. Section VIII at 33 seconds is, however, no longer present.

musical material and its temporal formation."[7] (ibid.). A reflection on temporality also forms the basis of *Transición II* for piano, percussion and two tapes, which despite the name has no obvious similarity with the previous work.[8]

The score – published by Universal Edition in 1963 – is conceived for a pianist and a percussionist who produces sounds directly on the strings of a grand piano. Some sections must be recorded beforehand (tape 1); some, if the technical conditions can guarantee a satisfactory result, should be recorded live during the performance on a second tape (tape 2) conceived and played back later in a shortened form, i.e., with its duration halved, equal to a third or a quarter of the durations of the original sections. Kagel refers to these as 'structures', but without modifying either the pitch or the duration of the sounds (id. 1963: 4). The composer states that three different layers overlap timewise:

> While the interpreters always play in the present, they simultaneously record fragments for the future; these fragments, in turn, become the past when, later, they are made audible through loudspeakers in the hall. (Kagel quoted in Schwartz 1973: 115)

Despite the impressive variety of notational forms used in this work, such as action notation, traditional notation and graphic notation, the instructions to synchronise the three temporal layers in the final score and in particular the resulting interaction between the two tapes and the two musicians are quite minimal. Indeed, Kagel fixes some line segments at the bottom of some pages (which correspond to structures that interpreters must choose in their entirety), indicating the beginning and the end of any tape activities. This is the only information to tell the tape operator when to start the playback of tape number 1 and the recording or the playback of tape number 2 (see Figure 4.4).

Since the performers have the freedom to choose the order in which to perform the various parts of the piece (although a set of rules is prescribed which governs their choices),[9] these lines are the only possible form of writing

---

7   "In '*Transición I*' [...] war der Ausgangspunkt zur kompositorischen Arbeit die Untersuchung einiger Zusammenhänge des klanglichen Materials in Bezug auf seine zeitliche Formulierung." (Kagel 1962: 15).

8   Kagel began to work on the electronic piece *Transición I* as early as 1957, but the work was only completed in 1960 at the Studio for Electronic Music of the West German Radio (WDR) (see Steigerwald 2011: 127).

9   Kagel specifies in the score: "In preparing a version for performance, a selection may be made from among the 21 sections. The number of sections so selected must make up a version of at least 10 minutes duration (the version of maximum duration will include all sections). Structures must be performed only in their entirety and are to be played once. All pages of a version must be played 'attacca'.

to indicate a recording or a playback. For this reason, a written form of exact synchronisation fixed in the score once and for all remains elusive.

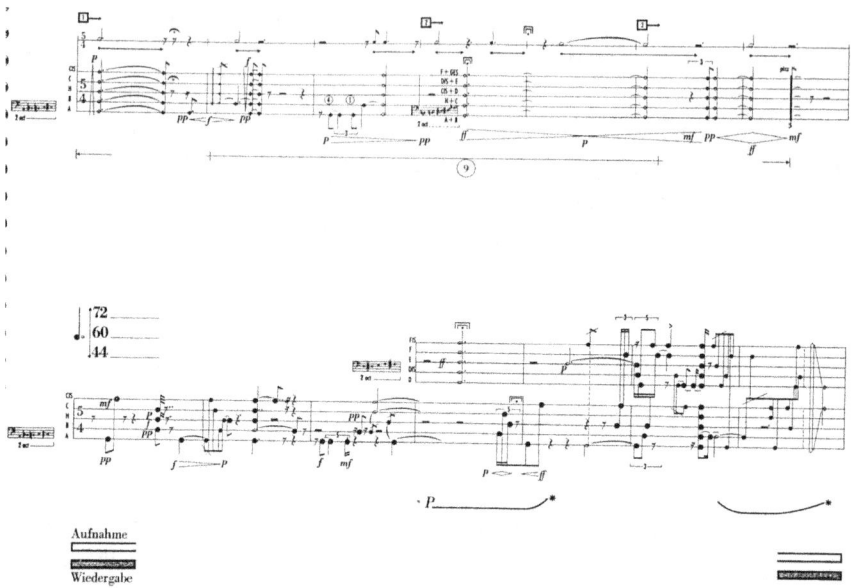

Figure 4.4: *Mauricio Kagel,* Transición II, *Structure 20 C, Universal Edition London Ltd.*

Similar to the consideration of archive materials of Xenakis's *Analogique A et B*, some sketches relating to Kagel's supervision of performances of *Transición II* also clearly reveal that each performance requires a prior elaboration – including the synchronisation – of the concrete version of the variable piece. On several pages kept in the Mauricio Kagel Collection at the Paul Sacher Stiftung and dated from 1959 to 1960 (thus prior to the printed score in 1963) the composer jotted down some synchronisation drafts. In these notes, often written on so-called *Band Begleitblätter* (tape accompanying sheets), or pre-printed templates generally used for tracking the studio recording work, there are several annotations concerning the synchronisation of '*ejecución*' (performance) and

---

The arrangement of A-, B- or C-structures is free (this includes the possibility of placing structures of the same type and to end in immediate succession) subject only to the following restrictions [...]" (Kagel 1963: 2).

'*bandas*' (tapes). In the diagram on a millimetre sheet reproduced here (see Figure 4.5), Kagel notes the final synchronisation of the composition sections, for the recording session for Time Records in New York in December 1960 with David Tudor (piano), Christoph Caskel (percussion), Mauricio Kagel and Earle Brown (sound engineers).[10]

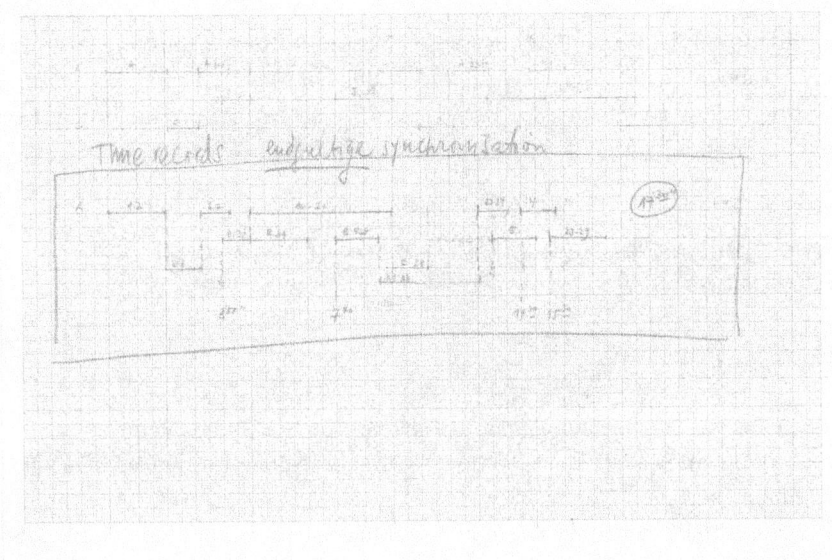

Figure 4.5: *Mauricio Kagel, sketch for the synchronisation of* Transición II *for Time Records, New York 1960, Paul Sacher Stiftung, Mauricio Kagel Collection.*

In the diagrammatic graph, the x-axis represents the temporal succession, in which each centimetre is equivalent to one minute. Although the entrances to certain sections are only roughly indicated in the diagram with arrows, Kagel precisely specifies with chronometric indications at what point in time these sections enter: section B 35 at 3'55", B 8–9 at 7'40", A 4 at 14'30" and B 25 at 15'30"

---

10   In the annotation concerning the musicians of this performance, Kagel designates himself as "Tonmeister" while referring to Brown as "Toningenieur" (see also Steigerwald 2011: 127). The performance was released on Time Records in 1961 as a 33 1/3 rpm LP combined with Karlheinz Stockhausen's compositions *Zyklus* and *Refrain*. In 2013, Naxos Classical Archives re-released it on CD, remastered by David Lennick and Joe Salerno. It is available on YouTube: https://www.youtube.com/watch?v=l3AwyNTVERQ (accessed October 7, 2022).

for a total of 17'30". The y-axis represents the three types of sections A, B and C, which Kagel refers to in the introduction to the score as "three types of structure" (Kagel 1963: 2). In total there are 21 structures in the piece (nine of type A, seven of type B and finally five of type C). According to certain rules explained in the introduction, performers must choose which structures to play for a total duration of no less than ten minutes (Kagel 1963: 2–4). Furthermore, Kagel explains that on the first tape, B or C structures should be recorded before the performance, while on the second tape, A or C structures should be recorded during the performance. This diagram – quite similar to the Xenakis sketch described above – shows the necessity of working out a performance score during the preparation to visualise the concrete order of the sections including their synchronisation.

Synchronising through a High Density of Notational Inscriptions

Rimes by Pousseur

The genesis of *Rimes pour différentes sources sonores* (1958–59) began in 1957 when Hermann Scherchen asked Henri Pousseur to compose a piece for a small ensemble and tape.[11] The piece was then premiered the following year on the occasion of the Congress of the Jeunesses Musicales Internationales at the 1958 Brussels World's Fair, for which Iannis Xenakis designed the Philips Pavilion.

As programmatically indicated in the title, sounds from the instruments 'rhyme' with sounds from magnetic tape until a unified dimension of the originally heterogeneous sound material is achieved. Pousseur writes:

> To "rhyme" "natural" sounds (emitted by orchestral instruments) and "artificial" sounds (played from the magnetic tape through loudspeakers), means to establish a correspondence between them, an exchange and sometimes a confusion of the origin, up to a *trompe-l'oeil*.[12] (Pousseur quoted in Decroupet 2018: 139)

---

11   The first version was followed by two further versions, the last of which, defined by Pousseur himself as the "*version régénérée*" and regarded as definitive, was written in the studio of Tempo Reale in Florence and performed in Turin in 2006.

12   "Faire 'rimer' des sons 'naturels' (émis par les instruments de l'orchestre) et des sons 'artificiels' (émis par la bande magnétique à travers les haut-parleurs), soit établir entre eux une correspondance, un échange et parfois une confusion des caractères, pouvant aller jusqu'au trompe-l'œil." (Pousseur, transcription of typescript dated November 29, 1961, quoted in Decroupet 2018: 139).

In the score published by Suvini Zerboni (see Pousseur 1962), synchronisation of 'natural' and 'artificial' sounds is achieved by presenting both the instrumental parts in standard notation and sections that more or less accurately represent the events on tape on the same page. This occurs indeed through three different notational typologies. The first one is a very precise standard musical notation, which is used at the beginning when orchestral sounds are emitted, previously recorded by the same instrumentalists participating in the performance. By doing so the composer intends to introduce the recorded part imperceptibly (see Figure 4.6). It is likely that these sections do not constitute a proper 'transcription' of the events of the tape, but rather a re-use possibly with corrections of the parts already read by the musicians for the recording before the performance. The second type consists of the transcription of tape-only parts in which dynamic indications, amplitude envelopes and frequency fields are indicated through elongated triangles, inscribed in standard stave systems with even some pitches of the pre-recorded sounds by the performers (see Figure 4.7). And finally, the third one is "an approximate transcription of harmonies and rhythms" (ibid.: 19) in standard notation as stated in the score, which is not as precise as the first one, but is intended to give a rough guide to the events on the tape (see Figure 4.8). Pousseur then uses the flexible forms for the recorded parts in light of their features, in particular he resorts to standard notation whenever the pitches and values of the recorded sounds remain rather defined. For electronically transformed sounds, however, he makes use of elongated triangles and similar forms to provide a visual track for the musicians during the performance.

Figure 4.6: Henri Pousseur, Rimes, p. 1, section Altoparlanti soli (loudspeaker only)

Figure 4.7: *Henri Pousseur, Rimes, p. 18, detail, section Altoparlanti soli (loud-speaker only), Sugarmusic S.p.A., Edizioni Suvini Zerboni, Milano.*

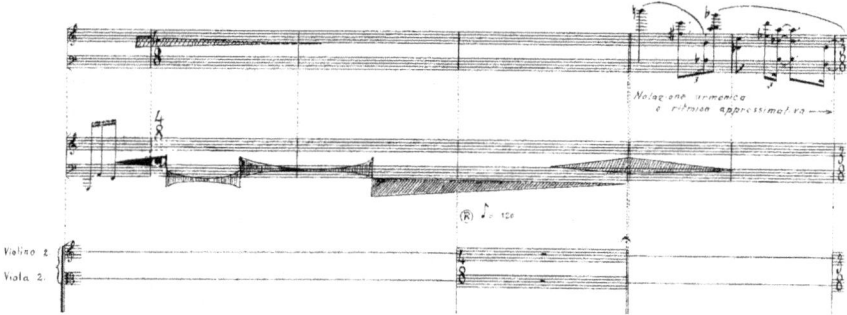

Figure 4.8: *Henri Pousseur, Rimes, p. 19, detail, Sugarmusic S.p.A., Edizioni Suvini Zerboni, Milano.*

Kontakte by Stockhausen

The use of writing to coordinate live and recorded events is particularly elaborated in the performance score of Stockhausen's *Kontakte* Nr. 12 $\frac{1}{2}$ for electronic sounds, piano and percussion, which is explicitly written for the "instrumentalists for the synchronisation of their music with the tape playback" (see Stockhausen 1995).

In October 1958, Stockhausen stated in *Elektronische und instrumentale Musik* that his works for electronic and instrumental music that had premiered that year focussed on "finding the superordinate laws of connection instead of using contrast as the most primitive type of form"[13] (id. 1963: 151). The idea of 'contacts' between the two parts and also between the practices of "composing electronic music" and "writing instrumental music" (ibid.: 150) forms the basis of *Kontakte*.[14]

The work was premiered on 11 July 1960 in Cologne at the World Music Festival of the International Society for Contemporary Music. In an interview on that occasion, Stockhausen explained how he tried for the first time to merge the domains of instrumental and electronic music, thus producing an interaction between something totally fixed and something depending on the flexible performance of musicians.

In this interview, Stockhausen also gave some significant information about the function of the performance score, which can to some extent also be found in the introduction to the score:

> Here [showing a page of the score, corresponding to page 33 in Stockhausen 1995], at the top of each sheet, I drew a schematic diagram of what happens in the loudspeakers, and the musicians got used to deciphering the graphic figures during the rehearsals. The time is precisely indicated. Here above, for example, they [the interpreters] have numbers of seconds [...]. Here is written what the percussionist with his various instruments does and what the pianist does. Musicians must constantly listen to what comes from the loudspeaker and react to it appropriately in time and intensity.[15] (id. 1960).

---

13 "Es geht darum, über den Kontrast hinaus – der die primitivste Art einer Form darstellt – die übergeordneten Gesetzmäßigkeiten einer Verbindung zu finden." (Stockhausen 1963: 150).

14 Stockhausen uses the terms "composing" respectively "writing" in relation to "electronic music" and to "instrumental music" (see Stockhausen 1963: 150).

15 The interview *Karlheinz Stockhausen explains "Kontakte"* is available at this link: https://youtu.be/7XWNR_TcPFI (accessed October 2022). The interviewer could not yet be identified. Transcription of the original language: "Da habe ich dann jeweils auf jedem Blatt oben ein bisschen schematisch aufgezeichnet was in den Lautsprechern passiert, und die Musiker haben sich im Verlauf der Probe daran gewöhnt, das grafische Bild zu entziffern. Die Zeit ist genau angegeben. Hier oben haben sie zum Beispiel Sekundenzahlen [...]. Hier ist dann jeweils geschrieben das, was der Schlagzeuger macht mit seinen verschiedenen Instrumenten und was der Pianist macht. Die Musiker müssen dauernd hören auf das, was vom Lautsprecher kommt und entsprechend zeitlich und in der Intensität darauf reagieren."

Stockhausen denotes the events recorded on tape in the upper system, and indicates the minutes, seconds, and tenths of a second with the help of a proportional timeline. Other numbers specify the durations of certain sections circumscribed by vertical lines, and smaller numbers refer to the duration of the tape in centimetres. Numbers in brackets indicate decibels, and roman numerals stand for the four loudspeakers, and the quadrophonic spatialisation. For example, the word 'alternierend' (see Figure 4.9, Section 'IC') means that the sounds should alternate between the indicated speakers. The composer mixes standard notation, graphical figures, and numbers, visualising the musical events on tape as precisely as possible.

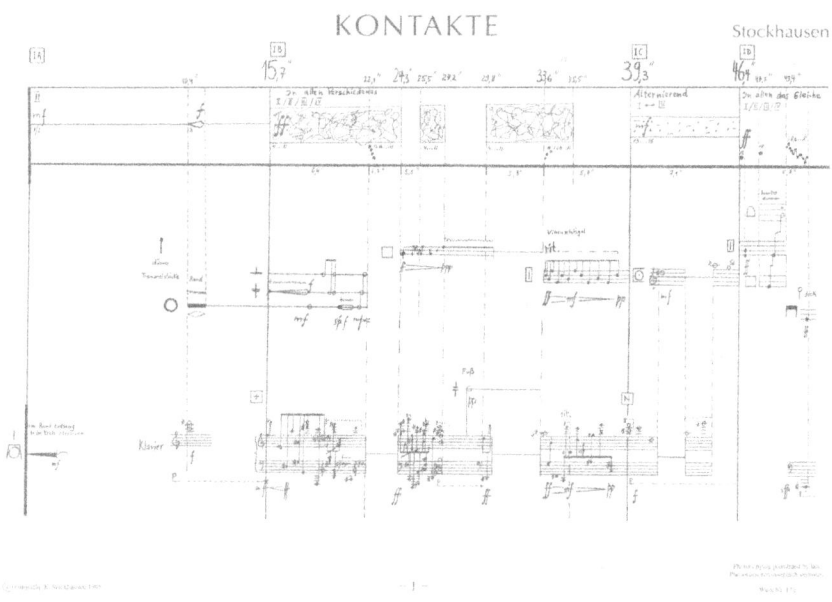

Figure 4.9: *Karlheinz Stockhausen,* Kontakte, *performance score for electronic sounds, piano and percussion, p. 1,* I_A – I_D, *Stockhausen-Verlag, Kürten, Germany.*

At the end of the already quoted interview, the interviewer asks Stockhausen quite ironically who might be able to read such a score. This question may have been prompted by the fact that the performance score for *Kontakte* does not seem 'traditional'. Even though the musical events on tape are measurable in seconds or centimetres (a kind of exactness), the interviewer must have imagined that this would have brought about a major interpretative change for performers accustomed to counting in beats but not necessarily in standard clock time. Such a score must have somehow required a new approach to 'reading music', even if the performers of the premiere of *Kontakte* – the pianist David Tudor and the percussionist Christoph Caskel (the same musicians of the cited performance of Kagel's *Transición II*) – were already renowned performers of New Music and, as Stockhausen promptly replies, could already successfully read that score.

Writing Temporal Contact Points

Based on paradigmatic performance scores of *musique mixte*, I have described how some composers made the coordination and the synchronisation between live musicians and electroacoustic parts visible and traceable in the late 1950s. Two approaches emerged from this comparison: Some scores, such as those of *Analogique A et B* by Xenakis and of *Transición II* by Kagel, synchronise the two sound dimensions by means of a few essential signs like arrows and lines, i.e. with a low density of synchronisation instructions. Others, such as the scores of *Rimes* by Pousseur and of *Kontakte* by Stockhausen testify to a more intense search of the composers in finding notational strategies to effectively enable the performers to coordinate with the pre-recorded electronic sections.

Beyond the observation of these two tendencies, all *musique mixte* scores have one fundamental aspect in common: By nature, they have a hybrid configuration. Consequently, they give information to performers in two very different ways.

On the one hand, standard western notation allows musicians to read, understand and transform the signs into music, namely in a future musical event subsequent to the act of writing. Standard notation descending from mensural notation indicates time in a measured way: the values of the notes are specified by their form according to the time unit and defined in relation to each other.

On the other hand, visual inscriptions on a timeline offer the musicians a visual trace, often rather minimal, of a pre-existing sonic track, in which sometimes graphic signs provide cues to follow the events on tape. This type of notation can be defined as 'chronometric'.

The performance score becomes the point of contact between two ways of writing down the fluid course of time, both however inscribed in the x-axis of the imaginary Cartesian coordinate system. In her concept of 'flattening' as an epistemic and aesthetic function of inscribed surfaces, Sybille Krämer reflects that a certain impulse in human beings "to transform time-bounded processes into spatial relations" may indicate that as soon as "we move in complex areas of knowledge, we privilege space and spatiality as a medium and instrument over temporality" (Krämer 2017: 244). The difference between these forms of time spatialisation, of the "flattening of time-bounded processes", leads to a reflection on the creative processes and compositional approaches from which they derive.

Considering the four chosen works, writing of mensural time derives from a compositional process mainly undertaken with pen and paper. On the contrary, writing of chronometric time is strictly connected to the process of the studio production of tape for electroacoustic music and to the preparation of a specific performance. To use an expression by Philippe Manoury, within this genre we are faced with the encounter of "la note et le son" (Manoury 1990), of the written note and the produced sound. *Musique mixte* brings together two different compositional approaches, one linked to the use of writing and one linked to electronic sound production and recording. The scores of *musique mixte* represent intriguing examples of how writing represents a key tool for understanding complex musical configurations such as the synchronisation between different temporalities and also between different compositional approaches which increasingly overlap and influence each other.

As attempted in this essay with a focus on the synchronisation between different temporalities, a philology of electroacoustic music (of which *musique mixte* is only one of many configurations) should consider the coexistence of and interaction between 'writing' in the composer's own workplace and 'recording' in the electroacoustic studio. These are two cultural techniques with which Xenakis and the other composers mentioned here were strongly confronted and whose analysis is indispensable for the understanding of their creative processes.

* * *

This essay is part of the research for my doctoral thesis entitled *Schrift als Werkzeug. Schriftbildliche Operativität in Kompositionsprozessen früher musique mixte (1949–1959)* (Minetti 2023), which was carried out within the framework of the project "Writing Music. Iconic, performative, operative, and material aspects in musical notation(s)". I would like to gratefully thank the organisers and participants of the symposium "Xenakis 2022: Back to the Roots" (May 19–21, 2022, University of Music and Performing Arts Vienna) for their valuable comments on the topic of this paper. Translations are my own unless otherwise specified.

Bibliography

Blondeau, Julia (2017) *Espaces compositionnels et temps multiples : de la relation forme/matériau*, Paris: Université Pierre et Marie Curie (Paris VI); https:// tel.archives-ouvertes.fr/tel-01717249 (accessed March 27, 2024).

Celestini, Federico, Nanni, Matteo, Obert, Simon, and Urbanek, Nikolaus, eds. (2020): "Zu einer Theorie der musikalischen Schrift. Materiale, operative, ikonische und performative Aspekte musikalischer Notationen", in *Musik und Schrift: interdisziplinäre Perspektiven auf musikalische Notationen*, ed. by Carolin Ratzinger, Nikolaus Urbanek, and Sophie Zehetmayer, Paderborn: Wilhelm Fink, 1–50.

Chion, Michel (1991) *L'art des sons fixés ou la musique concrètement*, Fontaine: Metamkine.

Cont, Arshia (2012) "Synchronisme musical et musiques mixtes: du temps écrit au temps produit", in *Circuit* 22/1, 9–24; https://doi.org/10.7202/100896 5ar (accessed March 27, 2024).

Decroupet, Pascal (2018) "Henri Pousseur. Three source texts concerning *Rimes pour differentes sources sonores*", in *The Performance Practice of Electroacoustic Music: The Studio di Fonologia years*, ed. by Lucas Bennett and Germán Toro Pérez, Bern/Vienna: Peter Lang, 137–147.

Di Scipio, Agostino (2005) "Formalization and Intuition in *Analogique* A et B (with some remarks on the historical-mathematical sources of Xenakis)", in *Definitive Proceedings: International Symposium Iannis Xenakis*, ed. by Makis Solomos, Anastasia Georgaki, and Giorgos Zervos, Athens: University of Athens: https://cicm.univ-paris8.fr/ColloqueXenakis/papers/Di%20S cipio.pdf (accessed September 10, 2023).

Harley, James (2004) *Xenakis: His Life in Music*, New York: Routledge.

Jordheim, Helge (2017) "Synchronizing the World: Synchronism as Historiographical Practice, Then and Now", in *History of the Present* 7/1/, 59–95, ht tps://doi.org/10.5406/historypresent.7.1.0059 (accessed March 27, 2024).

Kagel, Mauricio (1962) "Transición I: Elektronische Musik 1958–60. Bemerkungen", in *Neue Musik: kunst- und gesellschaftskritische Beiträge* 5/6, [15–17].

Kittler, Friedrich (1993) *Draculas Vermächtnis: Technische Schriften*, Leipzig: Reclam.

Krämer, Sybille (2006) "The Cultural Techniques of Time Axis Manipulation. On Friedrich Kittler's Conception of Media", in *Theory, Culture & Society* 23/7–8, 93–109.

Krämer, Sybille (2017) "Flattening as Cultural Technique: Epistemic and Aesthetic Functions of Inscribed Surfaces", in *Journal of the American Musicological Society* 70/1, 239–245.

Luque, Sergio (2009) "The Stochastic Synthesis of Iannis Xenakis", in *Leonardo Music Journal* 19, 77–84, https://doi.org/10.1162/lmj.2009.19.77 (accessed September 10, 2023).

Manoury, Philippe (1990) "La note et le son : un carnet de bord", in *Musiques Électroniques: Revue Contrechamps, Essais historiques ou thématiques* 11, ed. by Philippe Albèra, 151–164; https://doi.org/10.4000/books.contrechamp s.1589 (accessed March 27, 2024).

Minetti, Elena (2023) *Schrift als Werkzeug. Schriftbildliche Operativität in Kompositionsprozessen früher* musique mixte (1949–1959), PhD thesis, mdw – University of Music and Performing Arts Vienna.

Pendelton, Edmund J. (1960) "Paris Festival of Research", in *The New York Herald Tribune*. Centre Iannis Xenakis 2703, Fonds Sharon Kanach, https://www .centre-iannis-xenakis.org/items/show/242 (accessed October 31, 2022).

Sallis, Friedemann, Bertolani, Valentina, Burle, Jan, and Zattra, Laura, eds. (2018) *Live Electronic Music: Composition, Performance, Study*, London/New York: Routledge.

Scaldaferri, Nicola (2002) "Montage und Synchronisation: Ein neues musikalisches Denken in der Musik von Luciano Berio und Bruno Maderna", in *Handbuch der Musik im 20. Jahrhundert: 5. Elektroakustische Musik*, ed. by Elena Ungeheuer, Laaber: Laaber-Verlag, 66–82.

Schwartz, Elliott (1973) *Electronic Music: A Listener's Guide*, New York: Praeger.

Solomos, Makis (2017) "Notes sur la musique mixte de Xenakis", in *Analyser la musique mixte*, ed. by Alain Bonardi, Bruno Bossis, Pierre Couprie, and Vincent Tiffon, Sampzon: Delatour, 163–178.

Steigerwald, Pia (2011) *"An Tasten": Studien zur Klaviermusik von Mauricio Kagel*, Hofheim: Wolke.

Stockhausen, Karlheinz (1960) "Karlheinz Stockhausen explains 'Kontakte'", interview at the WDR Cologne: https://youtu.be/7XWNR_TcPFI (accessed October 31, 2022).

Stockhausen, Karlheinz (1963) "Elektronische und instrumentale Musik", in *Texte zur elektronischen und instrumentalen Musik*, ed. by Dieter Schnebel, Cologne: DuMont, 140–151.

Tiffon, Vincent (1994) *Recherches sur les musiques mixtes*, Marseille: Université d'Aix-Marseille I.

Tiffon, Vincent (2005) "Les musiques mixtes : entre pérennité et obsolescence", in *Musurgia* 12/3, 23–45.

Tiffon, Vincent (2013) "Musique Mixte", in *Théories dela composition musicale au XXe siècle*, ed. by Nicolas Donin and Laurent Feneyrou, Lyon: Symétrie, 1297–1314.

Xenakis, Iannis (1963) "Musiques formelles: nouveaux principes formels de composition musicale", in *La revue musicale*, special double issue no. 253–254, Paris: Editions Richard-Masse.

Xenakis, Iannis (1971) *Musique, architecture*, Tournai: Casterman.

Xenakis, Iannis (1992) *Formalized Music. Thought and Mathematics in Composition*, ed. by Sharon Kanach, Stuyvesant N.Y.: Pendragon Press.

Musical scores

Kagel, Mauricio (1963) *Transición II für Klavier, Schlagzeug und zwei Tonbänder* (1958–59) (UE 13809), London: Universal Edition.

Pousseur, Henri (1962) *Rimes pour différentes sources sonores* [1958–59] (S. 5520 Z.), Milano: Edizioni Suvini Zerboni.

Stockhausen, Karlheinz (1995) *Kontakte für elektronische Klänge, Klavier und Schlagzeug Nr. 12 $\frac{1}{2}$, Aufführungspartitur*, Kürten: Stockhausen-Verlag.

Xenakis, Iannis (1968) *Analogique A: Partition d'orchestre*. Vol. E.A.S. 17169, Paris: Éditions Salabert.

List of Figures

Figure 4.1: Iannis Xenakis, *Analogique* A, orchestra score, p. 3, detail, Durand Salabert Eschig, Paris.

Figure 4.2: Iannis Xenakis, *Analogique* A, orchestra score, p. 5, detail, Durand Salabert Eschig, Paris.

Figure 4.3: Iannis Xenakis, *Analogique* A et B, sketch, Collection Famille Xenakis DR, OM 5–5, p. 5.

Figure 4.4: Mauricio Kagel, *Transición II, Structure* 20 C, Universal Edition London Ltd.

Figure 4.5: Mauricio Kagel, sketch for the synchronisation of *Transición II* for Time Records, New York 1960, Paul Sacher Stiftung, Mauricio Kagel Collection.

Figure 4.6: Henri Pousseur, *Rimes*, p. 1, detail, Sugarmusic S.p.A., Edizioni Suvini Zerboni, Milano.

Figure 4.7: Henri Pousseur, *Rimes*, p. 18, detail, section *Altoparlanti soli* (loudspeaker only), Sugarmusic S.p.A., Edizioni Suvini Zerboni, Milano.

Figure 4.8: Henri Pousseur, *Rimes*, p. 19, detail, Sugarmusic S.p.A., Edizioni Suvini Zerboni, Milano.

Figure 4.9: Karlheinz Stockhausen, *Kontakte*, performance score for electronic sounds, piano and percussion, p. 1, I_A – I_D, Stockhausen-Stiftung für Musik, Kürten, Germany.

Common Sonic Entities in the Electroacoustic and Orchestral Music of Iannis Xenakis

James Harley

Introduction

At approximately the same time as Iannis Xenakis was penning his radical early scores such as *Metastaseis* (1954) and *Pithoprakta* (1956) that changed the history of orchestral music, he was embarking on his apprenticeship at what became known as GRM (Groupe de recherches musicales), producing his first electroacoustic work, *Diamorphoses*, in 1957. In his theoretical conceptions of music, as detailed in *Formalized Music* (Xenakis 1971), was the notion of "sonic entity", replacing traditional structures built from pitch and rhythm. The sliding string glissando textures in *Metastaseis* are reflected in the sliding "engine" sounds in *Diamorphoses*, and the pointillistic textures of *Pithoprakta* (knocking, plucking, bowing, etc.) are reflected in the granular "embers" of *Concret PH* (1958). The dense 8-channel textures of *Bohor* (1962) surrounding the listeners are mirrored in the swirling spatial densities in *Terretektorh* (1966) where the audience is interspersed amongst the musicians. With the *Polytope de Montréal* (1967), the highly textural score for four spatially-separated ensembles was conceived as an electroacoustic work, broadcast over loudspeakers as part of a multimedia installation. Other of Xenakis's electroacoustic works are created entirely from instrumental sources, more or less processed in the studio. Perhaps the most radical "crossover" of these works is *Kraanerg* (1969), with a live instrumental ensemble (23 players) performing together with pre-recorded material (equally substantial) produced from studio recordings of the same ensemble, divided between winds and strings, distributed amongst four channels surrounding the audience. Xenakis continued to use instrumental sonorities in his electroacoustic works until he turned definitively to computer-generated works with *Gendy 3* in 1991. Interestingly, in the 1990s his orchestral works moved away from more obvious sonic explorations, with glissandi and pizzicati giving way to modal melodies and less opaque vertical structures, as in *Dämmerschein* (1994). The common ontological conception of his music appears to have to some extent bifurcated, with computer-generated sonorities bearing little sonic overlap with simplified acoustic sounds, but perhaps with conceptual connections.

Sonic Entities

Iannis Xenakis (1922–2001) completed his first significant composition, *Metastaseis* for orchestra, in 1954. His primary training was in engineering, and from 1947 he worked as an engineer and architect in the studio of acclaimed artist and architect Le Corbusier. In 1955, he began working in the studios of what has become known as the GRM. His first electroacoustic composition, *Diamorphoses*, was completed in 1957. This was a fertile period for Xenakis: he completed *Pithoprakta* for orchestra; and the Philips Pavilion (architect, project manager) for the 1958 World Fair in Brussels. Having striven to apply mathematical tools from engineering and architecture to music and sound, Xenakis also undertook a process of formalisation, integrating his ideas into a theoretical framework that was unlike any other. In his approach, which encapsulated his current sense of musical form, he outlined what he called "fundamental phases of a musical work". He listed them as follows:

1.   Initial conceptions;
2.   Definition of the sonic entities;
3.   Definition of the transformations;
4.   Microcomposition;
5.   Sequential programming of 3 and 4 – the schema of the work in its entirety;
6.   Implementation of calculations;
7.   Final symbolic result;
8.   Sonic realisation (Xenakis 1971: 22).

While some of his 'phases' are better exemplified through musical scores, and he definitely focused on notated scores in his discussions in *Formalized Music*, Xenakis included the possibility of electroacoustic conceptions. In his definition of 'sonic entities', he discusses "symbolism communicable with the limits of possible means (sounds of musical instruments, electronic sounds, noises, sets of ordered sonic elements, granular or continuous formations, etc.)" (ibid.). He also posits a definition of the transformations which these sonic entities must undergo in the course of the composition, and the arrangement of these operations in lexicographic time with the aid of succession and simultaneity. (ibid.: 23f.)

Crossovers: Acoustic–Electroacoustic

In *Metastaseis* for orchestra, Xenakis looked to sliding glissando textures (individual strings and trombones) as a core sonic entity, one he went on to use in numerous other works (Harley 1996). This entity is mirrored in the sliding 'engine' sounds in *Diamorphoses*. The pointillistic string textures built from stochastic (random) distributions – timing, pitch, density – of *Pithoprakta* for orchestra are reflected in the granular electroacoustic 'embers' of *Concret PH*. In both these works, density of events was a primary compositional factor, along with global boundaries of parameters such as register, dynamics, etc. The conceptual relationship between acoustic and electroacoustic materials was made most explicit in *Analogique A et B* (1958–59), which alternates pointillistic music for strings with electronic sounds attempting to model granular synthesis, which Xenakis had conceived of but lacked the technical resources to truly achieve at the time (Di Scipio 2005).

In 1962, Xenakis created his largest electroacoustic work to-date, *Bohor*, for eight channels of sound surrounding the listeners. The music is built from layers of contrasting, relatively noisy materials, immersing the audience in a composite aural experience. The intensity of the music is heightened in the final minutes by a dramatic increase in noise and volume. Some of the concerns of *Bohor*, the immersive sound and the layers of unusual sonic textures, were explored in the orchestral domain in *Terretektorh* (1965–66). This work places the audience amongst the musicians, the epitome of an immersive acoustic experience (Santana 2001). The music includes glissandi, even more varied than in *Metastaseis* (a notable addition being slide whistles), and granular textures such as distributed maracas and percussion. *Nomos Gamma* (1968) expanded the spatialised orchestra-audience by surrounding everything with seven percussionists who spin rhythmic pulses around the space in an acoustic representation of studio panning techniques.

Incorporating Acoustic and Electroacoustic Entities

In *Polytope de Montréal*, Xenakis undertook his first multimedia project after his work on the Philips Pavilion in 1958, creating an installation of numerous angled cables stretched from ceiling to floor through a five-storey atrium space. The cables (forming patterns reminiscent of the string glissandi in *Metastaseis* which were conceived graphically before being turned into sound) had hundreds of flashbulbs attached to them that were triggered to form sequences of dynamic visual patterns. These were intended to be experienced in tandem with music that was scored for instruments but was presented during the installation at the French Pavilion at the World Exposition in Montreal (running for several months in 1967) as recorded material. The music was conceived for four identical ensembles, in the end projected through four channels through loudspeakers on each level of the atrium. Xenakis followed *Polytope de Montréal* with *Kraanerg*, where a live ensemble alternates with recorded segments on four channels of the same ensemble (23 players, winds and strings). The studio-produced segments are subject to a degree of signal processing but are clearly based on similar material as is presented by the acoustic instruments. The recorded elements are heard surrounding the audience while the musicians are onstage (or in the pit, as the commission was for a dance work) (Harley 2015).

Acoustic Sources for Electroacoustic Works

Xenakis followed these 'mixed' works with *Persephassa* (1969) for six percussionists surrounding the audience, and *Hibiki Hana Ma* (1970) for recorded sounds originally produced on 12 tracks to be projected over hundreds of loudspeakers. In this electroacoustic work for the 1970 World Fair in Osaka, Xenakis used entirely instrumental sources, but there is a great deal of studio manipulation applied, even while some sonic layers are easily recognisable as fragments from string orchestra, Japanese biwa, etc. (id. 2004: 67). Some of the more extensively developed sonorities Xenakis produced for *Hibiki Hana Ma* were recycled and elaborated in further electroacoustic works: *Persepolis* (1971), *Polytope de Cluny* (1972) and *La Légende d'Eer* (1978). At the same time, similar sonic entities are heard in his instrumental music, including string glissandi (numerous works from orchestral to chamber formations), clarinet multiphonics (*Synaphaï* for piano and orchestra, 1969, and *Antikhthon* for orchestra, 1971), low-register complex textures (*Antikhthon*).

Graphic Sources

With the establishment of a computer music research facility in Paris in 1966, operational in 1972, the CEMAMu (Centre d'Études de Mathématique et Automatique Musicales), Xenakis added computer-generated sounds to the layers of sonic entities in *Polytope de Cluny* and *La Légende d'Eer*. These digital textures were mostly remote from instrumentally-derived sonorities, but Xenakis explored conceptual relationships between them, primarily through graphic design. With the introduction of his computer music graphic interface system in 1978, the UPIC (Unité Polyagogique Informatique CEMAMu), he was able to transfer graphic designs into sound directly, notably with his computer-generated work, *Mycènes alpha* (1978). Since his earliest compositions, such as *Metastaseis* and *Pithoprakta*, Xenakis had 'composed' music based on graphic designs. With *Anémoessa* (1979) for choir and orchestra, he transcribed sketches used for *Mycènes alpha* into music notation for instruments and voices. The timbres are very different in these two works, but the generative process is the same, at least in part. In a similar way, identical 'arborescent' designs (branch-like shapes) are transcribed into string glissandi and into discrete textures played by the solo piano in *Erikhthon* (1974) for piano and orchestra. In the first section of *Jonchaies* (1977) for orchestra, the strings outline a slowly-unfolding wavelike design. Rather than mapping the shapes through glissandi, as in *Erikhthon*, Xenakis not only transfers the graphic design into discrete notes, he filters them through a pitch 'sieve', where only selected pitches are used, not the full chromatic complement (Harley 2012).

Focusing Inward

From *Jonchaies* on, Xenakis began to pay closer attention in his acoustic music to concerns of pitch: melodies, counterpoint, harmonies and clusters. As a consequence, instrumental textures became more focused, less reliant on the elements that had been predominant in earlier scores, such as glissandi, noisy complexity, etc. On the electroacoustic side, after the graphic-designed UPIC pieces – *Mycènes alpha, Pour la paix* (1981) with narration and choir, *Tauriphanie* (1987), *Voyage absolu des Unari vers Andromède* (1989) – Xenakis focused on extending his earlier compositional algorithms ("ST"-series, 1956–1962 and later) into the domain of generative sound synthesis (Hoffmann 2004). There is a great deal of variability in many of the compositional parameters, but the waveforms, eschewing curves in favour of straight-line segments, somewhat limit the timbral range. The algorithmic process was the primary concern. Xenakis produced two works generated in this way: *Gendy 3* (1991) and *S.709* (1994).

Conclusion

In his later works, Xenakis could be understood as following separate, rather than complementary, musical concerns, especially with regard to the limited timbral or textural palettes he explored in his electroacoustic and instrumental-vocal works. Where the computer-generated music implemented the earlier "phases" down to the level of sample values, his acoustic music concentrated on sonic density, often leaving aside glissandi, noisy timbres (such as percussion), layering of heterogenous textures. Rather than focus on the sonic entities themselves, though, might it be worthwhile considering the composer's concentration on generative processes? Xenakis became fascinated by the interior qualities and relations of dense but relatively controlled entities. The degree of contrapuntal activity in an orchestral score such as *Dämmerschein* could perhaps be compared to the number of 'voices' active in a section of *Gendy* 3. If so, perhaps there is a unity in his later works after all, one that is less obvious when comparing sonic entities directly. The concentration of all these works comes from the narrowing of sonic entities in order to focus on the inherent material qualities of the entities Xenakis chose to use, and the architectural design of the music overall.

Bibliography

Di Scipio, Agostino (2005) "Formalization and Intuition in *Analogique* A et B (with some remarks on the historical-mathematical sources of Xenakis)", in *International Symposium Iannis Xenakis Athens 18–20 May 2005, Conference Proceedings*, ed. by Anastasia Georgaki and Makis Solomos, 95–108.

Harley, James (1996) "Sonic and parametric entities on *Tetras*: an analytical approach to the music of Iannis Xenakis", in *Canadian University Music Review* 16/2, 72–99.

Harley, James (2004) *Xenakis: His Life in Music*, New York: Routledge.

Harley, James (2012) "Graphic conception of musical structure and sonority in *Jonchaies* by Iannis Xenakis", in *Xenakis Matters*, ed. by Sharon Kanach, Hillside: Pendragon Press, 205–217.

Harley, James (2015) *Iannis Xenakis: Kraanerg*, Farnham: Ashgate Publishing.

Hoffmann, Peter (2010) "'Something rich and strange': Exploring the Pitch Structure of GENDY3", in *Journal of New Music Research* 2004/2, 137–144.

Santana, Helena (2001) "*Terretektorh*: L'espace et le timbre, le timbre de l'espace", in *Présences de Iannis Xenakis*, ed. by Makis Solomos, 141–151.

Xenakis, Iannis (1971) *Formalized Music*, Bloomington: Indiana University Press.

Spatial Treatment of Sound in the *Polytope de Cluny*

Pierre Carré and François Delécluse

Introduction

During the 1960s and 1970s, Xenakis conceived several shows which mixed music, architecture and performance; he called them 'polytopes'. In the *Polytope de Cluny* (1972), in particular, the most advanced technologies of the time were employed to imagine a new synergy between music, space and light. During this 25-minute-long installation, concrete tape music flowed under the arches of the ancient Roman baths of Cluny (Paris) while interacting with visual patterns created by an array of hundreds of flashes and laser beams. In order to synchronise the diffusion of the different audio tracks among the many loudspeakers with the ballet of light, Xenakis had designed a customised technical apparatus that relied at its core on a monotasking computer to decode in real time the digital data stored on a command tape. However, the technologically avant-garde nature of this work, together with the temporary character of the show and its prohibitive cost were the very reasons why it was never played again. Due to the scarcity of the remaining original material, it was believed for a long time that the *Polytope* was lost. Nevertheless, the digital command tape of the show was recently rediscovered, and its cross-examination against archival documentation available at the Xenakis Archives (technical documentation, letters, photographs, videos, drawings, etc.) opened new perspectives for reconstructing the *Polytope* (see also Carré 2022).

The reconstruction of the spatial treatment of sound in the *Polytope de Cluny* provides insight into lost aspects of Xenakis's work. Spatialisation is of crucial importance in his work, both in his electronic and instrumental music. The latter has already been the subject of several studies in works such as *Persephassa* (1969) or *Terretektorh* (1966) (Da Silva Santana 2001; Hofmann 2008; Rimoldi and Schaub 2013). The spatial dimension of Xenakis's music has also been studied more generally (among others: Hoffmann 1998, 2008; Solomos 2015). Although space often plays a very important role, the scores of only three musical pieces contain a fixed spatialisation intended to be automated: *Concret PH* (1958), *Polytope de Cluny* and *La Légende d'Eer* (1978) as the musical part of the *Diatope*. In addition to general studies on this issue (see, e.g., Solomos 2001 and Harley 2015), the *Diatope* has been the subject of a particular investigation (Kiourtsoglou 2017) examining, among other things, the specificities of Xenakis's spatialisation of sound in his electronic music. Moreover, an existing multichannel spatialised version of *La Légende d'Eer* performed by Xenakis himself and two other colleagues can inform us about the composer's performance practice of spatialisation (Friedl 2015). Apart from these few studies, there is not much tangible literature on the spatial dimension of Xenakis's electronic music. From this perspective, the study of the archives and sketches linked with *Polytope de Cluny* sheds new light on spatialisation. It gives us a new perspective on the composer's thoughts about space – not so much from a philosophical point of view (already explored in the cited studies) – but specifically on his creative process and compositional approach. The exploration of Xenakis's compositional intentions through archival material makes it possible to understand, in particular, the complex relationship between the idea of a sound movement and its realisation. This relationship is nourished not only by an abstract concept of spatialisation, but also by the inherent possibilities of the specific devices available to the composer.

Description of the Sources and Apparatus

Sources

In order to reconstruct and understand the spatial treatment of sound in the *Polytope de Cluny*, it is necessary to refer to a set of sources, including the sound tapes produced by Xenakis for the *Polytope de Cluny*, but also the digital tape with the control data for the spatialisation. In addition, the sources essential to the understanding and reconstruction of the *Polytope de Cluny* include an important archive file documenting the entire period of its conception and production. These sources allow us to understand in particular the structure of the control tape and the processing by the various machines, which together constitute the *Polytope de Cluny*. These sources provide an opportunity not only to reconstruct the work's production process, but also to gain a deeper understanding of Xenakis's conception of sound space in the *Polytope de Cluny*.

Types of Sources	Sources	Location/Publication
Audio tape	8-track audio tape (audio on 7 tracks + 1 track synchronisation signal) = Official rental material for sound projection (1972)	Paris: Salabert, XE 105
Digital tape	9-track digital tape = Control tape (1973)	Paris: Bibliothèque Nationale de France, département de l'Audiovisuel, fonds Xenakis, DONAUD0602_000613
Technical drawings and tracing paper	Autograph drawings (p. 1) and tracing paper (pp. 2–4) on speaker placement and sound paths	Paris: Collection Famille Xenakis DR, OM 22-2
Photographs	Photographs of the *Polytope de Cluny* (1972–1974)	Paris: Collection Famille Xenakis DR
Notes, reports, correspondence	Autographic notes on the *Polytope de Cluny*, notably including: – pp. 13–19: project for the "armoire de commande" (electronic apparatus) –pp. 67–69: cost estimate –pp. 167–176: description of the control software by Robert Dupuy –pp. 218–220: instructions for the operator –pp. 221–227: description of the control tape data –pp. 237–238: improvements proposed by Bruce Rogers	Paris: Collection Famille Xenakis DR, OM 22–3
Advertising brochure	*Ampex: TM-7 Digital Tape Transport, TM-7200 Tape Memory System* = Advertising brochure for the tape machine Ampex TM-7 (1964)	Culver City: Ampex Corporation
Advertising poster	Advertising poster for the *Polytope de Cluny* (ca. 1973)	Paris: Collection Famille Xenakis DR

Table 6.1: *Sources of the* Polytope de Cluny *linked with the spatialisation device.*

The Command Chain

Figure 6.1a: *Sound diffusion system of* Polytope de Cluny, *Collection Famille Xenakis DR. The upper loudspeakers are highlighted by dashed lines, the lower ones by continuous lines. Annotations by the authors.*

The two main sources, the sound tape and the control tape, were read simultaneously and their output assembled by a rather complex electronic device. It linked the information of the control tape with the loudspeaker devices, which are an integral part of the spatial design.

Sound diffusion was provided by 12 2 × 2 m Tannoy 15″ loudspeakers distributed in two sets of six loudspeakers each, one mounted at 2.5 m from the floor, the other at 8.5 m, as shown in Figures 6.1a and 6.1b. This equipment was not free of defects: Several were reported in the technical documentation, especially concerning low-frequency reproduction, loudspeaker saturation, crackling and noise. Furthermore, even set at −∞ dB, the loudspeakers produced a low-volume sound, as several documents point out (Collection Famille Xenakis DR, OM 22–3).

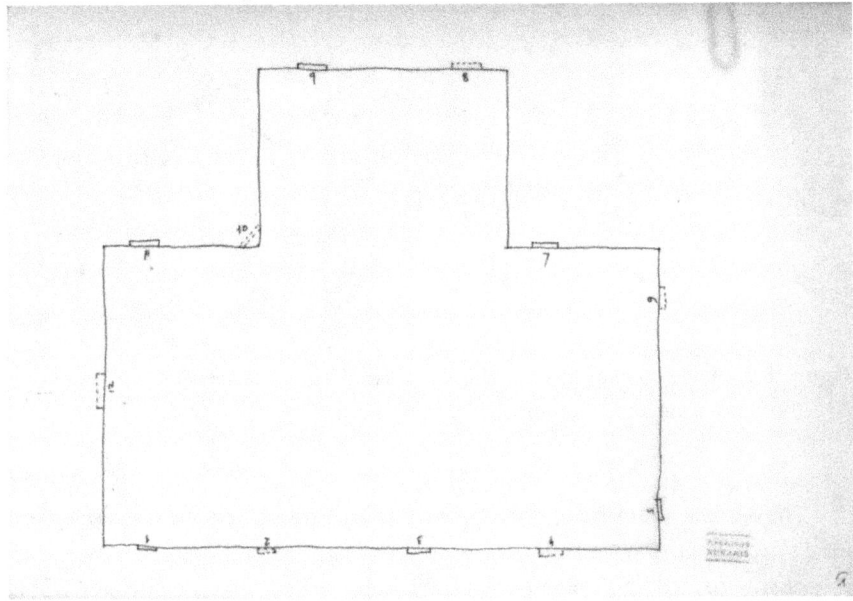

Figure 6.1b: Iannis Xenakis, top view of the loudspeaker positions of Polytope de Cluny, upper ones indicated by dotted lines, lower ones by continuous lines, Collection Famille Xenakis DR, OM 22–2, p. 1.

The playback system consisted of several devices linked together, allowing the synchronisation of the whole show: an Ampex MM-1000 8-track audio tape player (Figure 6.2, on the left in the foreground), an Ampex TM-7 9-track digital tape player (Figure 6.2, on the right in the foreground), as well as a "control cabinet" ("*armoire de commande*") – allowing us to interpret the data read by the latter (Figure 6.2, in the background on the right) – and 12 power amplifiers that send the computed sound signals to the loudspeakers (Figure 6.2, in the background on the left).

Figure 6.2: *Inside view of the control cabin, ca. 1972, collection Famille Xenakis DR. Photomontage and annotations by the authors.*

The 8-track audio is composed of seven audio tracks and one track reserved for a synchronisation signal for the other devices. The audio signal of the seven tracks was routed to 12 channels in real time and sent to the speakers. This dynamic routing made use of the digital devices (inside the "control cabinet") to interpret the spatialisation data contained on the control tape; thus, without the latter, the sound spatialisation could not be restored.

The control tape is a magnetic media intended to be read by a digital device, i.e., the signals it contains are interpreted as binary data. The medium is rather particular: a 9-track 1/2", tape, which was introduced by IBM in 1964, but had fallen into disuse by the end of the 20th century. It consists of eight data tracks and one so-called 'parity' track used for the correction of reading errors. For the *Polytope de Cluny*, the medium was used in a nonstandard way: The ninth track contained a signal delimiting data blocks of 150 bytes each to be read at a rate of 24 blocks per second. These data were used to control the "ballet of lights" (flashes and lasers), but also to spatialise the sound.

An electronic circuit converted the data written on the digital tape in order to transmit them to the optical and audio devices. The circuits as well as the construction plans of this data-conversion equipment have disappeared. Nevertheless, the notes and the specifications preserved in the archives make it possible to reconstruct the functioning of the missing parts. Figure 6.3 shows the functioning of the complete playback chain (for a description of the elements controlling the light equipment, see Carré 2022).

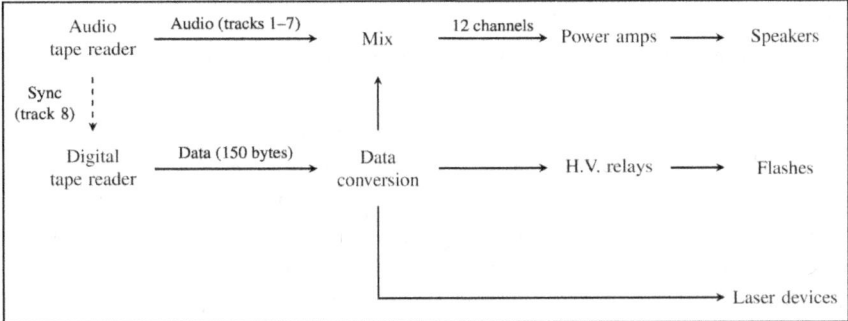

Figure 6.3: *Control chain. Diagram by the authors.*

Synchronisation

Various proposals for technical details drawn up in 1972 show that initially a synchronisation system between the two different Ampex tape machines – the analogue and the digital one – had been planned. The eighth track of the analogue audio tape, which had been reserved for this purpose, was to contain a continuous series of 1000 Hz pulses spaced at 1/25 s. This signal, monitored by an electronic circuit, would have triggered the playback function on the TM-7 digital player. The tape machine would then automatically stop after reading a 150-byte block, either by incrementing a counter or by detecting an end-of-block signal on the ninth track, and wait for the next pulse to start reading the next block, repeating the read/stop cycle 25 times per second. This system would have allowed precise coordination between the audio signals on the one hand, and the light and spatialisation control data on the other.

This solution was, however, not implemented, as Jacques Pervillé, design engineer on the second version of *Polytope de Cluny*, confirmed.[1] This was probably also the reason why the eighth track of the audio tape of Éditions Salabert is blank. Indeed, the drafts mention the use of a tape drive capable of playing at 45 ips (inch per second). The standard Ampex TM-7 tape machines are capable of 36 ips, but "special speeds [are] available to 45 ips maximum" (Ampex Corporation 1964: 4). The digital magnetic tape is encoded with a density of 800 bpi

---

1   Testimony of Jacques Pervillé, interview with Pierre Carré, March 17, 2021.

(bits per inch), so reading a 150-byte block of data required 1/30 s; however, the reader's manual indicates that starting and stopping the machine requires up to 10 ms, which means the reading time of a block of data would exceed the limit of 1/25 of a second. The envisaged synchronisation solution could probably not be implemented because of this technical limitation of the hardware, which was not fast enough to perform stop and resume reading cycles.

Regardless of the reason, no automatic synchronisation system was put in place.[2] Consequently, as we learn from the playback sheet of the operator who was in charge of launching the show, the synchronisation of the start was done manually.[3] Knowing that the two tape machines were not synchronised, the rate at which the control data was read still remains to be determined. The knowledge of the playback speed of the digital tape machine is fundamental for the appropriate rate of the lighting effects, and the exact correspondence between the sound material (the audio tracks) and their spatialisation. For a TM-7 player equipped with the "special speed" at 45 ips, the digital scroller would update the data 30 times per second for a total show duration of 18'40". On a standard player, on the other hand, the 36-ips playback results in a refresh rate of 24 cycles per second for a total duration of 23'30". The audio tape has a duration of approximately 24'30", so the 36 ips seem to be closer to this. Also a "25th of a second digital tape" playback was advertised on the show poster (Collection Famille Xenakis DR, not inventoried).

However, since there was no synchronisation between the devices, the timing between the sound material on the one hand, and its spatialisation on the other hand, was subject to the reading uncertainties of the control tape. The playback speed of the TM-7 could deviate up to eight per cent (Ampex Corporation 1964: 4), corresponding, in the worst-case scenario, to an advance or a delay of about 1'55" between the control tape and the soundtrack. Of course, these shifts would have had an impact on the spatialisation, since the mix data was stored on the control tape. Two cases were then possible: Either – if the digital tape was running too fast – the whole show finished too soon, the soundtrack not being played to the end, or – in the opposite case – the light show continued after the soundtrack had already stopped. This is exactly what happened in the concert situation: According to Jacques Pervillé, these shifts were indeed frequent.

---

2   Testimony of Bruce Rogers, interview with Pierre Carré, 30 November 2021.
3   The instruction sheet of the operator preserved in the Collection Famille Xenakis DR (OM 22-3, 218–220) does indeed indicate: "Send simultaneously the Ampex sound (play) [and] the Ampex light (remote)".

Command Data

In order to understand the storage of data on each frame of the digital control tape, it was necessary to refer to the technical documentation describing the data of the control tape (Collection Famille Xenakis DR, OM 22–3, pp. 221–227). This description gives us more precise details about the organisation of each frame (see Figure 6.4): The first 75 bytes of each frame control the flashes; the following ten control the lasers; five bytes are unused, then the following 18 control the deflectors of the three lasers. The last 42 bytes, organised in seven groups of six bytes, contain the information for the sound spatialisation: Each group of six bytes corresponds to the routing of one of the seven tracks on the 12 loudspeakers according to four possible sound levels described in the documentation (0 dB, –2 dB, –7 dB and –13 dB). The activation of one of these bytes sends the corresponding signal of the track to one of the 12 loudspeakers at one of the four given levels (which makes a total of $4 \times 12 = 48$ bits = 6 bytes). It should also be noted that by default (i.e., if no bit is set) the track is not sent to any loudspeaker, which in practice adds a fifth sound level at $-\infty$ dB. The interpretation of this data allows us to reconstruct the temporal evolution of the routing of the tracks throughout the show and thus to restore the original spatialisation.

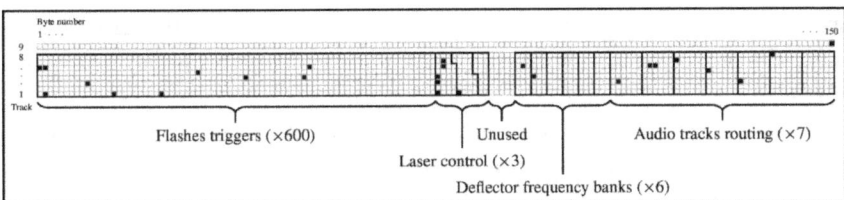

Figure 6.4: *Structure of the control tape frames, here: frame 820. Diagram by the authors.*

Thought of Sound Space

Notation of Sound Spatialisation: Tablature and Score

The understanding and reconstitution of a work such as the *Polytope de Cluny* are notably linked to the nature of the notation for machines. The Western musical writing tradition has two main categories of writing: tablature and score.

Tablature is a system of notation for an instrumental piece that indicates finger-ings and rhythms on a schematic representation of an instrument. In contrast, a music score brings together the different parts of a single work by indicating pitches, rhythms, timbres and intensity, without any concern as to how they are produced. This way of thinking about writing, which opposes tablature and score, corresponds to the opposition between machine thinking based on the device, on the one hand, and compositional thinking as a written sound inten-tion, on the other. In the case of the tablature, it is a question of how to play a particular device. In the case of the score, it is a question of thinking about the resulting positions and trajectories of the sound and light material.

The control tape used in *Polytope de Cluny* to command the ballet of lights and the sound trajectories is similar to a tablature. There is no score pointing out what movements Xenakis wanted; the control tape is a tablature, indicat-ing how to realise the different positions and trajectories. This tablature is in-tended for a single 'instrument', that of the light and sound device set up in 1972. In other compositions Xenakis alternates between the two types of no-tation: tablature and score. For *Concret PH*, created for the Philips Pavilion in 1958, Xenakis developed a notation of sound trajectories and not a tablature of loudspeaker signals (see Figure 6.5).

In this graphic score, we can observe a schematisation of the sound tra-jectories in space as well as a temporal sequence listing the different events. Thus, the slashes that can be seen on the right side of the example describe the movement of the different sound tracks according to a given trajectory, speed and recurrence; Xenakis created a graphic code to design his score and to make it readable for everyone.

The design of the sound movements is traceable in the sketches of some of the works. In particular, in regard to *La Légende d'Eer*, a piece composed about six years after *Polytope de Cluny*, several sketches allow us to under-stand how Xenakis thought about spatialisation. The sketches of *La Légende d'Eer* (Figure 6.6) show a thought from the sound source (i.e., an abstract com-positional thought) in the form of a movement of a track from one loudspeaker to another. In the upper sketch of Figure 6.6, each line (of different colours) shows the displacement of a track on different loudspeakers.

In the lower sketch, the data is not written track by track, but speaker by speaker, which is closer to a tablature, a pragmatic concept for a precise de-vice. In the conception phase, Xenakis seems to alternate between thinking in abstract movements of sound and concrete thinking regarding the available de-vice.

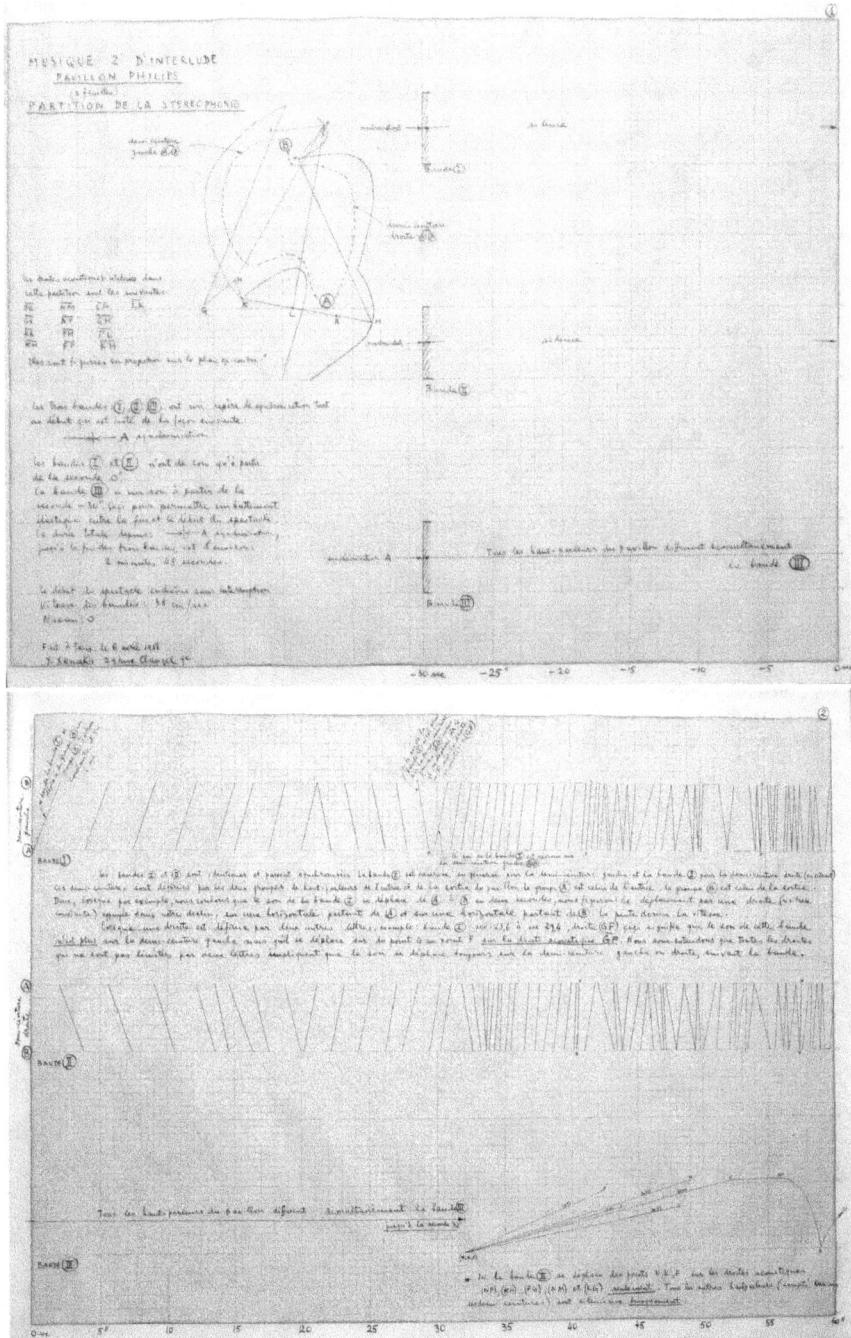

Figures 6.5a and 6.5b: *Iannis Xenakis,* Concret PH, *graphic scores for the sound spatialisation, Collection Famille Xenakis DR, pp. 1f.*

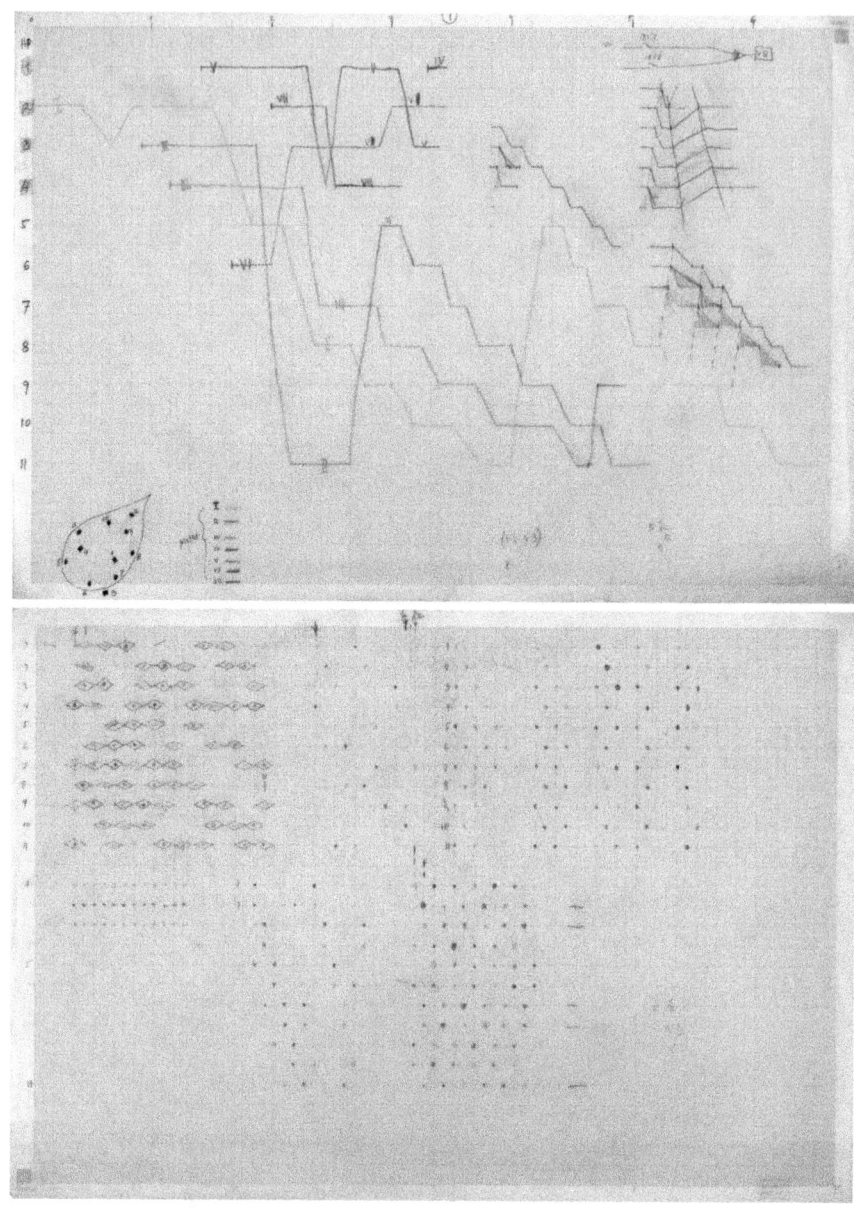

Figure 6.6a and 6.6b: *Iannis Xenakis,* La Légende d'Eer, *sketches for the sound spatialisation, collection Famille Xenakis DR, XA 11–7, pp. 27 and 25.*

Aspects of the Genesis of the Spatialisation in the *Polytope de Cluny*

Even if there are less traces of such work concerning the *Polytope de Cluny*, one can easily make the hypothesis that the genesis of the work must have been conceived, to a certain extent, through the abstract design of sound trajectories independent of the diffusion device. Several elements resulting from the analysis of the tape, the archive sources and the control program allow us to corroborate the back and forth between the imagination of the moving sounds on the one hand and a thought in respect to the unique 'instrument' for which Xenakis conceived the *Polytope de Cluny* on the other hand.

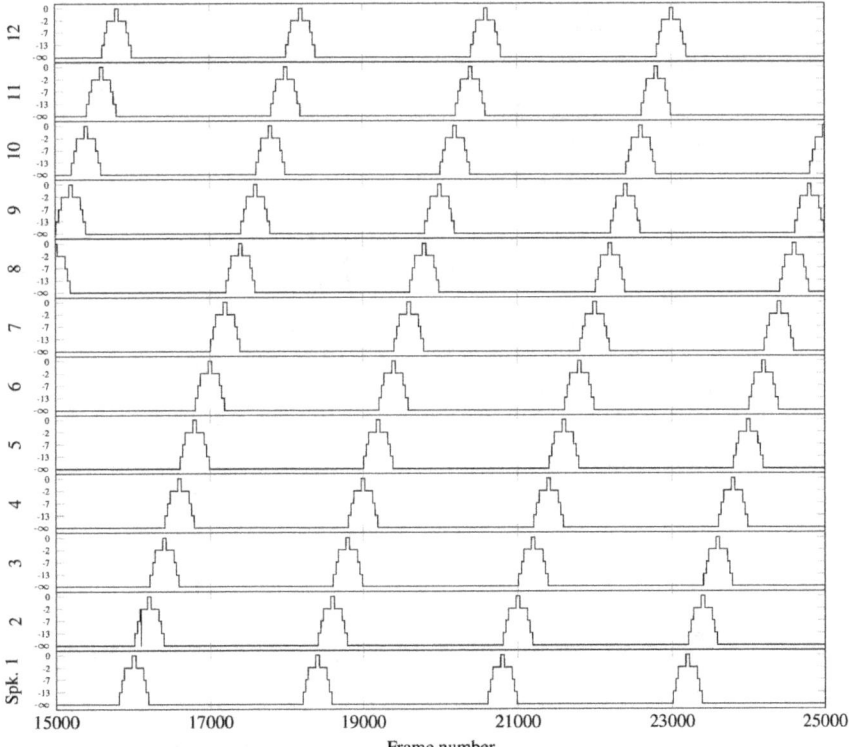

Figure 6.7a: *Automation curves on the command tape, Paris, Bibliothèque Nationale de France, département de l'Audiovisuel, fonds Xenakis, DONAUD0602_ 000613. Diagram by the authors.*

The analysis of the soundtrack clearly shows displacements of sound sources that must have been conceived by Xenakis at an earlier stage of the piece's conception. From the analysis of the control tape data, it is possible to identify regular patterns. For instance, for track 3, the data found between frames 15,000 and 25,000 (i.e., between 10'25" and 17'22") can easily be interpreted as the flow of a sound in an anticlockwise movement, jumping between the upper and lower rings of loudspeakers with a period of 1 min 45 s (Figure 6.7a).

Each line corresponds to a loudspeaker numbered from 1 to 12. Changes in each line represent intensity variations from silence to full amplitude. If we depict these data looking down on the hall (Figure 6.7b), we clearly see an anticlockwise movement. This type of movement, which can easily be reproduced on another device, bears witness to a way of thinking about the moving sound source that is not specific to the *Polytope de Cluny*.

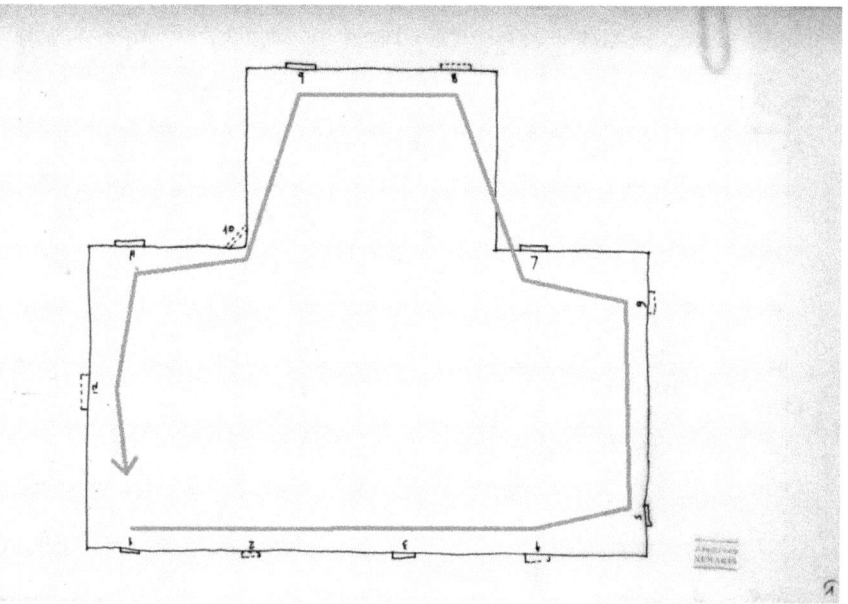

Figure 6.7b: *Anticlockwise motion of the sound spatialisation, Collection Famille Xenakis DR, OM 22–2, p. 1. Annotations in green by the authors.*

Moreover, it can even be said that certain sound movements would not be transcribed on a device other than the 12 loudspeakers used by Xenakis. Indeed, in the archives, there are several documents that represent the sound movements according to the specific device in place (Figure 6.8b). Xenakis connects the loudspeakers positioned at the top with a drawing, the layout of which can be found by interpreting the control tape. If we look at the spatialisation data of track 1 between frames 800 and 2,000 (i.e., between 33″ and 1′24″), we find complex movements of sound which, according to several patterns in the upper crown of the speakers, seem to bounce from wall to wall (Figure 6.8a).

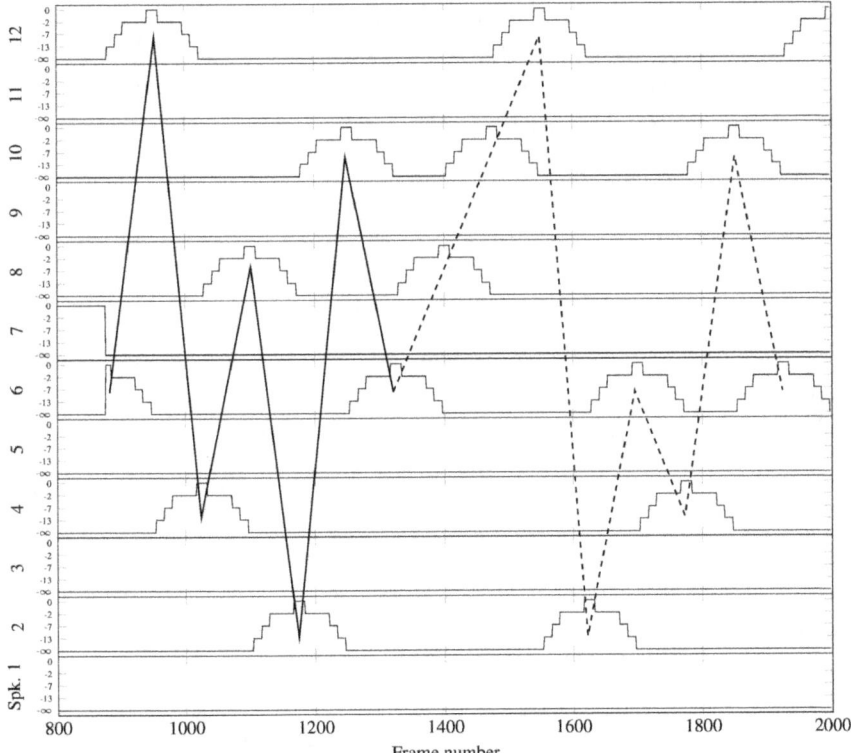

Figure 6.8a: *Automation curves on the command tape, Paris, Bibliothèque Nationale de France, département de l'Audiovisuel, fonds Xenakis, DONAUD0602_000613. Diagram by the authors.*

These patterns follow a displacement that can be found in graphic form in the sketches: The continuous lines correspond to a moving cycle between loudspeakers 6–12–4–8–2–10–6, while the dotted lines correspond to the displacement between loudspeakers 6–8–10–12–2–6–4–10–6 (Figure 6.8b). While there is a graphic design that documents the way in which Xenakis imagines sound movement, it demonstrates that Xenakis thinks of sound movement in terms of the device in place, namely the two loudspeaker crowns in specific places, and not as an abstract sound movement detached from the place and the 'instrument': the technical devices to realise that sound movement.

Finally, it seems particularly important to link the study of the spatial treatment of sound in the *Polytope de Cluny* to that of the *Diatope*, whose study of the sources (Kiourtsoglou 2017) has shown, among other things, that Xenakis's thought is strongly marked by a graphic and geometric conception of movement. The same graphic and geometric notions (see Figures 6.6, 6.7 and 6.8) allow Xenakis to imagine sound movements based sometimes on an abstract concept, sometimes on the specific possibilities of a device at his disposal, thus they can change from one project to another.

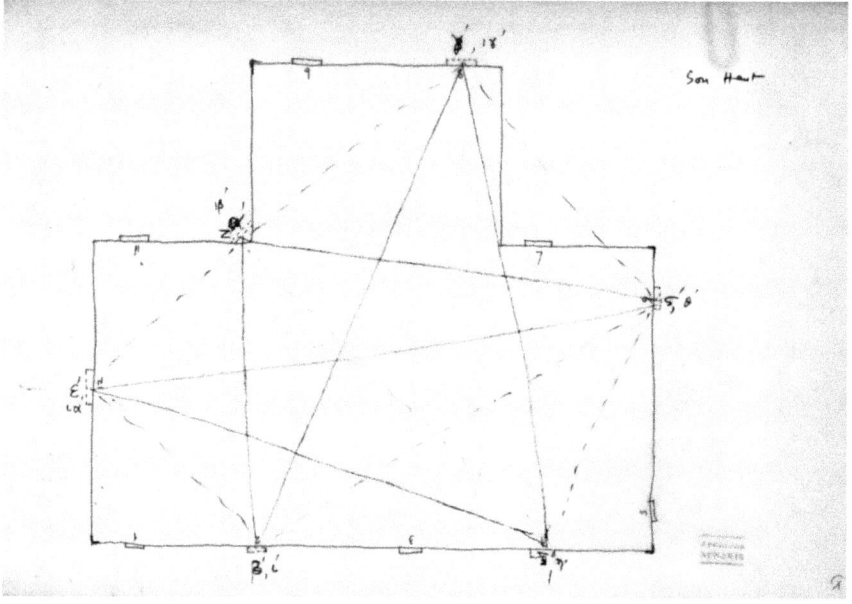

Figure 6.8b: *Iannis Xenakis,* Polytope de Cluny, *sound trajectories, Collection Famille Xenakis DR, OM 22–2, pp. 1f. Montage by the authors.*

The ambivalence of Xenakis's sound movement thinking is mirrored in the control program itself. In the description of the control program, Robert Dupuy, the computer engineer in charge of developing the programming tools for the

Polytope, defines an 'input language' used to provide computer functions for writing the various light and sound effects (Figure 6.9).

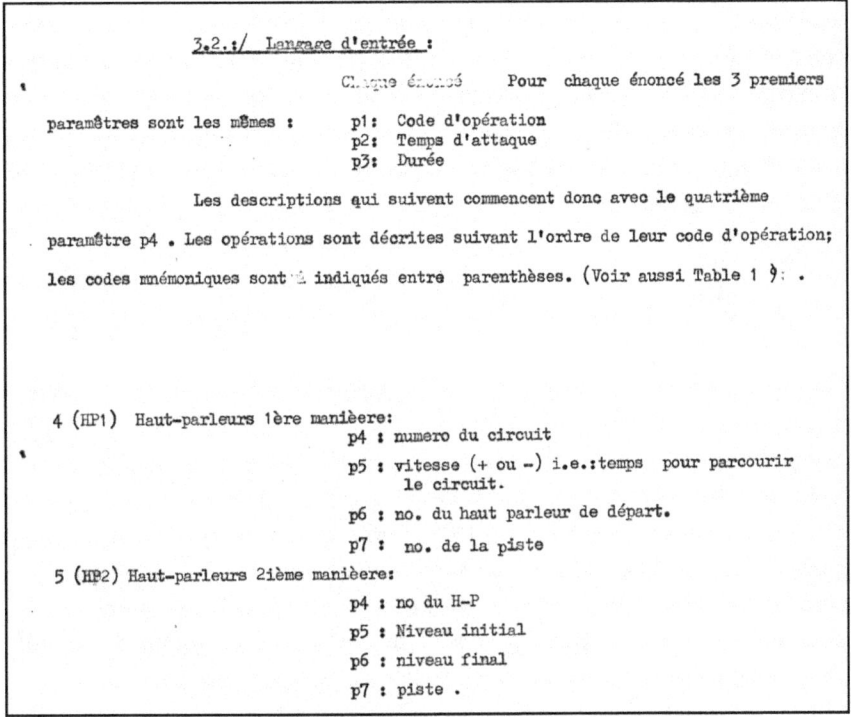

Figure 6.9: *Description of the control software by Robert Dupuy, Collection Famille Xenakis DR, OM 22–3, pp. 172f., detail.*

Two functions concern sound spatialisation, called "(HP1) Haut-parleurs 1ère manière" and "(HP2) Haut-parleurs 2ième manière". These two different functions permit spatialisation of sound either according to a trajectory or according to direct mixing. The first function (HP1) consists of translating the trajectory of a sound source (i.e., a track of the audio tape) onto a predefined loudspeaker circuit with a given speed. The user then enters, in addition to the date and duration of the effect, the identifier of a predefined loudspeaker circuit, the duration of a cycle and the starting point. The second function is used directly to route one of the tracks to a loudspeaker: The user assigns a track number to a loudspeaker as well as the start and end sound levels that will be interpolated for the defined duration. Even if this is only the provisional version of the program – the final program is not preserved – these two opposite approaches described by Robert Dupuy were probably each used by Xenakis depending on the effects he wished to achieve.

By analysing the control tape and the automation curves, it is possible to reimagine how Robert Dupuy's program was able to perform the spatialisation. For this purpose, let us reconsider the example given in Figure 6.7, which corresponds to the anticlockwise movement of audio track 3 over all the loudspeakers. Based on the description of the computer language reproduced in Figure 6.9, we could, for example, propose the following instructions for realising the above excerpt:

p1: 4 (HP1)
p2: 15,000
p3: 10,000
p4: [identifier for spatialisation circuit 1-2-3-4-5-6-7-8-9-10-11-12]
p5: 2,520
p6: 8
p7: 3

where the time variables are specified in frame units (1/24 s). The mixing of the tracks on the loudspeakers would then have been obtained by amplitude panning between two consecutive loudspeakers in the circuit, performed on the discrete scale of sound levels available on the control system (0 dB, –2 dB, –7 dB, –13 dB and –∞ dB). In other words, to simulate the movement of the sound source between two loudspeakers, the program would generate stepwise fade-in/fade-out effects, allowing the realisation of the acoustic idea of displacement on the limited system available to Xenakis for the *Polytope*. This would explain the crescendo/decrescendo relays occurring in the spatialisation data, of which Figures 6.7a and 6.8a are characteristic examples.

This reconstruction of the programming remains hypothetical, but it is not unlikely that the realisation of the sound movements was conceived in the manner described above. It enables us to distinguish Xenakis's artistic and musical idea from its realisation, that of the *Polytope de Cluny*. This concept of movement preceding the realisation through a specific program and device can then be compared with the ones in other instrumental or electronic works, notably orchestra compositions, like *Terretektorh*, or other spatialised compositions such as *Persephassa* or *Concret PH* and *La Légende d'Eer*.

Conclusion

Reconstituting both sound and visual aspects of the *Polytope de Cluny* led to a re-enactment of the show for a series of performances in the 'Espace de Projection' at IRCAM, Paris in July 2022. Further on, a concert version of the spatialised musical part was presented at the Klangtheater of the University of Music and Performing Arts Vienna during the Xenakis 2022 Conference 'Back to the Roots' in May 2022. These performances have made it possible for the first time in 50 years to rediscover a show of which only photographic traces and a stereophonic recording remained. Furthermore, the study of the sources and the analysis of the control tape offer insight into Xenakis's thinking about sound and space and can provide a framework for performers of his electroacoustic music. Finally, it is promising to compare the spatialisation concepts in his electroacoustic works such as *Polytope de Cluny* with those in his instrumental works such as *Persephassa* or *Terretektorh*: We find, for example, very characteristic circular sound movements at different speeds, which might be an indication of a common spatial concept in both fields.

Bibliography

Ampex Corporation (1964) *Ampex: TM-7 Digital Tape Transport, TM-7200 Tape Memory System*, Culver City: Ampex Corporation; https://archive.org/de tails/TNM_TM-7_digital_tape_transport_TM-7200_tape_memo_20171 204_0060/mode/1up (accessed March 20, 2023).

Carré, Pierre (2022) "*Polytope de Cluny*: Towards a Reconstitution", in *Proceedings of the Centenary International Symposium Xenakis 22. May 24–29, 2022, Athens and Nafplio*, ed. by Anastasia Georgaki and Makis Solomos, Athens: Spyridon Kostarakis, 454–466.

Da Silva Santana, Helena Maria (1998) "*Terretêktorh*: Space and Timbre, Timbre and Space", in *ExTempore, A journal of Compositional and Theoretical Research in Music*, 9/1, 12–36.

Friedl, Reinhold (2015) "Towards a Critical Edition of Electroacoustic Music: Xenakis – *La Légende d'Eer*", in *Iannis Xenakis. La musique électroacoustique/The electroacoustic music*, ed. by Makis Solomos, Paris: L'Harmattan, 109–122.

Harley, James (2015) "Orchestral Sources in the Electroacoustic Music of Iannis Xenakis: From *Polytope de Montréal* to *Kraanerg* and *Hibiki-Hana-Ma*", in *Iannis Xenakis. La musique électroacoustique/The electroacoustic music*, ed. by Makis Solomos, Paris: L'Harmattan, 15–18.

Hoffmann, Peter (1998) "L'espace abstrait dans la musique de Iannis Xenakis", in *L'espace: Musique/Philosophie*, ed. by Jean-Marc Chouvel and Makis Solomos, Paris: L'Harmattan, 141–152.

Hofmann, Boris (2008) *Mitten im Klang. Die Raumkompositionen von Iannis Xenakis aus den 1960er Jahren*, Hofheim: Wolke.

Kiourtsoglou, Elisavet (2017) "An Architect Draws Sound and Light: New Perspectives on Iannis Xenakis's *Diatope* and *La Légende d'Eer* (1978)", in *Computer Music Journal* 41/4, 8–31.

Rimoldi, Gabriel, and Schaub, Stéphan (2013) "Variações sobre o Espaço em *Terretektorh* (1965–66), de Iannis Xenakis", in *Opus* 20/2, 9–32.

Solomos, Makis (2001) "The unity of Xenakis's instrumental and electroacoustic music: The case for 'Brownian Movements'", in *Perspectives of New Music* 39/1, 244–254.

Solomos, Makis (2015) "The complexity of Xenakis's notion of space", in *Komposition für hörbaren Raum. Die frühe elektroakustische Musik und ihre Kontexte/Compositions for Audible Space. The Early Electroacoustic Music and its Contexts*, ed. by Martha Brech, and Ralph Paland, Bielefeld: transcript, 323–337.

List of Figures

Figure 6.1a: Sound diffusion system of *Polytope de Cluny*, ca. 1973–1974, Collection Famille Xenakis DR. Annotations by the authors.

Figure 6.1b: Iannis Xenakis, Top view of the loudspeaker positions of *Polytope de Cluny*, ca. 1972, Collection Famille Xenakis DR, OM 22–2, p. 1.

Figure 6.2: Inside view of the control cabin, ca. 1972, collection Famille Xenakis DR. Photomontage and annotations by the authors.

Figure 6.3: Control chain. Diagram by the authors.

Figure 6.4: Structure of the control tape frames, here frame 820. Diagram by the authors.

Figures 6.5a and 6.5b: Iannis Xenakis, *Concret PH*, graphic scores for the sound spatialisation, April 1958, Collection Famille Xenakis DR, pp. 1f.

Figure 6.6a and 6.6b: Iannis Xenakis, *La Légende d'Eer*, sketches for the sound spatialisation, Collection Famille Xenakis DR, XA 11–7, pp. 27 and 25.

Figure 6.7a. Automation curves on the command tape, Paris, Bibliothèque Nationale de France, département de l'Audiovisuel, fonds Xenakis, DONAUD0602_000613. Diagram by the authors.

Figure 6.7b: Anticlockwise motion of the sound spatialisation, 1972. Collection Famille Xenakis DR, OM 22–2, p. 1. Annotations in green by the authors.

Figure 6.8a: Automation curves on the command tape, Paris, Bibliothèque Nationale de France, département de l'Audiovisuel, fonds Xenakis, DO-NAUD0602_000613. Diagram by the authors.

Figure 6.8b: Iannis Xenakis, *Polytope de Cluny*, sound trajectories, 1972, Collection Famille Xenakis DR, OM 22–2, pp. 1f. Montage by the authors.

Figure 6.9: Description of the control software by Robert Dupuy, Collection Famille Xenakis DR, OM 22–3, detail pp. 172f.

Orchestrating Noise
Traces of *Mycènes alpha* in *Anémoessa*

Marko Slavíček

Background

From the earliest stages of his career, Iannis Xenakis was interested in two different approaches to composition: the definition of low-level material, or microcomposition, and the construction of high-level form, or macro-composition.
Having an engineering education and working experience, Xenakis turned to
graphic design as a means of achieving his goals. He would often sketch out
the music on graph paper, on which he would create various geometric shapes.
Reading them as a simple two-dimensional diagram – in which the horizontal
axis represents time and the vertical one pitch – he could use those sketches as
guidelines for creating a traditionally notated musical score. In contrast to composers of the past, who used notes as basic elements of their music material,
Xenakis was able to define and control the movements of large sound structures and then elaborate their scoring details *a posteriori*. Two early orchestra
examples, *Metastaseis* (1953–54) and *Pithoprakta* (1955–56) establish this method and are among Xenakis's most celebrated works (Bello 2001; Harley 2004).

UPIC

The idea of being able to *draw* music continued to intrigue Xenakis in the years to come. In 1966, he founded EMAMu (Equipe de Mathématique et Automatique Musicales), an institute aimed at designing equipment for computer-
aided sound synthesis and music production. In 1972, EMAMu became CEMA-
Mu (Centre d'Études de Mathématique et Automatique Musicales), a non-profit
organisation supported by the French Ministry of Culture. By 1977, Xenakis developed the so-called UPIC (Unité Polyagogique Informatique du CEMAMu), his

musical composition and sound-production system. It was conceived as a computer-based system with which the user could graphically describe different
levels of composition and synthesise sound from it (Valsamakis 2010).

Figure 7.1: *Iannis Xenakis and the UPIC board. Centre Iannis Xenakis.*

The UPIC consists of a digitising tablet with a vector display. As is the case with Xenakis's early sketches for *Metastaseis* and *Pithoprakta*, the tablet represents a two-dimensional pitch versus time diagram. The user can draw waveforms and store them in the internal memory. One then proceeds to trace a
graphic score and the computer uses the pre-assigned waveforms to render the
sound. Equally so, the dynamics and articulations can be defined by drawing envelopes. The speed at which the score is rendered can also be predefined by the
user. As the idea behind the UPIC system was to manipulate various aspects of
sound with a single intuitive drawing gesture, traditional musical parameters –
pitch, timbre, dynamics, articulation and tempo – find their analogies in the
new electronic context (Figure 7.1). The resulting score shows no details of timbre and dynamics but provides only information regarding the pitch and relati-
ve duration of the sounds. After more than two decades since the first graphic
experimentation, the UPIC finally allowed Xenakis to visualise and synthesise
sound directly from his freehand drawings without the need for further time-

consuming transcription (Harley 2004; Nelson 2010; Valsamakis 2000; Squibbs 1996).

Polytope de Mycènes

By the time the UPIC was finalised, Xenakis was preparing the largest multimedia spectacle in his œuvre: *Polytope de Mycènes* (1978). The first music to be created exclusively on the new system was a series of 'sound interpolations'[1] which would premiere at the ancient site of Mycenae. For this spectacle, Xenakis created several pages of graphic scores, which he placed between live music performances and narrations. The polytope included seven such interpolations in total, initially titled UPIC I–VII. The duration of the individual interpolations ranged from 30 seconds to two minutes.[2]

The early version of the UPIC had limitations which lingered in the compositional process. As there was no real-time synthesis, the composer needed to wait for the computer to render the drawing before he/she could hear the sound result, and this could take quite some time. There were also no mixing functions, so the pages needed to be prepared in such a way that they could be linked together. Such limitations could have prevented Xenakis from approaching the composition in any other way than as an exercise. Nevertheless, he was ultimately satisfied with the outcome and recognized the experiment not only as a suitable implementation in his polytope but as a new official composition as well: *Mycènes alpha* (1978) (Squibbs 1996; Valsamakis 2010). As a separate entry in Xenakis's catalogue of works, there was no need for the individual segments to be arranged in the same order as they occurred in *Polytope de Mycènes*. Indeed, Xenakis permutated the order of graphic scores to form a new structure consisting of the same blocks of sound.[3] In this way, the composer may have considered this work an electronic suite: a collection of shorter, interrelated movements, without any strict order.[4]

---

1   The term 'sound interpolation' was used in the programme catalogue of the polytope. The catalogue is available at the KSYME Archives.
2   For a detailed analysis of the concept and the formal structure of the *Polytope de Mycènes*, see Slavíček (2022).
3   The audio recordings of the *Polytope de Mycènes* performance are available at the KSYME Archives.
4   A percussion piece Xenakis completed earlier that year, *Pléïades* (1978), also consists of movements which can be performed in any desired order.

Mycènes alpha

The *Mycènes alpha* drawings exploited archetypal shapes which can be found in different arts and sciences. Xenakis determined two such shapes: 'clouds' and branching systems, which he called 'arborescences'.[5] He defined a 'cloud' as a form that occurs in many places, naming crowds and flocks as examples (Varga 1996: 206f.). He used stochastic functions to construct cloud-like musical events. The arborescent shape, on the other hand, resembles the growth of a tree and can be found in lightning or in the cardiovascular system. Arboricity is linked to causality, repetition and variation. Unlike clouds, it is deductive and includes temporal progression. To manipulate such shapes in music, Xenakis reached out for Markov chains and random walks. While the musical equivalent of clouds can be understood as a pointillistic multitude, he expressed arborescences using glissando tones. In *Mycènes alpha*, he explored the dichotomy and the possible connections between these archetypical shapes (Levy 2012; see Figure 7.2).

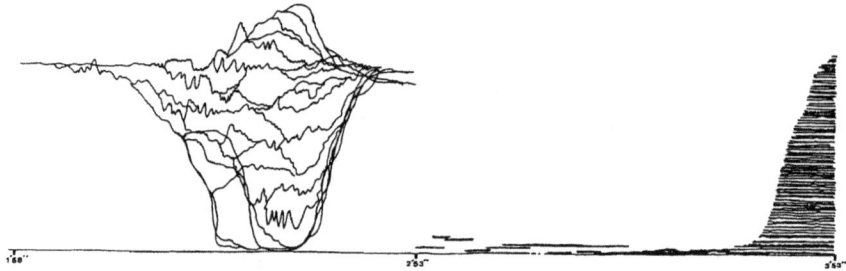

Figure 7.2: *Iannis Xenakis, Mycènes alpha, Segment 5 (1'58"-2'53") 'arborescences' and segment 6 (2'53"-3'53") 'clouds', Collection Famille Xenakis DR, score.*

The score consists of 13 segments, each having a characteristic graphic outline (Table 7.1).[6] Most of them are approximately one minute long. The shor-

---

5   Xenakis borrows the term 'arborescence' from mathematics, namely graph theory, in which it describes a directed graph form of a rooted tree.

6   Although not officially indicated in the score, Squibbs and Di Scipio agree on the numeration of the segments. The same division of the piece into 13 segments is used in this paper. The arguments for this are timestamps in the score and Xenakis's own sketches for the piece created on tracing paper. The scans of sketches are available on the official website of Centre Iannis Xenakis: http://www.centre-iannis-xenakis.org/upic_mycenae?lang=en (accessed September 22, 2022).

test segment (segment 4, timestamp 1′53″-1′58″) is only five seconds in durati-on. The score contains timestamps to mark where one segment ends and the new one begins.[7] Segments 7 and 13 are graphically identical but reproduced at different speeds (the former lasting around 20 seconds and the latter a full minute). Segment 3 and the beginning of segment 6 also resemble each other visually and audibly. Segments 11 and 12 differ in duration, lasting one minute and 20 seconds, respectively, but are visually similar as if the latter were a di-minution or a simplification of the former. The transition from segment 9 to 10 is uninterrupted and can be understood as a single block of sound (Squibbs 1996; Di Scipio 1998).[8]

Mycènes alpha		
Segment number	**Timestamps**	**Approximate duration**
1	0′00″–0′17″	20″
2	0′17″–0′55″	40″
3	0′55″–1′53″	60″
4	1′53″–1′58″	5″
5	1′58″–2′53″	60″
6	2′53″–3′53″	60″
7	3′53″–4′17″	20″
8	4′17″–5′16″	60″
9	5′16″–6′16″	60″
10	6′16″–7′16″	60″
11	7′16″–8′15″	60″
12	8′15″–8′35″	20″
13	8′35″–9′36″	60″

Table 7.1: *Sections of* Mycènes alpha. *Formal division by the author.*

---

7   The beginning of the published score contains an error: at the 0′17″ mark the timestamp wrongly reads 0′55″. The next timestamp, which should read 0′55″, was left blank.

8   These two segments also appeared one after another at the polytope perfor-mance, meaning Xenakis most probably imagined them as a unified whole.

Anémoessa

After a long period of high productivity, Xenakis created only one score for a large ensemble in the following year: *Anémoessa* (1979) for mixed choir (82 or 42 voices) and an orchestra of 90 musicians. The piece was commissioned for the Holland Festival and was performed in Amsterdam on 21 June 1979, by the Dutch Radio Choir and Orchestra under the baton of Richard Dufallo. The title stands for 'exposed to the wind' in Greek, and the choir sings exclusively vowel sounds throughout the piece (Harley 2004: 113f.). The difference between the material performed by the choir and the orchestra is minimal, as both singers and players mostly engage in creating typical Xenakian sonorities: clusters and glissandi. The score manuscript is written entirely in common time (4/4) with five measures on each page (225 measures in total). The tempo indication is 64 bpm or faster, so five measures per page add up to a duration of slightly less than 20 seconds, meaning that one measure is less than four seconds. The performance lasts between ten and 15 minutes.

In the Xenakis Archives there are 17 pages of sketches for *Anémoessa*, consisting of drawings, diagrams, calculations, and texts.[9] The composer assigned Ancient Greek numerals[10] with subscripts to various drawings and created three different versions of macro-structure:

1. $\alpha_{\alpha\beta\gamma} - \beta_{\alpha\beta\gamma} - \gamma_{\alpha\beta\gamma} - \chi_\alpha - \varepsilon_{\alpha\beta\gamma} - \chi_{\alpha\beta} - \varsigma_\alpha - \chi_\beta - \zeta_\alpha - \chi_\gamma - \eta_\alpha - \chi_\delta - \theta_{\alpha\beta\gamma} - \iota - \iota\alpha - \chi_\varepsilon - \delta_{\alpha\beta\gamma} - \iota\beta$;

2. $\gamma_{\alpha\beta\gamma} - \chi_\alpha - \varepsilon_{\alpha\beta\gamma} - \chi_{\alpha\beta} - \varsigma_\alpha - \chi_\beta - \alpha_{\alpha\beta\gamma} - \beta_{\alpha\beta\gamma} - \zeta_\alpha - \chi_\gamma - \eta_\alpha - \chi_\delta - \theta_{\alpha\beta\gamma} - \chi_\varepsilon - \iota_{\alpha\beta} - \delta_{\alpha\beta\gamma} - \iota\alpha_{\alpha\beta\gamma} - \iota\beta_{\alpha\beta}$;

3. $\gamma_{\alpha\beta\gamma} - \chi_\alpha - \varepsilon_{\alpha\beta\gamma} - \chi_{\alpha\beta} - \varsigma_\alpha - \chi_\beta - \zeta_\alpha - \chi_\gamma - \eta_\alpha - \chi_\delta - \theta_{\alpha\beta\gamma} - \iota_{\alpha\beta} - \iota\alpha_{\alpha\beta\gamma} - \chi_\varepsilon - \alpha_{\alpha\beta\gamma} - \beta_{\alpha\beta\gamma} - \delta_{\alpha\beta\gamma} - \iota\beta_{\alpha\beta}$.[11]

While he crossed out the first two versions, he underlined the third one and wrote ‚bon' (good) underneath. In the score, Xenakis also marked the same numerals for each segment that corresponds to the ones in the sketches, only this time serving as rehearsal marks for the conductor. The 'bon' order of numerals from the sketches corresponds to the one written in the score.

---

9   Collection Famille Xenakis DR, folder OM 26–2.

10   α (alpha) = 1; β (beta) = 2; γ (gamma) = 3; δ (delta) = 4; ε (epsilon) = 5; ϛ (digamma) = 6; ζ (zeta) = 7; η (eta) = 8; θ (theta) = 9; ι (iota) = 10. The combinations result in higher numbers, for example: iota (ι = 10) and alpha (α = 1) equal 11 (ια). Transliterated to Latin, these values are traditionally converted to Roman numerals.

11   Found on the first and last page of the sketches, Collection Famille Xenakis DR, OM 26–2, pp. 1, 17.

All three versions consist of 18 segments. Apart from the δ (delta) segment, which occurs before the last one, the original version follows the alphabetical order of 12 numerals (α, β, γ, ... ιβ), intersected six times by the numeral χ (khi). Although χ denotes the number 600 in the ancient numeral system, it is unlikely that Xenakis meant anything numerical in this case. Instead, χ stands for chorus (χορός; khorós), as each of the six such segments are scored for voices a cappella.[12] The second and third versions maintained the intersecting χ between the segments but further rearranged the original alphabetical order. Unlike the last two versions, the original one also has a single ι (iota) which likely corresponded to ιαβ in the other two versions. The second and third versions are almost identical, only with different positions of segments $α_{αβγ}$, $β_{αβγ}$ and $ια_{αβγ}$. The sections of the third and final version are ordered according to the following proportions:

$$γ_{αβγ} [3(1+1+1)] - χ_α [5] - ε_{αβγ} [3(1+1+1)] - χ_{αβ} [2(1+1)] - ç_α [1] - χ_β [3+2/5] - ζ_α [1/5]$$
$$- χ_γ [2/5] - η_α [1] - χ_δ [1] - θ_{αβγ} [3(1+1+1)] - ι_{αβ} [2(1+1)] - ια_{αβγ} [3(1+1+1)] - χ_ε [6] -$$
$$α_{αβγ} [3(1+1+1)] - β_{αβγ} [3(1+1+1)] - δ_{αβγ} [3(1+1+1)] - ιβ_{αβ} [2(1+1)].^{13}$$

The majority of subscripts of the segments represent exactly five measures in the score. The exceptions are $χ_α$ (25 measures), $χ_β$ (17 measures), $ζ_α$ (one measure), $χ_γ$ (two measures), and $χ_ε$ (30 measures) with no subdivisions. While there is nothing unusual about Xenakis's shaping of the macro-form using the blocks of material, his drawings in the sketches must be taken seriously. Out of 17 pages, 12 of them – the ones which correspond to 12 segments annotated by the Greek numerals – are copied directly from the graphic score of *Mycènes alpha* (see Figures 7.3 and 7.4; Gibson 2011: 208).

This is not an isolated example of self-borrowing in Xenakis's œuvre, and Xenakis is far from being the only composer to reuse his own material. His early electronic music and polytopes have many common passages drawn from acoustic sources. In other works, he would select certain fragments for their sonic qualities and transfer them to create new ones. Once these fragments were removed from their original context, they became independent entities, which he would further manipulate as desired. Such manipulations include everything from literal repetition, transpositions, inversions, arrangements for different instrumentation and other transformations (Di Scipio 2004; Gibson 2005).

---

12   Xenakis also wrote the Greek word χορός on the ninth page of the sketches, where he drew the vocal lines for the $χ_α$ segment.

13   Author's analysis: One unit in the representation stands for five measures in the score.

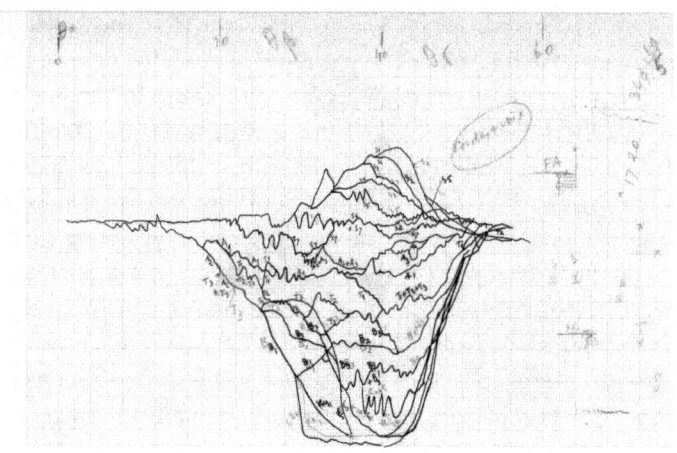

Figure 7.3: *Iannis Xenakis, sketches for* Anémoessa, *Collection Famille Xenakis DR, OM 26–2, p. 15.*

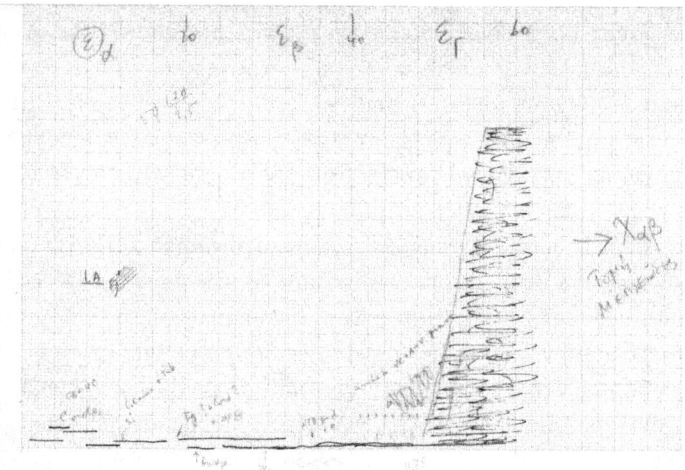

Figure 7.4: *Iannis Xenakis, sketches for* Anémoessa, *Collection Famille Xenakis DR, OM 26–2, p. 11.*

Even *Polytope de Mycènes* – within which *Mycènes alpha* material was first performed – contained five existing pieces from the composer's catalogue. But unlike his early *musique concrète* works, in which the recordings of various instruments and ensembles became building blocks for further electronic manipulation, the situation here is reversed: An electronic piece is transformed into an acoustic one.

A particularly interesting page among the *Anémoessa* sketches is the very last one, which is also the only one created on blank paper without a millimetre grid (Figure 7.5).

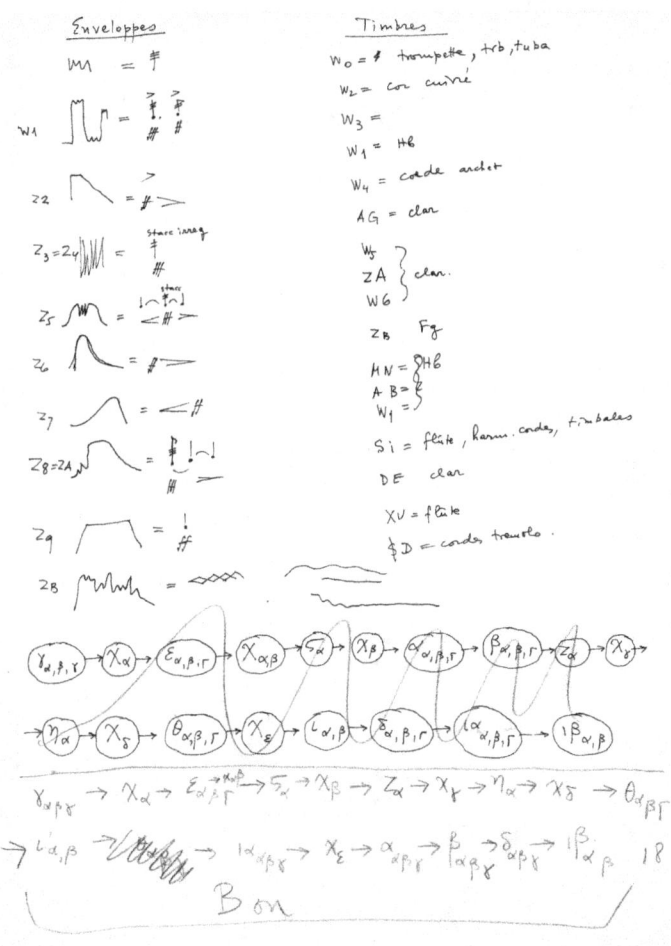

Figure 7.5: *Iannis Xenakis, sketches for* Anémoessa, *Collection Famille Xenakis DR, OM 26–2, p. 17.*

Above the previously explained three versions of a macro-structure, Xenakis wrote down a list of various envelopes and timbres and their musical analogies. For example, he compared a square wave in electronics to a tremolo technique in instrumental performance and a sharp random walk envelope to an irregular staccato. The list of timbres includes the list of instruments, groups of instruments or instrumental techniques such as 'strings tremolo'. All envelopes and timbres are assigned a code name which Xenakis used as a memo for the creation of UPIC scores. This list equally served as a memo for the transcription of UPIC material to the orchestra. By consistently assigning ancient numerals in both the sketches and the final score of *Anémoessa*, Xenakis made it possible to detect each of the corresponding segments transcribed from *Mycènes alpha* (Table 7.2). At times, one is even able to visually track analogous sections in the scores, for example, segment 3 of *Anémoessa* and segment 6 of *Mycènes alpha* (Figure 7.6).

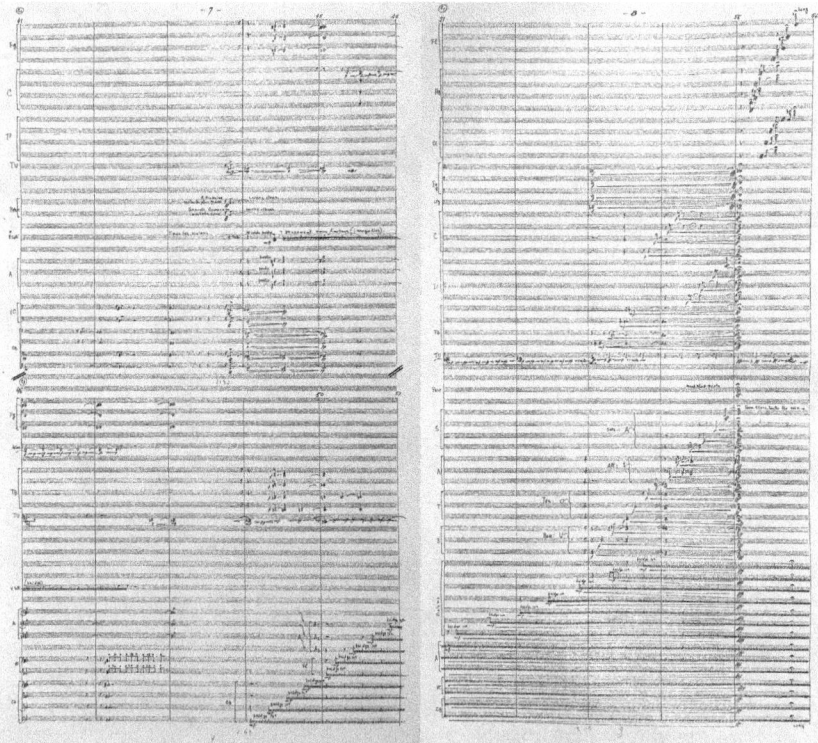

Figure 7.6: *Iannis Xenakis,* Anémoessa, *pp. 7f., (bars 44–55) as analogous to segment 6 of* Mycènes alpha *(Fig. 7.2, 1'58"-2'53"), Durand Salabert Eschig, Paris.*

Anémoessa				Mycènes alpha	
Segment number	Rehearsal mark(s)	Bar(s)	Maximal duration	Segment number	Times-tamps
1	$\gamma_{\alpha,\beta,\gamma}$	1–15	60″	11	7′16″–8′15″
2	χ_α	16	90″	–	–
3	$\epsilon_{\alpha,\beta,\gamma}$	41–55	60″	6	2′53″–3′53″
4	$\chi_{\alpha,\beta}$	56–65	40″	–	–
5	ς_α	66–70	20″	4	1′53″–1′58″
6	χ_β	71–87	68″	–	–
7	ζ_α	88	4″	4	1′53″–1′58″
8	χ_γ	89–90	8″	–	–
9	η_α	91–95	20″	1	0′00″–0′17″
10	χ_δ	96–100	20″	–	–
11	$\theta_{\alpha,\beta,\gamma}$	101–115	60″	5	1′58″–2′53″
12	$\iota_{\alpha,\beta}$	116–125	40″	2	0′17″–0′55″
13	$\iota\alpha_{\alpha,\beta,\gamma}$	126–140	60″	8	4′17″–5′16″
14	χ_ϵ	141–170	120″	–	–
15	$\alpha_{\alpha,\beta,\gamma}$	171–185	60″	9	5′16″–6′16″
16	$\beta_{\alpha,\beta,\gamma}$	186–200	60″	10	6′16″–7′16″
17	$\delta_{\alpha,\beta,\gamma}$	201–215	60″	13	8′35″–9′36″
18	$\iota\beta_{\alpha,\beta}$	216–225	40″	12	8′15″–8′35″

Table 7.2: *Corresponding segments of* Anémoessa *and* Mycènes alpha. *List by the author.*[14]

The Self-borrowing Method

Xenakis's intention to transfer the electronic material to orchestra and choir is revealed in an interview with Enzo Restagno (Restagno 1988: 56, 58). Another hint can be found on page 3 of the *Anémoessa* sketches, where Xenakis wrote a memo in Greek mentioning *Mycènes alpha* (Collection Famille Xenakis DR, OM 26-2). But one can find other quotations in *Anémoessa* as well, namely

---

14   Segments 9 and 10 of *Mycènes alpha* follow one another in *Anémoessa*, just as they did in the *Polytope de Mycènes*.

that of a percussion piece Pléïades (1978). An adaptation from the Claviers (keyboards) movement is identified in sopranos and altos in bars 161–170 (Harley 2004: 113; Gibson 2011: 208). Another possible source is a composition similar to Anémoessa in instrumentation, Cendrées (1973), scored for choir and orchestra. On page 13 of the Anémoessa sketches, above the indication for Pléïades implementation, Xenakis simply wrote Cendrées (Collection Famille Xenakis DR, OM 26-2). Indeed, some choral passages of Anémoessa seem to resemble the vocalising style of its precursor.[15] All six a cappella segments of Anémoessa – those assigned the numeral χ (khi) – are composed of random walks, which is also evident in the curvy lines in the sketches.[16]

Gibson compared various instances of self-borrowing in Xenakis's instrumental works and pointed out the similarities between the pieces N'Shima (1975) and Nyuyo (1985). Xenakis transferred 69 bars from N'Shima, which occupies almost a third of the Nyuyo score. As an extreme example of such an approach, Gibson stated that it is probably the longest excerpt that Xenakis transcribed (Gibson 2005: 270f.). In the case of Mycènes alpha and Anémoessa one could argue the contrary: Out of 225 bars, 136 of them have been taken from Mycènes alpha, thus comprising approximately two thirds of the piece. What makes this example unique is the fact that the entire Mycènes alpha material is present in Anémoessa instead of selected sections only.[17] One must acknowledge, however, that Gibson (2005) focused exclusively on Xenakis's instrumental music in his paper. The instances of self-borrowing in electronic pieces (for example, those in the polytopes) could cover more, but that was never the point. In addition, the case of Mycènes alpha and Anémoessa is specific because Xenakis did not (and could not) simply copy the notes from one piece to the other. Until the creation of Anémoessa, Mycènes alpha was not composed with notes but with lines on a UPIC board. That means Xenakis had

---

15   As the focus of this paper is the transfer of the electronic material into an acoustic context, an in-depth analysis of possible connections between Anémoessa and Cendrées is omitted. If there should be any correlation, the transfer is likely not direct and without manipulation of the material. It is also possible that there is no instance of self-borrowing in this case, but Xenakis wrote a memo to describe the vocalising style he wished to achieve. Whatever the reason for the appearance of Cendrées in the sketches, there is still plenty of room for further research on the Anémoessa sources.

16   See Collection Famille Xenakis DR, OM 26-2, pp. 1, 2, 9, 12, 13 and 14.

17   The only exception is segment 3 of Mycènes alpha. However, this segment's material (at least partially) appears in segment 6, so one could argue that no material has been omitted.

to interpret the drawings first before he could take any further steps, which is assuredly a creative process in its own right.

Conclusion

All three instances of the same music – the sound interpolations of *Polytope de Mycènes*, the electronic piece *Mycènes alpha*, and *Anémoessa* – were created in the span of approximately one year. Although they share the same material, the order of individual segments differs in each instance. Xenakis's reasons for reaching out for existing material and applying it in other works could be explained by the shortage of time to produce a score. However, in the aforementioned interview with Restagno, Xenakis stated that to him transcription is not merely a mechanical operation. Whether or not such a method was a time-saver is a matter of debate, but in the case of *Anémoessa*, Xenakis intentionally tested his techniques and experimented with a single sonic material in diverse contexts.

It is crucial to understand that in his early years, Xenakis used drawing as a compositional tool, not to produce scores with graphic notation. Once the graphics were finished, he would transcribe them into conventional music notation. With the development of the UPIC, this process was eliminated. One did not need to transcribe anything because the drawings *were* the score. There was no need for live performers because the computer did all the work. After decades of experimentation, Xenakis's architectural dream to draw music by hand came true. And yet, he repeated the same transcription process with *Anémoessa*, despite the fact that he had already finalised the recording of an electronic piece. Such a procedural enantiodromia indicates that there is no difference of value between electronic and acoustic music in Xenakis's reasoning. They are genres of equal worth, sharing aesthetics and compositional techniques.

* * *

I would like to thank Mâkhi Xenakis and Costas Mantzoros of the KSYME (Contemporary Music Research Centre) for their kind help in providing me with archival material.

Audio-visual Presentation

The audio-visual presentation of all corresponding segments of the *Anémoessa* and *Mycènes alpha* scores is available under the following link: https://vimeo. com/751070889 (accessed March 27, 2024).

Bibliography

Bello, Angelo (2001) "Notes on Composing with the UPIC System: The Equipment of Iannis Xenakis", in *Présences de Iannis Xenakis*, ed. by Makis Solomos, Paris: Centre de documentation de la musique contemporaire, 93–98.

Di Scipio, Agostino (1998) "Compositional models in Xenakis's electroacoustic music", in *Perspectives of New Music* 36/2, 201–243.

Di Scipio, Agostino (2004) "The Orchestra as a Resource for Electroacoustic Music/On some works by Iannis Xenakis and Paul Dolden", in *Journal of new music research*, 33/2, 173–183.

Gibson, Benoît (2005) "Self-borrowings in the instrumental music of Iannis Xenakis", in *Definitive Proceedings of the "International Symposium Iannis Xenakis" (Athens, May 2005)*, ed. by Makis Solomos, Anastasia Georgaki, and Giorgos Zervos, 265–274, https://cicm.univ-paris8.fr/ColloqueXenakis/p apers/Gibson.pdf (accessed April 4, 2024).

Gibson, Benoît (2011) *The Instrumental Music of Iannis Xenakis. Theory, Practice, Self-Borrowing*, Hillsdale N.Y.: Pendragon Press.

Harley, James (2004) *Xenakis: His Life in Music*, New York/London: Taylor & Francis.

Levy, Benjamin R. (2012) "Clouds and Arborescences in Mycenae Alpha and the Polytope de Mycènes", in *Xenakis Matters*, ed. by Sharon Kanach, Hillsdale N.Y.: Pendragon Press, 173–184.

Nelson, Peter (2010) "Performing the UPIC system of Iannis Xenakis", in *Performing Xenakis*, ed. by Sharon Kanach, Hillsdale N.Y.: Pendragon Press, 373–390.

Restagno, Enzo, ed. (1988) *Xenakis*, Torino: E.D.T. Edizioni di Torino.

Slavíček, Marko (2022) "The Narrative of the Mycenae Polytope", in *Centenary International Symposium XENAKIS 22: Lectures Workshops Concerts*, 467–475; https://xenakis2022.uoa.gr (accessed March 27, 2024).

Squibbs, Ronald (1996) "Images of Sound in Xenakis's *Mycenae-Alpha*", in *Troisièmes journées d'informatique musicale JIM* 96/4, 208–219.

Valsamakis, Nikolas (2000) "Aesthetics and techniques in the electroacoustic music of Iannis Xenakis", in *Journal of the Hellenic diaspora* 26, 7–58.

Varga, Bálint-András (1996) *Conversations with Iannis Xenakis*, London: Faber & Faber.

List of Figures

Figure 7.1: Iannis Xenakis and the UPIC board. Centre Iannis Xenakis.

Figure 7.2: Iannis Xenakis, *Mycènes alpha*, Segment 5 (1'58"-2'53") 'arborescences' and segment 6 (2'53"-3'53") 'clouds', Collection Famille Xenakis DR, score.

Figure 7.3: Iannis Xenakis, sketches for *Anémoessa*, Collection Famille Xenakis DR, OM 26–2, p. 15.

Figure 7.4: Iannis Xenakis, sketches for *Anémoessa*, Collection Famille Xenakis DR, OM 26–2, p. 11.

Figure 7.5: Iannis Xenakis, sketches for *Anémoessa*, Collection Famille Xenakis DR, OM 26–2, p. 17.

Figure 7.6: Iannis Xenakis, *Anémoessa*, pp. 7f., detail (bars 44–55) as analogous to segment 6 of *Mycènes alpha* (Fig. 7.2, 1'58"-2'53"), Durand Salabert Eschig, Paris.

Sonic Otherness. Traces of Traditional Musics in Xenakis's Electroacoustic Œuvre

Reinhold Friedl

> No expedition to Amazonia, Sikkim or Kilimamdjaro without a tape recorder. No tape experiments, no phonogène or electronic music in Paris, Milan or New York without Zulus, sorcerers and lamas.[1] (Schaeffer 1960: 300)

Introduction

This article discusses a hitherto little-noticed aspect of Xenakis's œuvre: the use of recordings of instruments from traditional music cultures in his electroacoustic music. "Traditional musics" shall in this article denote – according to Jaap Kunst's definition of ethnomusicology as a subject of study – "all tribal and folk music and every kind of non-European art music" (Rice 2014: 7). This is exactly, what Xenakis was interested in: folk musics, European included, and art music from other cultures (especially Japan), or in other words: every traditional music beyond Western art music (with the exception of contemporary popular music).

Already in his youth Xenakis was interested in folk music. In his first steps as a composer, he tried to follow Béla Bartók. In the beginning of the 1950s, Xenakis started to discover non-European music and studied with Olivier Messiaen – an avowed lover of Indian Classical music. Having trained in the late 1950s with Pierre Schaeffer at the GRM (Groupe de recherches musicales) in Paris, Xenakis was – after his experience in the class of Messiaen – once more

---

1 "Pas d'expédition en Amazonie, au Sikkim, au Kilimamdjaro, sans magnétophone. Pas d'exploration magnétique, pas de phonogène ni de musique électronique à Paris, à Milan ou à New York sans zoulous, sans sorciers, sans lamas." Unless otherwise stated, all translations by the author.

in an environment very open for traditional music from all over the world. Schaeffer had not only founded the GRM, but also Radio France's own record label Ocora to collect and preserve traditional music heritage especially in Africa. Xenakis had a considerable private collection: The Xenakis Archives in the Bibliothèque nationale in Paris list more than 90 tapes and audio cassettes with traditional music from Zaire to Japan, from Central Africa to Bali, from Norway to Corsica. Xenakis's first commission was to compose film music for *Orient-Occident* (1960), a film dedicated to the cultural connection between East and West.

Xenakis was attracted by unusual sounds: In his first tape piece *Diamorphoses* (1957) he used the noise of airplanes and wind, and later included in his electroacoustic music – especially in his polytopes – sounds of non-European instruments, like African thumb pianos, kalimbas or a Japanese biwa in *Hibiki Hana Ma* (1970). The characteristic bass bourdon of *Bohor* (1962) is a transposed Laotian mouth organ. Almost all of his polytopes include recordings of what he calls 'Jew's harps' ('guimbardes'). Even in his late electronic computer music, he could not resist the temptation of sound material from other continents: Thanks to the second generation of the UPIC system (Unité Polyagogique Informatique du CEMAMu) Xenakis was able to use samples, probably doing so in *Voyage absolu des Unari vers Andromède* (1989).

It is difficult to determine the exact provenance of the recordings of traditional musics and sounds used by Xenakis: Sometimes they are treated with tape manipulation techniques or cumulated in overlays and eventually used as samples; Xenakis hardly ever listed the sources. Recordings and production tapes as well as paper drafts from the work in the studio were often lost. But listening comparisons and Xenakis's naming in preserved sketches and scores is unequivocal: We must revise our notion (derived largely from the rare publications on this topic mostly related to his instrumental music) that Xenakis used traditional musics only as an inspiration for structural goals. Certainly, he used large-scale recordings of traditional instruments, perhaps even parts of existing traditional music recordings. If Xenakis did some recordings himself, the question arises whether or not he 'improvised', thus contradicting his explicit rejection of improvisation.

The use of recordings of traditional musics in Xenakis's electroacoustic compositions has for pragmatic reasons not been studied extensively to date: Analogue recordings in archives are hardly accessible, and if already digitised, copies are difficult to get within the normal procedure of libraries. This makes it almost impossible to compare different sources. But even if that were the case, a methodological problem arises: Musicological research is mostly based on written sources and rarely on auditive ones. In this context, re-evaluation becomes necessary, as does comparative listening.

The influence of traditional musics on Xenakis's work has been discussed first by Makis Solomos as an example of the broader use of "musical cultures indiscriminately referred to here as traditional, local or extra-European" (Solomos 2010: 228) in contemporary music (Stockhausen, Boulez, etc.). Solomos focusses on Xenakis's instrumental music and points out: "The integration [of non-European music] was mostly carried out for structural purposes – that is, precisely to radically renew the musical language"[2] (ibid.), and not only to get an "exotic look" [*optique d'exotisme*]. "His interest [in non-European music] is not heard much in his work, since the reference to local music is made in a structural way"[3] (ibid.: 229).

Ronan Gil de Morais calls this into question and gives a comparative listening example of an original gamelan piece from Bali that Xenakis transcribed (at least the scale) and "a conclusive section in the *Claviers* movement [a part of *Pléïades* (1978)]" (De Morais 2022: 336), as "hearing it at the BnF [Bibliothèque nationale de France], a direct correlation with the movement *Claviers* emerged" (ibid.). De Morais states: "Xenakis's relationship with Indonesian gamelan music cannot be described as appropriation but rather more of an influence" (ibid.). This influence is clearly audible, thus not only structural.

For Xenakis's electroacoustic music the influence is even stronger: Listening to his tape music – especially the single tracks of his multitrack compositions – shows that the composer extensively used recordings of traditional instruments, perhaps even some existing recordings of traditional musics. Even though this remains unclear, he was not the only one. Gianmario Borio described the long tradition of "solidarity between ethnology and avant-garde" in the 20th century (Borio 2011). And Romuald Vandelle stated as early as 1959:

> If [...] works of exotic music and works of experimental music are played to an unprepared audience, they might be confused. This is no coincidence but rather a result of the great similarities between the two types of music.[4] (Vandelle 1959: 35)

---

2   "l'intégration s'effectua le plus souvent à des fins structurelles – c'est-à-dire précisément pour renouveler radicalement le langage musical – et non pas dans une optique d'exotisme pour apporter une 'couleur' locale."

3   "Cet intérêt s'entend assez peu dans son œuvre, puisque la référence aux musiques locales s'effectue d'une manière structurelle".

4   "Si [...] on fait entendre à un auditoire non prévuenu des œuvres de musique exotique et des œuvres de musique éxperimentale, il peut arriver qu'on vienne à les confondre. Ce n'est pas un effet du hasard mais parce qu'il existe de grandes ressemblances entre les deux musiques."

Traditional Musics and Electroacoustic Music

Born in Brăila in Romania, Xenakis's first attempts as a composer have been in-fluenced by Béla Bartók, following his approach of using folk music as a source of inspiration (Baltensperger 1996; Matossian 2005). Xenakis's family returned to Greece when he was eight years old. Xenakis remained receptive to tradi-tional music throughout his life.

> I know it sounds silly, but sometimes a sentimental melody can move me to tears. [...] Music can even make me cry. It's crazy. But it still happens today. (Xenakis 1995: 17)

For a composer who is notorious for his rational concepts and who even tried to build an automatic composing machine towards the end of his life, this is surprising. But for Xenakis, rational design and emotional content of music were not opposites.

> I loved traditional music – Indian music, for example – and I always found the music of the Noh theatre to be extraordinary. Intuitively, I thought: It must be very close to the music of the first ancient tragedies. This wide-ranging interest that I have always had, comes perhaps from the fact that I was born in Romania and that very early on I heard Gypsy, Hungarian and Russian music ... (Xenakis 1994: 109)

Xenakis had to flee Greece because of his opposition to the British occupation. He arrived in Paris in 1947.

> I worked for Le Corbusier, first as an engineer and then as an architect, while starting to compose ... folkloric-post-Bartókian music.[5] (Xenakis 2003: 19)

And Xenakis opened his listening horizons to non-European music:

> In 1948 I was already a composer. But I was only writing somewhat folk-loristic mawkishness. Greek folklore helped me a lot. At the time this type of music sold well, thanks in particular to the Chant du Monde team, which was financed by the Soviet Union. This publisher distributed very beauti-

---

5   "J'ai donc travaillé chez Le Corbusier, d'abord comme ingénieur puis comme architecte, tout en commençant à composer... une musique folklorico-post-bartókienne..."

ful things. And I used to go to André Schaeffner, who introduced me to the music of Bali, Java and Japan. That was in 1950.[6] (Xenakis 2003: 41f.)

André Schaeffner founded the ethnomusicological department of the Musée de l'homme in Paris in 1929 and directed it until 1965. His influence on contemporary music was immense and, at least in France, well known; his correspondence with Pierre Boulez has been published (Boulez, Schaeffner 1998). Probably the same year, also in 1950[7] (Gerhards 1972: 366), Xenakis attended the composition class of Olivier Messiaen, who had a particularly strong interest in Indian classical music and its rhythmical structures. Xenakis discovered "Hindu music. The most civilised and perfect rhythmic organisation", as he noted in 1951 (Mâche 2011: 21). Francois-Bernard Mâche speculates that Xenakis might even already have been involved with Indian Classical music before he met Messiaen.[8] Subsequently Xenakis composed for Indian percussion instruments, as the recently discovered score of *Rythmes sur Tabla* (1953) shows (Declercq 2022: 338).

Since the beginning of ethnomusicology, audio recordings and the phonograph have been at the base of ethnomusicological research. Bartók especially preferred recordings of traditional music to transcriptions (Borio 2015: 136), which for him were more of an analytical tool as well as a way of providing materials for his activity as a composer. Xenakis profited early on from ethnomusicological audio recordings. He also listened to commercial records of traditional music and would have tape recorded some of them for his own personal use (De Marais 2022: 329); he might have obtained copies of unreleased recordings via Schaeffner.

I knew Noh because I discovered it at André Schaeffner's home in the attics of the Musée de l'Homme in 1951–1952. Schaeffner was as bald as he was

---

6   "En 1948, j'étais déjà compositeur. Mais je n'écrivais que des mièvreries quelque peu folklorisantes. Le folklore grec m'aidait beaucoup. A l'époque ce type de musique marchait bien, grâce notamment à l'équipe du Chant du Monde que finançait alors l'Union Soviétique. Cet éditeur diffusait de très belles choses. Et j'allais au Trocadéro chez André Schaeffner qui m'a fait découvrir les musiques de Bali, de Java, du Japon. C'était en 1950."

7   Concerning Xenakis visiting Messiaen's class, the sources differ: Seurat states 1948–1949 (Xenakis 2003: 45), Matossian 1951 (Matossian 1981: 59), Mâche 1952 (Mâche 2011: 22).

8   "Le carnet n° 1 sur lequel Xenakis a noté esquisses et réflexions de septembre 1951 à décembre 1952 porte la trace, en octobre 1951, d'un intérêt pour 'la musique hindoue'. Les remarques de Xenakis témoignent d'une admiration spontanée, probablement liée à un spectacle de ballet indien, et peut-être même antérieure à son contact avec Messiaen: Organisation la plus civilisée du rythme et la plus parfaite." (Mâche 2011: 21)

charming. He had a phenomenal curiosity and knowledge, and he received us in an appalling dust. I used to spend whole Sundays in his museum.[9] (Xenakis 2003: 93)

Many traditional musics and most electroacoustic musics are not notated. They are hard to transcribe as the traditional European notation systems often do not apply. Thus for both, it was repeatedly disputed if they were music at all. Friedrich Blume stated in 1958 about electronic music:

> [...] this fully denatured product of the montage of physical sounds has nothing to do with music [...]. Here, the border is definitely crossed.[10] (Blume 1959: 17)

In different contexts, neither Wendy Carlos nor Daphne Oram were allowed to call their electronic music "music". (Holmes 2016: 86) And still, in 2006 Martha Brech writes about early *musique concrète*:

> [...] the tonal content is not very reminiscent of music. According to today's criteria, one should rather speak of acoustic art.[11] (Brech 2006: 110)

A similar discussion took place about whether traditional musics are music, and if so, in which sense (see also Nettl 2006).

Xenakis was seduced by this common extra-musical charm. His interviews with François Delalande are entitled "You always have to be an immigrant" (Xenakis 1997). Xenakis was interested in foreign worlds and the otherness of traditional musics and *musique concrète*.

> Xenakis was probably present at the first concert of musique concrète in 1950, at a time when he was studying with Olivier Messiaen and composing music in the spirit of Bartók. In 1953, he tried to get access to Schaeffer's studio. Thanks to a recommendation by Messiaen, he met Schaeffer in 1954. (Solomos 2002: 2f.)

---

9   "Je connaissais le Nô pour l'avoir découvert chez André Schaeffner dans les greniers du musée de l'Homme en 1951–1952. Schaeffner était aussi chauve que charmant. Il avait une curiosité, une connaissance phénoménale et nous recevait dans une poussière effroyable. Je passais dans son musée des dimanches entiers."

10 "Mit Musik [...] hat dieses volldenaturierte Produkt aus der Montage physikalischer Schälle nichts mehr zu tun. Hier ist die Grenze entschieden überschritten."

11 "Doch der klangliche Gehalt erinnert wenig an Musik. Nach heutigen Kriterien müsste man eher von akustischer Kunst sprechen."

But Pierre Schaeffer did not welcome the young composer until 1957, when Xenakis got accepted to visit the 'grand stage', the initiation course at the GRMC, the Groupe de recherches de musique concrète at the French Radio. Subsequently he became a member of the group (Gayou 2007: 114).

Since the autumn of 1954, Pierre Schaffer had also started working for the RFOM (Radiodiffusion de la France d'outre-mer) and was less and less present at the GRMC. (Le Bail 2012: 165). Schaeffer is usually known as a pioneer of electroacoustic music and inventor of *musique concrète*, but his interests were much broader: Radio broadcasts in France's African colonies were made by people in Paris who had never been to Africa. Schaeffer developed a concept for an appropriate training for future African native radio producers to run local radio stations by themselves – decolonised, so to speak (Tournet-Lammer 2008: 61). For that purpose, he set up his Studio-école and in 1956 became director of the newly founded SORAFOM (Société de radiodiffusion de la France d'outre-mer). Schaeffer war impressed by the musical richness of traditional musics from Africa and immediately founded – quite a man of action – a record label: Local music and field recordings were released, the first one in 1957 being the 10″ record *Danses et chants de Bamoun* with music from Cameroon. The first releases were labelled "Collection radiodiffusion outre-mer", soon taking over the department's name SORAFOM (which changed to OCORA (Office de coopération radiophonique) in 1960, the new name of the same radio department). Ocora still exists today as one of the most well-known 'world music' labels and has a back catalogue of more than 1,000 releases.[12]

In October 1957, Pierre Schaeffer was fired due to a political change (Tournet-Lammer: 309) and took back the direction of the GRMC the following month (Robert 2000: 43). In order to redynamise the group, he pushed pedagogical and research activities and changed the name to express a new openness: GRM, Groupe de recherches musicales.[13] All kinds of music should henceforth serve as subjects of research, not only *musique concrète*.

Pierre Schaeffer was well aware of the already mentioned common problems of traditional musics and electroacoustic music:

> One of these dead ends is 'musical concepts'. It is now not only the scale and tonality that have come to be rejected by the most adventurous, as by the most primitive musics of our time, but the very first of these concepts: the musical note, the archetype of the musical object, the basis of all notation,

---

12   https://www.radiofrance.com/les-editions/collections/Ocaora (accessed March 20, 2023).

13   The name was changed to GRM, Groupe de recherches musicales, in 1958 (Gayou 2007: 107).

an element of every structure, melodic or rhythmic. No music theory, no harmony, even atonal, can take into account a certain general type of musical objects, and in particular those used in most African or Asian musics. (Schaeffer 2017: 4)

Xenakis himself collected 'world music'. The inventory list of the Xenakis Archive at the Bibliothèque nationale in Paris, where the family deposited Xenakis's personal sound recordings, includes 1,139 items (analogue tapes and analogue and digital cassettes only, no vinyl records). More than 90 of those tapes contain music from a wide variety of cultures. One finds, among others, recordings of traditional musics from Senegal, Burundi, Laos, Vietnam, Java, China, Japan, Korea, but also European musics from Crete, Corsica or Norway.

Most of the tapes are not dated. The oldest is dated 1951 and contains music from Java, Sumatra, Bali, Vietnam, Tibet, Upper Volta and Gabon. The most recent dates from 1991. Some of the recordings are probably copies of commercial releases, as titles and dates coincide with releases on Ocora or other labels.

Xenakis's Electroacoustic Compositions

It is widely known that Xenakis used instrumental recordings in his electroacoustic compositions. For his first tape composition *Diamorphoses* (1957) he had already recorded himself playing small bells and treated the recorded sounds in multifaceted – often systematic – ways, to create textures of different densities from single sounds.

Like most electroacoustic composers of his generation, Xenakis did not openly discuss the origin of his recorded sound sources: The production of one's own sounds was considered a craftsman's secret. Beatriz Ferreyra remembered using the sound of the Baschet-instruments:

Back then, we kept something like that to ourselves. We didn't have forty thousand possibilities. When we discovered something, we kept it to ourselves so that others wouldn't copy it. (Friedl 2018)

Xenakis for example did not list instrumental recordings in *Bohor* and *La Légende d'Eer* (1978); neither did he mention the eight minutes of what was probably a double bass solo improvisation hidden in the multitrack of *La Légende d'Eer*, nor contradict wrong interpretations of names in his drafts: The sound of huge thunder sheets at the end of *Bohor* has been denoted as 'white noise' and consequently taken as such in the musicological literature for years (Friedl 2019).

In this context it is important to keep in mind that statements of composers are almost always interested statements. Remembering the hard ideologic fights in Paris in Xenakis's time between different contemporary music groups, this applies all the more. In addition, Xenakis had made a great reputation for himself as a connector of mathematics and music, a reputation he did not want to risk. Official use of improvised pre-recorded material or existing recordings might have been compromising.

Orient-Occident (1960)

In 1960, Pierre Schaeffer managed to acquire the first official commission for Xenakis. The UNESCO engaged him to compose electro-acoustic film music for *Orient-Occident: images d'une exposition* by Enrico Fulchignoni (Fulchignoni 1960), presented at the Cannes Film Festival the same year. The film focuses on the relationship between oriental and occidental sculpture. What could have been more obvious than to include oriental-like sounds?

The film music comprises passages that presumably stem from recordings of folk music instruments: Extensive drum passages can be found throughout the piece (ibid., e.g., 2:04–2:56 or 6:27–6:37), oriental bells and metal percussion (ibid., 5:58–6:13), overblown flute sounds (ibid., e.g., 4:10–4:25), and a bourdon similar to the one in *Bohor*, which is made by a Laotian mouth organ. The provenance of the sounds used is unclear, a recording has not been found in the archives so far.

These hardly hidden, probably unedited ethnomusicological borrowings are combined with sounds of other origins. For the eponymous tape piece, Xenakis shortened the music by almost 50 percent, the mentioned sounds almost completely disappeared (Xenakis 2022: CD1).

Bohor (1962)

Even though the original recording has not yet been found in the archives, hardly anyone doubts that Xenakis used the sound of a khen, a Laotian mouth organ, for the 22-minute long *Bohor*. Transposing it two octaves down by reducing the playback speed of a tape machine to one quarter, the khen turns into a bass drone. This drone is very prominent throughout the piece, e.g., from 13:28–15:50 (Xenakis 2022: CD1).

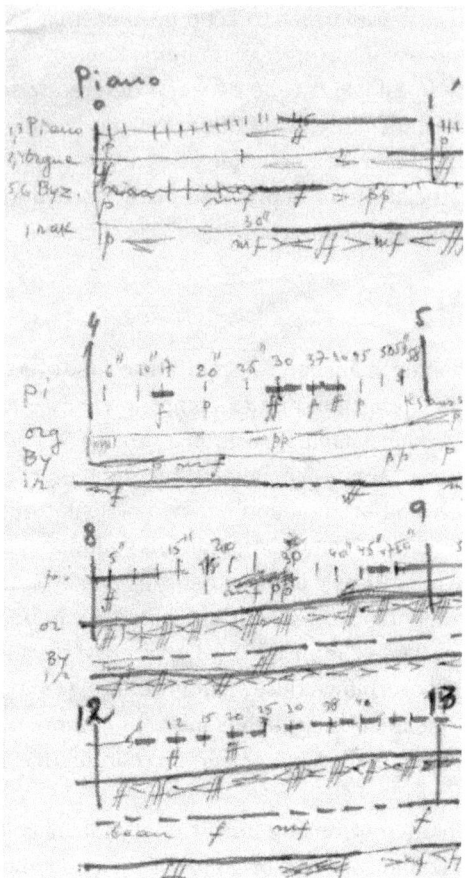

Figure 8.1: *Iannis Xenakis, Bohor, score, detail with the names of the four stereo tracks, Collection Famille Xenakis DR, OM 33–11, p. 10.*

Bohor is an eight-track composition, at that time conceived for four stereo tapes, as 8-track machines were not yet available then. Xenakis named the four tracks "piano", "orgue", "Byz." and "Irak". It is interesting that Xenakis did not mention a khen. It was James Brody who wrote on the LP cover of *Iannis Xenakis – Electroacoustic Music* that a Laotian mouth organ had been used (Brody 1970). Since then, this has been broadly quoted and 'orgue' [organ] interpreted as Xenakis's abbreviation for the Laotian Mouth Organ, in French '*orgue à bouche*' (Figure 8.1).

Benoît Gibson tried to reconstruct the original khen recording by transposing the bourdon sound and concluded: "In *Bohor*, Xenakis improvises by playing the khen himself" (Gibson 2015: 87). As Xenakis hardly played any instrument, and there is no known source saying that he used to do so in studio recordings, this remains unclear. Further on, I could not find any recording of a khen on the tapes related to *Bohor* in the Xenakis Archives (see Friedl 2019). Given that Xenakis had a solid collection of ethnological music, it also seems possible that he used an existing recording from Laos.

On the other hand, it is interesting that Gibson assumes that Xenakis "improvised". Not only did Xenakis reject improvisation in his music, he also made a clear distinction between improvisation and aleatoric techniques, arguing that is it not possible to delegate the latter to a performer:

> The interpreter is a highly conditioned being, so that it is not possible to accept the thesis of unconditioned choice, of an interpreter acting like a roulette game. (Xenakis 1992: 38)

In this sense Gibson is correct: Xenakis improvised. This might be interesting for further discussions, as Xenakis connected "trivial improvisation" with "imprecision and irresponsibility" (ibid.: 181).

"Irak" and "Byz." stand for jewellery and bells ("*grelots*") from Iraq and Byzantium respectively which Xenakis used as sound sources. It is interesting that some authors interpreted "Byzanz" as "Byzantine chant", but this is not mentioned in any source and no chant can be heard in the composition. Unusual sounds apparently made those authors mistakenly think of traditional music.

The *Polytopes* (1967–1978)

With *Bohor*, Xenakis explored the possibilities of multi-track composition for the first time, and he deepened his examination of this aspect in his subsequent polytopes (see Harley 1998). In the tape parts of these multimedia œuvres, Xenakis included numerous sounds of traditional music instruments:

- 1967 *Polytope de Montréal* (6 min) for four orchestras (pre-recorded)
- 1970 *Hibiki Hana Ma* (18 min) manipulated orchestra and biwa sounds, 8-track tape
- 1971 *Persepolis* (54 min) 8-track tape
- 1972 *Polytope de Cluny* (25 min) 7-track tape, automatised spatialisation
- 1978 *La Légende d'Eer* [*Le Diatope*] (45 min) 7-track tape, automatised spatialisation

Xenakis regarded this group of compositions as a kind of variation of the same work. Sounds used in earlier polytopes often reappear in the later ones.

Hibiki Hana Ma (1970)

In 1961, around the time *Bohor* was composed, Xenakis travelled to Japan for the first time. He met musicians such as the pianist and composer Yuji Takahashi, who was just 21 years old, as well as the composer Toru Takemitsu, through whose personal efforts he became a frequent guest in Japan. Xenakis became enthusiastic about traditional Japanese music.

> We were fortunate to be able to listen to Japanese music, to visit a Noh the-atre and to experience gagaku in the imperial theatre. I couldn't understand how young Japanese composers could write tonal or serial music. [...] During my conversations with Toru Takemitsu and other talented musicians, I found that most Japanese composers did not know their wonderful old-time music at all; they did not understand it and were not interested in it. They had all been trained at Western-style conservatories and despised their own tradition. (Xenakis 1995: 41)

Xenakis's enthusiasm for Japanese music spilled over to some young Japanese musicians: Toru Takemitsu is known today for his compositional synthesis of avant-garde orchestral technique with traditional Japanese music. He also developed a preference for the biwa. In 1967 Takemitsu composed *November Steps* for the three-stringed instrument, shakuhachi and orchestra. Xenakis remembers:

> I contributed to their rediscovery of Noh and their traditional music. I felt that their cultural revolution was leading them to reject their traditions too categorically. When I asked them to attend Noh performances, they laughed in my face.[14] (Xenakis 2003: 93)

The otherness of Japanese music fascinated Xenakis deeply. In particular, the biwa caught his attention: a three-stringed instrument played with a large plec-trum and which accompanies sprawling narrative chants with its noisy sound. It was probably Xenakis who made the release of biwa music on Chants du Monde possible, as he knew the label since the early 1950s (see above). His handwritten dedication was printed inside the gatefold cover of the LP:

---

14   "J'ai contribué à leur redécouverte du Nô et de leur musique traditionnelle. J'estimais en effet que leur révolution culturelle les conduisait à rejeter trop catégoriquement leurs traditions. Lorsque je leur ai demandé d'assister à des spectacles Nô, ils m'ont ri au nez."

In 1966, I had a revelation in Tokyo through the art of Kinshi Tsuruta: the Japanese troubadour singing, preserved with love for generations. It enchants you even if you don't understand the lyrics; you can listen to this music for hours, fascinated. (Xenakis 1972)

Figure 8.2: *Iannis Xenakis, orchestra score to be recorded for* Hibiki Hana Ma, *p. 3, detail, Collection Famille Xenakis DR, OM 12.*

Xenakis wanted to include these sounds in his music. The opportunity arose in 1970 on the occasion of the World Exhibition in Osaka. In the electronic music studio of Japan's Broadcasting Corporation NHK, Xenakis composed the 12-track tape piece *Hibiki Hana Ma* for the pavilion of the Japan Iron and Steel Federation. As sound material, Xenakis recorded some musical sketches (for orchestra, biwa, etc.) with the National Japan Philharmonic Symphony Orchestra under Seiji Ozawa and with Kinshi Tsuruta, whom he held in high esteem, playing the biwa (Figure 8.2).

On the individual tracks of *Hibiki Hana Ma*, the biwa sounds can be clearly discerned (Xenakis 1970: track 1, 5:00–5:50), the same holds for recorded Japanese tone woods (ibid., track 8, 3:12–4:00). These ingredients amalgamate into a dense mass of sound whose individual elements, however, emerge again and again and can still be well distinguished in the stereo releases (Xenakis 2022: CD2, 2:20–10:00).

In *Hibiki Hana Ma*, Xenakis adapted the new fascinating sounds, but not as clearly recognisable quotations or in an eclectic sense; instead, he incorporates single notes but also treated sound by using techniques of '*musique concrète*': recording, editing, alienating, cutting, looping, superimposing, etc.

Persepolis (1971)

Xenakis's concept for *Persepolis* was more reduced. There was no special recording session anymore, but a limited list of sounds he assembled in a modular way: Each sound module appears once in each of the eight tracks, always for exactly the same length of time. As the drafts for the composition are well preserved, there is an almost full list of the sounds he superposed in a modular way, including a distorted "Japanese gong" (Collection Famille Xenakis DR: OM 27-4-3, 01). It is well perceptible in the commercial stereo versions of *Persepolis* as a kind of drone, similar to the transposed khen in *Bohor* (Xenakis 2022, CD3, e.g., after 7:32).

Polytope de Cluny (1972)

In *Polytope de Cluny*, Xenakis used mostly recordings of African instruments which he called "guimbardes". The Collection Famille Xenakis DR contains extensive material including mixing plans, scores and lists of the sounds for the montage of each of the seven tracks (Figure 8.3; "Guimbarde" 1 to 5). Xenakis named five different guimbardes recordings.

Only one of them, most prominent on track 7, sounds like a – probably African – wooden Jew's harp, as used, for example, in Namibia. The other recordings denoted as "guimbardes" do not sound like a Jew's harp, but much more like a senza, a Central African thumb piano often also called a kalimba. The recordings seem to be made by an amateur. The instruments are played in an arhythmical way and do not show clear musical structure or virtuosity, and no great recording quality either. It is quite possible that Xenakis played on these recordings himself or used some historic recordings.

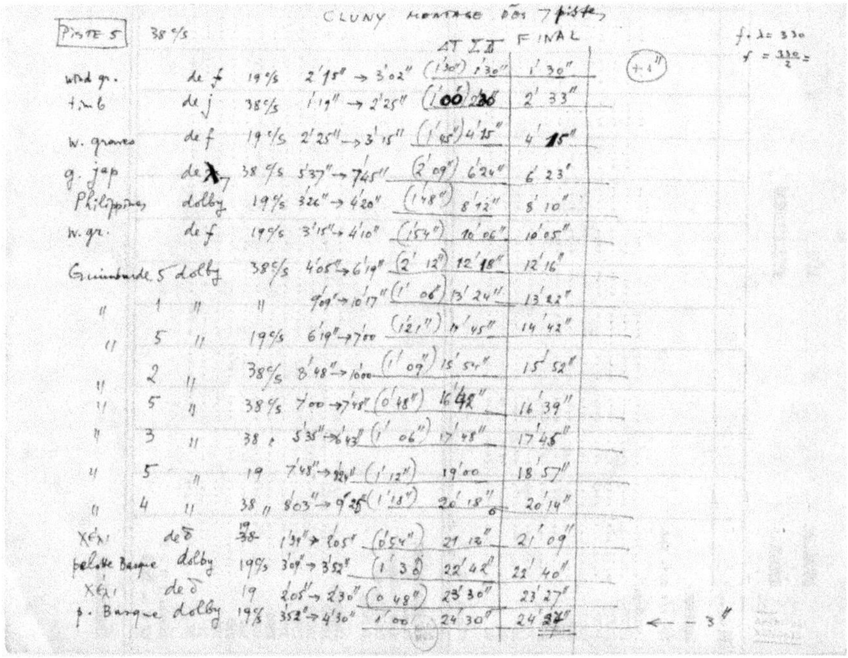

Figure 8.3: *Iannis Xenakis, montage list for track 5 of* Hibiki Hana Ma, *names of the sounds on the left side, Collection Famille Xenakis DR, OM 4–3, p. 7.*

Where his sound material came from, who recorded it and when, apparently mattered little to Xenakis. He seemed to regard these recordings merely as raw material from which new sound material could be formed. In *Polytope de Cluny*, he layers seven 'guimbardes' recordings for several minutes (Figure 8.4) and creates a kind of an imaginary senza/Jew's harp orchestra (Xenakis 2022: CD 2, e.g., 16:00–20:00).

This can sound very 'electronic', as composer Trân Quang Hai described it in respect to his tape music *Vê Nguôn* composed in 1975: "The Jew's harp can produce electronic sounds. It can give me the impression of synthetic speech. I've used it in cartoon sound effects to imitate the robot."[15] (Quang Hai 2001: 298).

---

15 "La guimbarde permet de donner des sons de type électronique. Elle peut me donner l'impression d'une parole synthétique. Je l'ai ainsi utilisé dans le bruitage de dessin animé pour imiter le robot."

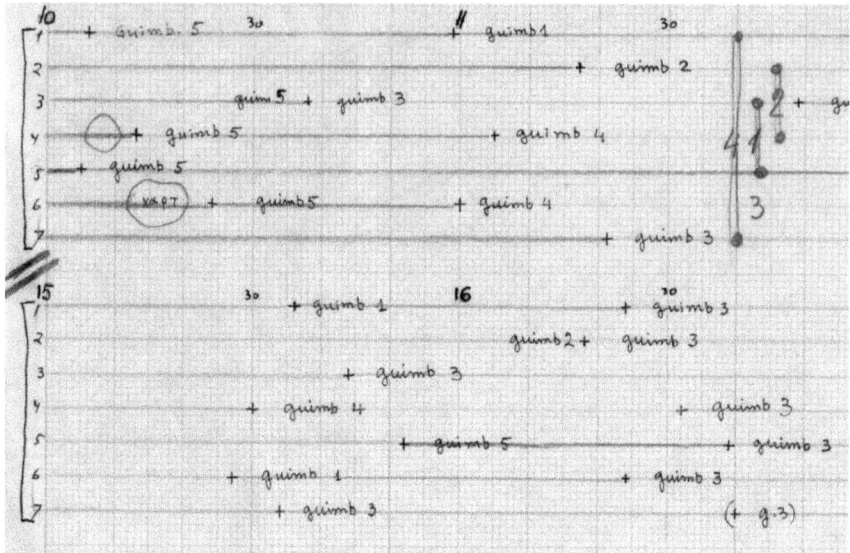

Figure 8.4: *Iannis Xenakis, Montage plan for* Polytope de Cluny, *p. 1, detail, Collection Famille Xenakis DR, OM 4-3.*

In that period, traditional musics were pretty popular and were also used prominently in movies, as for example in the soundtracks for Federico Fellini's *Satyricon* (1969) or Pier Paolo Pasolini's *Medea* (1969). African sanza music had been released among others by the label Ocora, as for example *Chant et sanza – Musiques traditionnelles de Burundi* (1968).

Xenakis even discovered similarities between his stochastic approach and African music:

> Authentic African music is not primitive. It has undoubtedly undergone a development that we know only very poorly or not at all. [...] African music corresponds more to a probabilistic, stochastic approach [...]. That is, it is unpredictable, while at the same time it is predictable: a kind of unpredictability in detail. (Solomos 2010)

La Légende d'Eer (1978)

The musical part of the *Diatope*, produced at Westdeutscher Rundfunk, shows the same concept as *Polytope de Cluny*: Seven tracks are fixed on an 8-track tape in order to be spatialised automatically. Xenakis reused the sounds he had already included in *Polytope de Cluny*, but for the first time he added his new electronic sounds created by stochastic synthesis (Friedl 2015).

Xenakis did not mind combining all these heterogeneous influences:

My music is not a revolution. My greatest achievement would be to compose music that embraces all forms of expression. However, it requires me to break free from all ties and preconditions that make me unfree. Tonal music is such a bondage, serial music, Indian music, Japanese music, and so on. They all represent worlds separate from each other, continents or islands, each with its own self-contained system of rules. The task is to find out what these islands have in common, what common structure of thought underlies them all; whether one can find access to each of them and whether the creation of a higher level of abstraction is possible. (Xenakis 1995: 52)

Xenakis's solution was pragmatic: In his electroacoustic music, especially in the multi-channel polytopes, he simply used recorded sounds, also combining them with electronic sounds and orchestral recordings, and weaving all of this into complex sound layers. Xenakis loved the view of the foreign. It is not for nothing that the interviews Francois Delalande did with Xenakis bear the title "One must always be a migrant" (Xenakis 1997).

Xenakis even stated that he has no relation with Western music:

"My music has no roots in Western music except for the instrumentation." (Solomos 2010)

Consequently, he also used non-western instrumentation, as in, e.g., *Okho* (1989) for African percussion instruments: three djembes, West African tin drums, and a "big African skin". Xenakis attempted a kind of new synthesis: stochastically organised music on non-European instruments. The same holds for *Nyuyo* (1985) (*nyuyo* = sinking sun) for shakuhachi, a Japanese bamboo flute, and three stringed instruments: shamisen and two kotos, composed for Ensemble Yonin No Kaï from Tokyo and commissioned by the Festival d'Angers, France. We might be tempted – at least in the first part – to think it is Japanese music.

Voyage absolu des Unari vers Andromède (1989)

Xenakis composed *Voyage absolu des Unari vers Andromède* in 1989 for a Japanese kite festival with an exhibition of flying objects organised by the Goethe Institute in Osaka. To compose this piece, he used the UPIC system he had developed as a graphical interface at his research centre CEMAMu (Centre d'Études de Mathématique et Automatique Musicales) in Paris. Its interface allows electronic sounds to be drawn on a touch-sensitive screen with a special pen.

In the Xenakis Archives there is an audio cassette from 8 January 1989, labelled "Sound of Unari (Kites)" (Xenakis 1054, DONAUD 0604–999) and accompanied by a business card of "Ikuko Matsumoto, Goethe Institute Osaka". Obviously, Xenakis had requested sound recordings of Japanese stunt kites from Japan in advance: These kites are equipped with wooden bows that start singing and humming with the airstream.

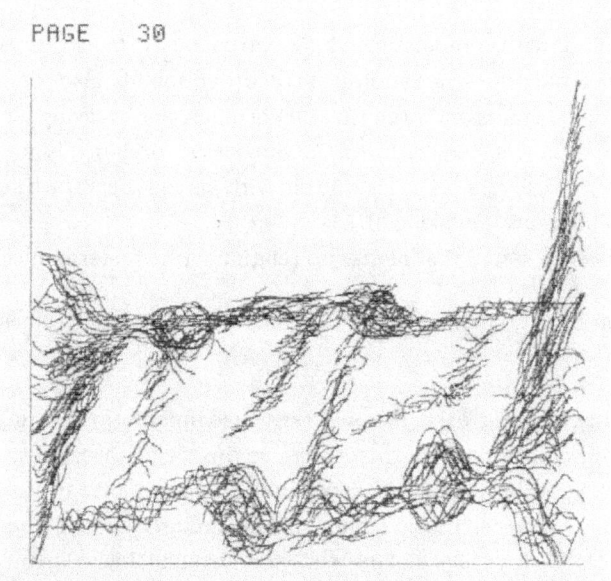

Figure 8.5: *Iannis Xenakis*, Voyage absolu des Unari vers Andromède, *screenshot UPIC, p. 6, Collection Famille Xenakis DR, OM 33–12.*

Xenakis finished *Voyage absolu des Unari vers Andromède* ('Journey of the Kites towards the Andromeda Galaxy'; see Figure 8.5) the same year, and the music sounds very similar to kite sounds.

The second generation of the UPIC system allowed it to work with recorded samples – or at least the waveform of existing samples. As Pierre Couprie assumes, Xenakis already did so in *Taurhiphanie* (1987), a composition for a bull arena in Southern France: "I realized that the waveforms used in UPIC probably all come from recordings of bull's roars" (Couprie 2020: 450). If this is right, it would be obvious to assume the same for *Voyage absolu des Unari vers Andromède*: Xenakis might have used the kite recordings he got from Japan as waveforms for the composition. This would explain why the sounds are so similar to the real kite sounds.

Conclusion

Recording sounds on tape, manipulating the playback speed or direction, assembling new sequences is reminiscent of Xenakis's origins in *musique concrète*. His sound material – especially in compositions like *Polytope de Cluny* – largely uses recordings of instruments of other cultures, often simply layering long passages on top of each other, even though Xenakis had great respect for the music of other cultures.

> When we say 'developed country', we think only of washing machines, cars or the A or H bomb, but we forget that civilisations – such as those of India, for example, or Africa – are far more developed than the artistic civilisations of capitalist or socialist countries. There is no comparison between the traditional arts of India – music, dance, architecture – or those of China, Indonesia, Africa, which are the heritage of all humanity and what exists in the artistic field in Europe, the United States, or the Soviet Union. (Xenakis 1994: 129)

Xenakis puts himself in a tradition of "solidarity between ethnology and avant-garde" in the 20th century that "shows how cultural 'appropriation' can also occur beyond categories of domination and transgression"[16] (Borio 2011: 127).

Most of Xenakis's electroacoustic compositions comprise more or less treated recordings of instruments and further sound objects of other cultures (bells, jewels, kites, etc.). But there are a lot of open questions: Who played the instruments? Who made the recordings and where? Is it at all possible to find out the exact roots? Did he sometimes use existing commercial records or original field recordings?

This article shows that comparative listening and historical context in conjunction with meta-information of sources can provide a new point of view on an œuvre. This holds especially true for electroacoustic music, where most sources are auditive. Even knowing only some classification or the nature of existing sources can already enable us to deduce some theses. These theses

---

16   "Die Solidarität zwischen Ethnologie und Avantgarde [...] zeigt, wie kulturelle Aneignung auch jenseits der Kategorien von Herrschaft und Überschreitung stattfinden."

allow us to go back to the sources with concrete questions and thus provide important clues for studying some aspects more precisely.

Xenakis himself rejected any association with musical sources:

> I don't want to have roots. Of course, I have some too. I too was exposed to influences, but fortunately so many that none of them could prove to be decisive. I have already mentioned them: Romanian and Greek folk music, Byzantine church singing, Western music, extra-European music. I tried to understand them, some I liked more, others less; but I let each of them approach me, none of them I claimed was not music. In this way, I gave myself the freedom to be without roots. (Xenakis 1995: 53)

Bibliography

Baltensperger, André (1996) Iannis Xenakis und die stochastische Musik. Komposition im Spannungsfeld von Architektur und Mathematik, Bern: Haupt.

Blume, Friedrich (1959) Was ist Musik? Ein Vortrag, Kassel: Bärenreiter (Musikalische Zeitfragen 5).

Borio, Gianmario (2011) "Vom Ende des Exotismus oder: der Einbruch des Anderen in die westliche Musik des 20. Jahrhunderts", in Was bleibt? 100 Jahre Neue Musik, ed. by Andreas Meyer, Mainz: Schott, 114–134.

Borio, Gianmario (2015) "Die Darstellung des Undarstellbaren. Zum Verhältnis von Zeichen und Performanz in der Musik des 20. Jahrhunderts", in Die Schrift des Ephemeren. Konzepte musikalischer Notationen, ed. by Matteo Nanni, Basel: Schwabe (Resonanzen 2), 129–146.

Boulez, Pierre, and Schaeffner, André (1998) Correspondance 1954–1970, Paris: Fayard.

Brech, Martha (2006) Können eiserne Brücken nicht schön sein? Über das Zusammenwachsen von Technik und Musik im 20. Jahrhundert, Hofheim: Wolke.

Brody, James (1970) Iannis Xenakis – Electroacoustic Music, liner notes on LP Cover, New York: Nonesuch Records.

Couprie, Pierre (2020) "Analytical Approaches to Taurhiphanie and Voyage absolu des unari vers Andromède by Iannis Xenakis", in From Xenakis's UPIC to graphic notation today, ed. by Peter Weibel, Ludger Brümmer, and Sharon Kanach, Karlsruhe/Berlin: ZKM, Hatje Cantz Verlag, 434–457.

De Morais, Ronan Gil (2022) "Xenakis' journey to Indonesia: Influence on Jonchaies (1977) and Pléïades (1978)", in Centenary International Symposium XENAKIS 22, ed. by Anastasia Georgaki, Makis Solomos, Areti Andreopoulou, Dimitris Exarchos, Elisavet Kiourtsoglou, and Iakovos Stein-

hauer, Athens: Spyridon Kostarakis, 328–337; https://xenakis2022.uoa.gr
/wp-content/uploads/2022/05/Xenakis-22_Proceedings.pdf (accessed
August 30, 2023).

Declercq, Zoé (2022) "The score of *Rythmes sur Tabla*, a 'key document' in the
work of Iannis Xenakis?", in *Centenary International Symposium XENAKIS
22*, ed. by Anastasia Georgaki, Makis Solomos, Areti Andreopoulou, Dimitris
Exarchos, Elisavet Kiourtsoglou, and Iakovos Steinhauer, Athens: Spyridon
Kostarakis, 338–359; https://xenakis2022.uoa.gr/wp-content/uploads/2
022/05/Xenakis-22_Proceedings.pdf (accessed August 30, 2023).

Friedl, Reinhold (2015) "Towards a Critical Edition of Electroacoustic Music: Xenakis – La Légende d'Eer", in *Iannis Xenakis – La musique électroacoustique*,
ed. by Makis Solomos, Paris: L'Harmattan, 109–122.

Friedl, Reinhold (2018) *Die Baschet-Instrumente und die GRM*, Radio Feature,
Westdeutscher Rundfunk, WDR3, Studio elektronische Musik, Cologne,
September 29, 2018.

Friedl, Reinhold (2019) "Performance in Iannis Xenakis's Electroacoustic Music",
in *Exploring Xenakis. Performance, practice, philosophy*, ed. by Alfia Nakipbekova, Wilmington: Vernon Press (Vernon series in music), 69–88.

Gayou, Évelyne (2007) *Le GRM, Groupe de recherches musicales. Cinquante ans
d'histoire*, Paris: Fayard.

Gerhards, Hugues, ed. (1972) *Iannis Xenakis*, Paris: Discothèque de France.

Gibson, Benoît (2015) "À propos de Bohor (1962) de Iannis Xenakis", in *Iannis
Xenakis – La musique électroacoustique*, ed. by Makis Solomos, Paris: L'Harmattan, 84–96.

Harley, Maria Anna (1998) "Music of Sound and Light: Xenakis's Polytopes", in
Leonardo 31/1, Cambridge: MIT Press, 55–65.

Holmes, Thom (2016) *Electronic and experimental music. Technology, music, and
culture*, New York: Routledge.

Le Bail, Karine, and Kaltenecker, Martin (2012) *Pierre Schaeffer. Les constructions
impatientes*, Paris: CNRS.

Mâche, François-Bernard (2011) "Xenakis et la musique indienne", in *Filigrane.
Musique, esthétique, sciences, société* 10/2, Paris: Delatour, 21–26; https://
revues.mshparisnord.fr:443/filigrane/index.php?id=320 (accessed August
30, 2023).

Matossian, Nouritza (1981) *Iannis Xenakis*, Paris: Fayard.

Nettl, Bruno (2006) "Was ist Musik? Ethnomusikologische Perspektive", in *Musik – Zu Begriff und Konzepten: Berliner Symposion zum Andenken an Hans
Heinrich Eggebrecht*, ed. by Michael Beiche and Albrecht Riethmüller, Stuttgart: Franz Steiner Verlag, 9–18.

Oswald, John (1985) *Plunderphonics, or Audio Piracy as a Compositional Prerog-ative*, Wired Society Electro-Acoustic Conference, Toronto; http://www .bitwisemusic.com/wp-content/uploads/2015/08/Plunderphonics-or-Audio-Piracy-as-a-Compositional-Prerogative.pdf (accessed August 30, 2023).

Quang Hai, Trân (2001) "Un dialogue occident-orient : l'exemple de Vê Nguôn (1975)", in *Du sonore au musicale – Cinquante années de recherches concrètes (1948–1998)*, ed. by Sylvie Dallet and Anne Veitl, Paris: L'Harmattan.

Rice, Timothy (2014) *Ethnomusicology. A Very Short Introduction*, New York: Oxford University Press.

Schaeffer, Pierre (1960) in "Cahiers d'études de la Radio-Télévision", numéro 27/28. Quoted from Quang Hai, Trân (2001) "Un dialogue occident-orient: l'exemple de Vê Nguôn (1975)", in *Du sonore au musicale – Cinquante années de recherches concrètes (1948–1998)*, ed. by Sylvie Dallet and Anne Veitl, Paris: L'Harmattan.

Schaeffer, Pierre (2017) *Treatise on Musical Objects. An Essay across Disciplines*, transl. by Christine North and John Dack, Berkeley: University of California Press.

Solomos, Makis (2002) "Analysing the First Electroacoustic Music of Iannis Xenakis", in *5th European Music Analysis Conference*, Bristol; https://hal.scie nce/hal-02055242/document (accessed August 30, 2023).

Solomos, Makis (2010) "Xenakis, du Japon à l'Afrique", in Musique et globalisation: musicologie-ethnomusicologie, ed. by Jacques Bouët and Makis Solomos, Paris: L'Harmattan, 227–240.

Tournet-Lammer, Jocelyne (2006) *Sur les traces de Pierre Schaeffer. Archives 1942–1995*, Paris: Institut national de l'audiovisuel.

Vandelle, Romuald (1959) "Musique exotique et musique expérimentale", in *Expériences musicales, musiques concrète électronique exotique* (La revue musicale 244), 35–37.

Xenakis, Iannis (1972) Facsimile printed on LP cover: *Kinshi Tsuruta Et Katsuya Yokoyama, Japon: Biwa Et Shakuhachi*, Paris: Le Chant Du Monde.

Xenakis, Iannis (1992) *Formalized Music*, Stuyvesant: Pendragon Press.

Xenakis, Iannis (1994) "Culture et créativité", in *Kéleütha*, ed. by Iannis Xenakis and Benoît Gibson, Paris: L'Arche.

Xenakis, Iannis, and Delalande, François (1997) *Il faut être constamment un immigré. Entretiens avec Xenakis*, Paris/Bry-sur-Marne: Buchet/Chastel.

Xenakis, Iannis, and Serrou, Bruno (2003) *Iannis Xenakis – l'homme des défis, les entretiens de Bruno Serrou*, Paris: Editions Cig'art/Jobert.

Xenakis, Iannis, and Szendy, Peter (1994), "Ici et là. Entretien avec Iannis Xenakis", in *Les Cahiers de l'IRCAM 5*, Paris.

Xenakis, Iannis, and Varga, Bálint András (1995): *Gespräche mit Iannis Xenakis*, Zürich: Atlantis.

Xenakis, Iannis, and Varga, Bálint András (1996) *Conversations with Iannis Xenakis*, London: Faber & Faber.

Audio and Video Sources

Fulchigoni, Enrico (1960) *Orient-Occident. images d'une exposition*, https://www.youtube.com/watch?v=7siM9_9GSiI&t=6s (accessed August 30, 2023).

Xenakis, Iannis (1970) *Hibiki Hana Ma*, 8-track version, Paris: Durand Salabert Eschig.

Xenakis, Iannis (2022) *Iannis Xenakis – The Complete Electroacoustic Works*, 5CD/5LP-Box, Berlin: Karlrecords.

List of Figures

Figure 8.1: Iannis Xenakis, *Bohor*, score, detail with the names of the four stereo tracks, Collection Famille Xenakis DR, OM 33–11, p. 10.

Figure 8.2: Iannis Xenakis, orchestra score to be recorded for *Hibiki Hana Ma*, p. 3, detail, Collection Famille Xenakis DR, OM 12.

Figure 8.3: Iannis Xenakis, montage list for track 5 of *Hibiki Hana Ma*, Collection Famille Xenakis DR, OM 4–3, p. 7.

Figure 8.4: Iannis Xenakis, montage plan for *Polytope de Cluny*, p. 1, detail, Collection Famille Xenakis DR, OM 4–3.

Figure 8.5: Iannis Xenakis, *Voyage absolu des Unari vers Andromède*, UPIC screenshot, p. 6, Collection Famille Xenakis DR, OM 33–12.

The Voice of the UPIC: Technology as Utterance

Peter Nelson

Iannis Xenakis, in his predilection for the ancient rather than the modern, has always proved a puzzle for theorisation focused on notions of the avant-garde. His own early critique of serialism (Xenakis 1955, 1956) already marked him as being on a different path to the generation of European and American composers who shaped the discourses of post-war music. Furthermore, Xenakis's aesthetic outlook was deeply informed by non-Western cultures, particularly following his trip to Indonesia in 1972 (cf. Andreyev 2022), as well as by ancient Greek thought (cf. Xenakis 2001). This led him to repurpose the practices of music away from Eurocentric concerns with works of art created in the aesthetics of modernity, and from the technocratic development of more or less esoteric musical structures, opening up the possibilities of sound and music in ways that offer a positive counter to the standard tropes of modernism through their recognition of a specific and material correspondence between the real forces of existence and the creative insights of the imagination. This correspondence is of course fundamental to the ancient philosophical traditions of Greek thought, and in an interview given at the Huddersfield Festival in 1987, Xenakis stated quite clearly: "I brought myself up into the ancient Greek tradition, that's for sure", (Xenakis 1987) and in a published interview with Bálint András Varga he says, "I felt I was born too late – I had missed two millennia" (Varga 1996: 15).

What are we to make, then, of Xenakis's consistent concern for new technological means, particularly his use of the digital computer? Starting with his collaboration with engineers at IBM France in 1962, through the establishment of the CEMAMu (Centre d'Études de Mathématique et Automatique Musicales)[1] in Paris in 1966, and his work at Indiana University in Illinois, all the way to his later development of the stochastic granular synthesis programme GENDY (cf. Serra 1993), the digital computer was a constant in Xenakis's creative endeavour.

---

1   CEMAMu was founded in 1965 at CNET (Centre national d'études des télécommunications), Issy-les-Moulineaux, France, with grants from the French Ministry of Culture.

Here, I want to consider the computer music system, he developed between – roughly speaking – 1977 and 1992, the UPIC (Unité Polyagogique[2] Informatique du CEMAMu), and I want to think of it both as a modern technological innovation, and as a producer of sound with a specific and, I will argue, *non*-modern intent. The discussion of sound, in a historical context, is tricky, and I intend to attempt a sort of philological approach to the matter, in order to trace a narrative of listening in relation to the material resources and sonic effects of the UPIC.

This volume specifically proposes the development of a *philology* of electroacoustic music. That term sets up as a primary area of research "the specific material situation of the sources of electroacoustic music."[3] The digital computer must figure here as one of these critical 'sources', a source with its own materials and histories which, in fact, include sound almost from its beginning. However, that is not the source I want to consider: I am concerned here with the source not of sound but of listening. In the process, I will ask how a resolutely non-modern approach, such as that of Xenakis, can encounter a radically modern technological device such as the digital computer in a manner that opens up listening to different opportunities.

So, first I will consider some of the implications of taking a philological approach: How does a disciplinary paradigm based on words, books, and language map onto something which, while language-like, is constituted rather differently, not just as *music* but as music rooted in specific sorts of technological and communicative practice? Next, I will consider the notion of listening from within that philological perspective, drawing on some insights of the Scottish philosopher Thomas Reid, to attempt to get a sense of what we might hear when we listen to certain of Xenakis's electroacoustic works. Finally, I will take Xenakis's UPIC computer music system as a case-study, trying to link together histories of practice and histories of listening, from this philological perspective, to see what sort of 'renovation' might be possible for the UPIC – now a rather historical method of music production – and its musical repertoire.

Music Philology

Nikolaus Urbanek asks, "What is a music-philological question?" (Urbanek 2013) and I want to begin by considering some approaches to that puzzle, in order to

---

2   'Polyagogic' is a sort of plural of pedagogic (cf. Varga 1996: 121).
3   Call for Papers: *Xenakis 2022: Back to the Roots.* 19–21 May 2022, University of Music and Performing Arts Vienna, Austria.

lay out the terms of my own discussion here. Editorial and performance practices in traditionally notated music have undergone a process of more or less rigorous and self-critical development over the last 200 years or so: The application of similar insights to electroacoustic music is a fairly recent development, focused on specific repertoires. Thus, Sean Williams has sought to establish the relationship between the studio practice of Karlheinz Stockhausen as annotated in the published score for *Electronic Study II*, and the physical realities of that studio practice, both as remembered by Stockhausen's collaborator, Gottfried Michael Koenig, and as experienced by Williams himself in his attempts to reconstruct Stockhausen's work on reconditioned equipment from the era. This might be close to what, for other repertoire, can be called historically informed performance practice, and it raises, for Williams, the central issue of "the agency of technology" (Williams 2016: 445). To what extent is technology an active participant in music creation, and how can that agency be registered across a historical gap in time? What is lost, what remains, and what can be reconstructed? This does seem like a music-philological question, insofar as it is at least metaphorically related to similar questions concerning textual sources. In this reading, technology becomes text. Williams identifies three key themes in his reading of this 'technological text': first, technology as material presence, then a theme of temporality, and lastly the notion of ontology: Where do sound and music come from? (ibid.) Williams sources these themes in Georgina Born's theorisation of relational musicology (Born 2010: 62), though he omits Born's fourth theme, sociality, which is arguably present anyway in his discussion of studio practice. Since the agency of technology establishes itself in the discussion through historical narratives, Williams writes:

> I use temporality as a way of categorizing elements, characteristics or problems that change their nature over time: for example, the composer's differing attitudes to the use of particular technologies used in the realization process; and the different capabilities and affordances of technologies of the 1950s, on the one hand, and of the second decade of the twenty-first century, on the other. (Williams 2016: 446)

In this account, temporality is a key element in the philological enterprise since it is the trajectory of changes that philology undertakes to map. Technologies, in Williams's sense, refer to actual pieces of machinery, like tape recorders and electronic filters, as well as to the practices that are developed in their physical operation. But, of course, there are other sorts of technology, specifically thoughtful methods and processes for identifying and organising sounds: Stockhausen's use in *Electronic Study II* of a basic frequency step that never produces octave relations might be one such technology. Thus, technology and ontology are deeply bound together, even if, following Philip Bohlman (Bohlman 1999), one must acknowledge that music has multiple ontologies.

The ontology of music is also a key concern of Xenakis; the principal foundation of his book *Formalized Music* (Xenakis 1992). Indeed, he says explicitly that "it is incumbent on music to serve as a medium for the confrontation of philosophic or scientific ideas on ... being" (ibid.: 261). Insofar as ontology is concerned with stories of origin, it must be seen as a key philological concern: Not only does philology seek to identify the originary sources of the material it investigates, but the very notion of 'material' includes the narratives by which that material itself comes to be identified, as well as its "elements, characteristics or problems that change their nature over time" (ibid.: 201). These narratives are explored by Xenakis as "an 'unveiling of the historical tradition' of music" alongside the attempt "to construct a music" (ibid.). Thus temporality figures here, as in Williams's work, as a grounding thematic strand in order to develop narrative as a key strategy for investigation. This is a strategy I want to develop here.

Williams's concern with technology, in a material sense, is also a concern with sound, and I now want to make my own approach to sound explicit. As the nascent discipline of Sound Studies has shown, sound is tricky to talk about, its history even more so. However, sound clearly has a history,[4] and I would claim that that history is as prone to gaps, inconsistencies, and misunderstandings as other textual constructs. My specific interest here is the sound of the UPIC computer music system. I will leave the material technology aside,[5] apart from some brief discussion of the graphic nature of the UPIC's interface, and concentrate instead on its sound. In particular, I am interested in how that sound is and was heard. As Georg Feder remarks, in the introduction to his book on music philology, "Philology is love of words and the mental images manifested in words" (Feder 2011: 1). Sound also produces mental images, both through what we could, by analogy, call 'syntactic structure', and through its sheer presence to our senses. The sound of the UPIC has always been marked as somehow 'unsatisfactory', raw, or rebarbative, even by its creator. When Brigitte Condorcet (Robindoré) refers to the perception of the UPIC's sound as being "somewhat harsh" (Condorcet 2020: 403), she is registering the frequent sense of disappointment of people using the device for the first time. I want to interrogate that response, and to try to construct a narrative of listening to the UPIC, both as itself, and in a context of other sonorous images, in order to attempt both

---

4   An attempt at such a history is made in R. Murray Schafer's book, *The Tuning of the World* (1977).

5   For further information on the UPIC see Weibel et al. (2020).

a reconstruction of the birth of a particular sound world, and a reassessment of how that sound world appears to us. Urbanek remarks on the difficulty of assessing aspects of a text that seem unhappy or unlikely when he says: "Is a problematic moment in a text to be interpreted as a textual error, or as a moment of compositional audacity?"[6] (Urbanek 2013: 161). This remark may have been made of text as notation, but in the context of the UPIC, a certain *sound* might in fact appear as "eine problematische Textstelle". How is one to assess the possible "audacity" that this seeming sonic "error" proposes? Barbara Johnson suggests that, indeed, one of the tasks of philology is "to read in such a way as to break through preconceived notions of meaning in order to encounter unexpected otherness – in order to learn something one doesn't already know – in order to encounter the other" (Johnson 1990: 29). So now I want to consider the sound of the UPIC as 'sonic other'.

Listening

Listening turns out to be a complex phenomenon.[7] Discussions of listening, particularly in relation to sound disseminated through loudspeakers, were dominated, until the last 20 years or so, by the theorisation of Pierre Schaeffer, with its attempt, inspired by Husserl's phenomenology and its notion of the *epoché*, to cut off mediated sound from what surrounds it. More recently, however, several scholars including Jean-Luc Nancy, Peter Szendy, Georgina Born, and others have opened up a different sort of discourse that centres on, in Born's terms "the *relations* [my emphasis] between musical object and listening subject, where the latter demands an analysis of the social and historical conditions and the mediation of listening, as well as the changing forms of subjectivity brought to music" (Born 2010: 80f.). In order to get a sense of how listening might figure in a philological enterprise, I want to consider listening to the UPIC from a number of perspectives. The basis for this is the thought – crazy perhaps – that, just as we have come to value 'historically informed performance', we could also attempt a 'historically informed listening'.

The first move in my argument is to recall a line of thought from the Scottish Enlightenment philosopher Thomas Reid. Reid traverses an intriguing path between pragmatic realism and a transcendental idealism that finds strong parallels in contemporary neuroscientific notions of mirroring systems: What hap-

---

6   "Ist eine problematische Textstelle als Textfehler oder als kompositorische Kühnheit zu werten?" Unless otherwise stated, all translations by the author.

7   This is an understatement! But see, for example, Nancy (2007).

pens outside the body is induced to also happen inside the body. This allows sound a particular sort of reality, that does not deny the psychological and philosophical subject-formation described by Born, but that also implies a stronger connection between sound and the social and material network than Born and others have implied.

In his *Essays on the Active Powers of Man* (1788), Reid writes:

> I call those operations social, which necessarily imply social intercourse with some other intelligent being who bears a part in them. ... Between the operations of the mind, which, for want of a more proper name, I have called solitary, and those I have called social, there is this very remarkable distinction that, in the solitary, the expression of them by words, or any other sensible sign, is accidental. They may exist, and be complete, without being expressed, without being known to any other person. But, in the social operations, the expression is essential. They cannot exist without being expressed by words or signs, and known to the other party. (Reid 2010: 330)

This presents the social act as a moment of inter-subjectivity, where there is a sort of co-creation by the social group of something that takes place out in the open, not in the inner sanctum of anyone's mind. Moreover, Reid's assertion that the words or signs uttered must be "known to the other party" stems from his belief in some sense before language, "by which we are sensitive to our world and to one another. It is not learnt as a matter of habit and customs, but exists as an *a priori* condition of our experience" (Reid 1983: 41). Thus, the co-forming of the matter presented in social signs is underwritten by some sort of foundational representation of a sense of selves, within which acts may be undertaken and understood as *counting* for the participants. How can sound figure within such a representation of a recognised world?

The social understanding of sound is at least partly present in historical record. It is not just music criticism that concerns itself with the description and discussion of sound. Thus, for example, Douglas Kahn, in his book *Earth Sound Earth Signal* (Kahn 2013), surveys the historical record of accounts of the sounds registered by telephone lines, radio antennae, seismic monitors, and electrical devices. An early example he gives comes from the 1893 manual *Practical Information for Telephonists* in which different sorts of line noise are categorised in a manner strikingly similar to the aesthetic categorisation of sounds attempted by Luigi Russolo in his manifesto of 1913, *The Art of Noises* (Russolo 1986). Some 40 years later, Hugo Benioff's long-playing record, *Out of this World* presented recordings of just these sorts of sounds, like earthquakes, the atmospheric phenomena called 'whistlers,' and ionospheric radio signals, described by Eric D. Barry as a sort of "audiophile spectacle" (Barry 2009: 120) of the sonic wonders of the universe. These historical accounts of sound, in their mundane as well as their artistic manifestations, give us a narrative of common understanding in relation to sound: They register the sort of co-creation of a listening-sense that allows us insight into traditions of social intercourse and social meaning concerning sounds that came within the collective consciousness during specific historical time periods. The configuration of the experiences thus registered is consistent, and presents a critical context for the appearance in the 1940s and 1950s of concrete, electronic, and electroacoustic musics. I would represent that configuration as: First, the presence of an apparatus – usually a metal cable or stylus attached to some registering device, configured for purposes of communication, like a sort of stethoscope applied to the surface or the atmosphere of the earth; second, a narrative of discovery and exploration, as epitomised in the novels of the 19th century French writer Jules Verne, in which the Universe and planet earth figure as mysteries to be uncovered for the progressive development of scientific, industrial colonialism. In this network, the device itself is a conduit, rather than an instrument: In the narrative of its operation, it conveys and collects rather than produces, and the common imaginary of the listening experience it provides is one of colonial exploration and science fictive appropriation. Thus, Karlheinz Stockhausen can characterise his work *Hymnen* as opening with "the international gibberish of short-wave transmissions" (Wörner 1976: 59) and as moving towards a "Utopian realm" centred on the harmony of the spheres as an image of the collected sounds of the world.

I have tried to indicate here how a philological narrative of 'historically informed listening' might be developed, considering listening, in Reid's terms, as an inter-subjective moment of subject-formation in relation to sound experiences with a specific historical availability, configured through particular types of apparatus with their own material presence, practices of operation, and narratives of existence and purpose. I could now try to relate this listening to a specific historical canon of sound and music practice, particularly as developed within the genres of concrete, electronic and electroacoustic music. But instead, I want to try to show how Xenakis, both in principle, and specifically through the development of the UPIC and its sound world, is in fact concerned with a totally different sort of enterprise.

Writing and Sounding

There is a moment, in an interview given at the Huddersfield Festival in 1987 where the UPIC was showcased, when Xenakis seems to express some regret about its functioning. In answer to a question about the quality of computer-generated sound, he said the following:

> The natural sounds, yes, they are, indeed they are richer. Of course, the instruments for instance have still a very fine sound which can be very complex, [...] and the computer is still poor in that domain. I think it's not a matter already of the technology, but also of thinking and theories. (Xenakis 1987)

He then goes on to speak about what, as formulated in the 1970s by Steve Holtzman, has come to be known as 'non-standard sound synthesis', that is, in the case of Xenakis, the direct transcription, either by hand or by calculation, of the instantaneous pressure differences that lead to the perception of sound. Holtzman describes non-standard synthesis as an approach which,

> given a set of instructions, relates them one to another in terms of a system which makes no reference to some super-ordinated model, [...] and the relationships formed are themselves the description of the sound. (Holtzman 1978: 1)

More recently, Luc Döbereiner has explored the implications of this approach to sound, noting not just the technical but also the poetic and ontological narratives that underpin it. Thus, he cites Rainer Maria Rilke's text of 1919, *Ur-Geräusch* ('Primal-sound') which presents the groove of the gramophone as a sort of terrain of radical possibility:

> What if one changed the needle and directed it on its return journey along a tracing which was not derived from a graphic translation of a sound, but existed of itself, naturally – well: to put it plainly, the coronal suture, for example. What would happen? A sound would necessarily result [...] which of all the feelings here possible prevents me from suggesting a name for the primal sound which would then make its appearance in the world ... (Rilke 2001: 23)

This reconfigured apparatus becomes, in Döbereiner's words "an extension of our senses in that it renders perceptible otherwise imperceptible structures" (Döbereiner 2011: 30). Döbereiner connects this notion of extending the senses explicitly with the act of listening when he asserts that the act of synthesis is "understood as generating a unique sonority [...] actively transforming listening habits" (ibid.: 34). This is reminiscent of Barbara Johnson's suggestion, mentioned above, that one of the tasks of philology is "to read in such a way as to break through preconceived notions of meaning in order to encounter unexpected otherness" (Johnson 1990: 29). In this case, however, the text being interrogated is a material reality registered as a sequence of instantaneous pressure differences. In what sense could this *be* a 'text' open to a philological reading?

The analysis of listening I outlined earlier, based on Reid's avowal of inter-subjectivity, might seem to preclude this sort of "unexpected otherness", yet if music is not social, what else is it? Reid's explicit formulation of the social as in-corporating "any other intelligent being" prefigures the sort of open, non-hier-archical ontologies proposed by Latour and others, and in this instance would seem to allow the "primal sound" or 'unique sonority' the opportunity to be heard: Indeed, in so far as it is heard – rather than remaining obscure and unin-telligible, below the threshold of our perception – it must, in Reid's account, be *recognised* within a social, if not within an acoustic sensibility. It is recognised because of its impact on us as a particular social construction that counts for us. But what could it be recognised *as*?

Here we have to stop for a moment to take account of Xenakis's attributi-on of a certain 'poverty' in the sound quality of synthesised sounds. It is clear that this 'poverty' does not relate to the unlike-ness of the sounds to previously known sounds. The whole purpose of non-standard synthesis, as exemplified in the apparatus of the UPIC, is the *extension* of the domain of sound, not in the exploratory sense I described a moment ago, where a sort of palpating of the world and its inter-stellar location is undertaken with an acquisitive intent, but more in a revelatory sense, where the requirement is – in a manner of spea-king – to engage with moments of enunciation. In this context, the 'poverty' described by Xenakis is a registering of the import of the enunciation: The ora-cle has spoken, but has not yet – for Xenakis – uttered a completely compelling message. This is to say that, in these works, Xenakis is not so much *making wi-th* as *listening for*. The compositional effort, as is clear in all of the early works with their detailed mathematical working out, is not a putting together of ma-terials found but the registering of a trajectory or track that is sought for in the terrain of the created universe. This *seeking* is a detailed investigation that is at the heart of Xenakis's compositional process; it uses logic and mathematics in an ancient sense as a sort of *divination*, uncovering or bringing forth into social reality the imprints of creation. Thus, the computer becomes a sort of apparatus like Rilke's altered gramophone, a modern manifestation of ancient concerns. As Xenakis put it, in the interview he gave in Huddersfield:

> whenever you say computer, you must put in the computer all these fan-tastic experiences that mankind has acquired during these millennia. So, when you deal with these things even if you don't have computer, I mean when you deal with problems, deep problems in music, you have to deal wi-

th the things that the computer makes easier to handle you see. So, when you have a computer it's very natural to use it. (Xenakis 1987)

In this sense, Xenakis shares a certain attitude with the American composer John Cage, although their methods and aesthetics could not be more different. Where Cage listens for the imprint of chance events, Xenakis seeks out and registers flows and forces, transitions and transformations. Cage approaches the oracle with dice and yarrow stalks, Xenakis with tracings of the imprints made by elemental forces.[8]

Here, in this invocation of the oracular, we might think for a moment about the relation between Rilke's "coronal suture" and the graphism of the UPIC. One of the key moments of philology is the tracing of genealogies; the narratives that contextualise words and their meanings. Thus, Plato has Socrates remark, in *Cratylus*, "The name of the Muses and of music would seem to be derived from searching and their making philosophical enquiries (μῶσθαι)" (Plato 1961: 406a). The coronal suture is a material manifestation of a being, and the implication of its 'primal sound' is the hearing of a voice from beyond: It is oracular, in the sense that it interprets a sign – the suture – and the sign is emblematic and prophetic of the person who bears it and their evolution as both individual and species. One could see a similarity to other oracular methods, such as the examining of entrails or tea leaves. These are all sorts of graphism. The UPIC, in Xenakis's hand, explores a number of graphic potentials, but I will use just one here as an example: the arborescence. Xenakis was fascinated by arborescent structures. In one of the conversations with Bálint András Varga, he says:

> I believe that is what is lacking today, a theory about shapes. [...] (A) fantastic shape is that of trees. Arborescences. Veins and nerves have that shape. Lightning has it. (Varga 1996: 207)

And river deltas: The wall of the UPIC atelier had satellite images of river deltas pinned to it. The arborescence is a material structure, like the coronal suture, that can be traced to reveal primal forces that allow a sort of oracular enunciation: the sound, not of the world as a resource for sonic accumulation and exploitation, but of the world as inter-subjective co-respondent to our supplication and interrogation.

---

8   For another account of such 'tracings' see Morton (2013).

Conclusion

The aim of this discussion has been to reconsider the UPIC as an apparatus, where, following Giorgio Agamben, an apparatus is "a heterogeneous set that includes virtually anything. [...] The apparatus itself is the network that is established between these elements" (Agamben 2009: 2f.). Thus, *listening* seems to me to be a critical component of the network that extends around the UPIC. Following Reid's characterisation of communication within the social network as a sort of apparatus of inter-subjectivity, the *philological* project has been to try to trace the narrative of a root of common understanding that allows the UPIC to be heard, not as a poor version of something it is not, but in its own voice: an oracular voice that speaks from behind appearances. This is not just a historical project: an attempt to hear with the ears of the 1970s, but also a project of renovation, attempting to uncover, by narrative means, what it might mean to listen to the UPIC as a radically different approach to the acousmatic project. I have tried to characterise the voice of the UPIC as a voice of enunciation, rather than replication or presentation, and I have tied the notion of enunciation to an oracular moment. This is partly in acknowledgment of the commitment of Xenakis to an ancient, rather than a modern mindset, but of course the oracle is not just ancient, and never really about foretelling the future. Its predictions are always ambiguous (see Kindt 2017): It is about the revelation of unlikely correspondences, between human narratives and the contingent narratives of events – a drawing together of humans and the teeming life around them in nodes of sympathetic and inter-subjective connection.

Bibliography

Agamben, Giorgio (2009) "What Is an Apparatus?", in *What Is an Apparatus? And Other Essays*, trans. by David Kishik and Stefan Pedatella, ed. by Werner Hamacher, Stanford: Stanford University Press, 1–24.

Andreyev, Samuel (2022) *The Samuel Andreyev Podcast – Betsy Jolas: My Trip to Bali with Xenakis and Takemitsu*; https://podcasts.apple.com/gb/podcast/betsy-jolas-my-trip-to-bali-with-xenakis-and-takemitsu/id1455789353?i=1000530410090 (accessed March 27, 2024).

Barry, Eric D. (2009) "High-Fidelity Sound as Spectacle and Sublime 1950–1961", in *Sound in the Age of Mechanical Reproduction*, ed. by David Suisman and Susan Strasser, Philadelphia: University of Pennsylvania Press, 115–138.

Bohlman, Philip V. (1999) "Ontologies of Music", in *Rethinking Music*, ed. by Nicholas Cook and Mark Everist, Oxford: Oxford University Press, 17–34.

Born, Georgina (2010) "For a Relational Musicology: Music and Interdisciplinarity, Beyond the Practice Turn", in *Journal of the Royal Musical Association* 135/2, 205–243.

Condorcet (Robindoré), Brigitte (2020) "Beyond the Continuum: The Undiscovered Terrains of the UPIC", in *From Xenakis's UPIC to Graphic Notation Today*, ed. by Peter Weibel, Ludger Brümmer, and Sharon Kanach, Berlin: Hatje Kantz, 296–415.

Döbereiner, Luc (2011) "Models of Constructed Sound: Nonstandard Synthesis as an Aesthetic Perspective", in *Computer Music Journal* 35/3, 28–39.

Feder, Georg (2011) *Music Philology: An Introduction to Musical Textual Criticism, Hermeneutics, and Editorial Technique*, Hillsdale: Pendragon Press.

Holtzman, Steven R. (1978) "A Description of an Automatic Digital Sound Synthesis Instrument", in *DAI Research Report No. 59*, Edinburgh: University of Edinburgh Department of Artificial Intelligence.

Johnson, Barbara (1990) "Philology: What Is at Stake?", in *Comparative Literature Studies* 27/1 (What Is Philology?), 26–30.

Kahn, Douglas (2013) *Earth Sound Earth Signal: Energies and Earth Magnitude in the Arts*, Berkeley: University of California Press.

Kindt, Julia (2017) "The Inspired Voice: Enigmatic Oracular Communication", in *Mercury's Wings: Exploring Modes of Communication in the Ancient World*, ed. by Richard J. A. Talbert and Fred S. Naiden, Oxford: Oxford University Press, 211–229.

Morton, Timothy (2013) *Hyperobjects: Philosophy and Ecology after the End of the World*, Minneapolis: University of Minnesota Press.

Nancy, Jean-Luc (2007) *Listening*, trans. by Charlotte Mandell, New York: Fordham University Press.

Plato (1961 [1892]) "Cratylus", trans. by Benjamin Jowett, in *Plato: the Collected Dialogues*, ed. by Edith Hamilton and Huntington Cairns, Princeton: Princeton University Press, 421–474.

Reid, Thomas (1983) *Inquiry and Essays*, ed. Ronald Beanblossom and Keith Lehrer, Indianapolis: Hackett.

Reid, Thomas (2010 [1788]) *Essays on the Active Powers of Man*, ed. by Knud Haakonssen and James A. Harris, Edinburgh: Edinburgh University Press.

Rilke, Rainer Maria (2001 [1919]) "Primal Sound", in *The Book of Music and Nature*, ed. by David Rothenberg and Marta Ulvaeus, Middletown: Wesleyan University Press, 21–24.

Russolo, Luigi (1986 [1913/1916]) *The art of noises*, trans. with an introduction by Barclay Brown, Hillsdale: Pendragon Press.

Schafer, R. Murray (1977) *The Tuning of the World*, New York: Knopf.

Serra, Marie-Hélène (1993) "Stochastic Composition and Stochastic Timbre: GENDY3 by Iannis Xenakis", in *Perspectives of New Music* 31/1, 236–257.

Urbanek, Nikolaus (2013) "Was ist eine musikphilologische Frage?", in *Historische Musikwissenschaft, Grundlagen und Perspektiven*, ed. by Michele Calella and Nikolaus Urbanek, Stuttgart: Metzler, 147–183.

Varga, Bálint András (1996) *Conversations with Iannis Xenakis*, London: Faber & Faber.

Weibel, Peter, Brümmer, Ludger, and Kanach Sharon, eds. (2020) *From Xenakis's UPIC to Graphic Notation Today*, Berlin: Hatje Cantz.

Williams, Sean (2016) "Interpretation and Performance Practice in Realizing Stockhausen's Studie II", in *Journal of the Royal Musical Association* 141/2, 445–481; https://doi.org/10.1080/02690403.2016.1216059 (accessed March 27, 2024).

Wörner, Karl H. (1976) *Stockhausen. Life and Work*, introduced, ed. and trans. by Bill Hopkins, Berkeley: University of California Press.

Xenakis, Iannis (1955) "La Crise de la Musique Serielle", in *Gravesaner Blätter* 1, Mainz: Ars Viva.

Xenakis, Iannis (1956) "Wahrscheinlichkeitstheorie und Musik", in *Gravesaner Blätter* 6, Mainz: Ars Viva.

Xenakis, Iannis (1987) Interview with Richard Steinitz. Huddersfield Festival of Contemporary Music 1987, 21 November 1987, recorded and transcribed by the author.

Xenakis, Iannis (1992) *Formalized Music: Thought and Mathematics in Music*, rev. ed. compiled and ed. by Sharon Kanach, Stuyvesant [NY]: Pendragon Press.

Xenakis, Iannis (2001 [1958]) "Problèmes de Composition Musicale Grecque", in *Présences de Iannis Xenakis*, ed. by Makis Solomos, Paris: Centre de documentation de la musique contemporaine, 11–14.

La légende de Xenakis

Curtis Roads

This is a personal account of the impact Xenakis had on my life over several decades.[1] To be clear, I am not an expert on Xenakis's life. These recollections view Xenakis through the narrow lens of my encounters with him. It has been wonderful to sift through my memories to reconstruct this narrative. To begin, it is important to describe the historical milieu of my earliest encounters with Xenakis. In 1970 I was a 19-year-old musician living in a commune in Urbana-Champaign, Illinois (home of the University of Illinois) with 24 other people. I was learning a great deal about the music business and becoming more and more disillusioned. At the same time, my aesthetic perspective was rapidly evolving. I was going to concerts of classical music at the university but also concerts of new experimental music. On my own I was experimenting with new sounds using available equipment.

By chance, in this period the University of Illinois was a pioneering centre for research in computer music. At the invitation of a graduate student friend, I started working in the EMS (University of Illinois Experimental Music Studio). The EMS was an excellent facility with an API mixing console, 4-track tape recorders, a large Moog synthesizer, and quadraphonic playback. This was a state-of-the-art analogue studio. My friend and I started making tape music pieces that we would play in various venues.

The EMS also had a Digital Equipment Corporation (DEC) PDP-8 computer. It was the model with glass doors displaying the circuit boards. It was love at first sight for me. I saw the computer as a way to combine my intellectual and musical aspirations. I met Professor Herbert Brün, a pioneer of algorithmic composition and experimental digital synthesis, Professor James Beauchamp, a pioneer of computer sound analysis and synthesis, and researcher Edward Kobrin, a pioneer of real-time interactive composition. They were all generous with their time. I was given a printout of Max Mathews's Music V program, written in Fortran, which I still have.

---

1   A later version of this chapter also available as Roads 2024.

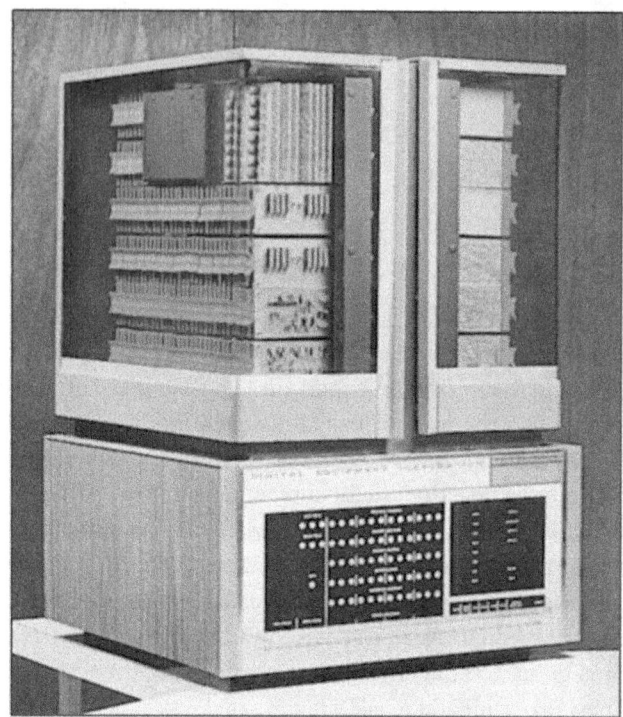

Figure 10.1: DEC PDP-8 *computer. Photographer unknown.*

Through recordings I became familiar with the music of Iannis Xenakis, beginning with *Metastaseis* (1954), *Pithoprakta* (1956), and *Eonta* (1964), the electronic works *Concret PH* (1958), *Diamorphosis* (1957), *Orient-Occident* (1960), and *Bohor* (1962), and the orchestra plus tape piece *Kraanerg* (1969).

First Encounter with Xenakis

In 1972 I saw a poster for Xenakis's short course in Formalized Music at Indiana University. I decided to enrol. Xenakis lectured at a blackboard, detailing his theories in mathematical terms. In between the lectures he played his pieces at considerable volume over four Altec-Lansing Voice of the Theatre loudspeakers. Xenakis's computer programming assistant, Cornelia Colyer, took us to the campus computer centre to show us plots of waveforms produced by dynamic stochastic synthesis (Xenakis 1971: 247).

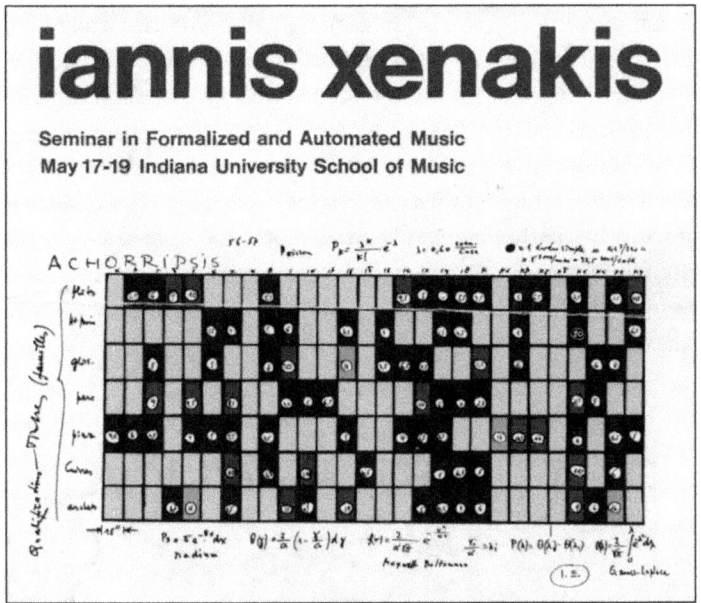

Figure 10.2: *Poster for the Seminar on Formalized and Automated Music at Indiana University, 1972. Courtesy of the Author.*

My encounter with Xenakis was life-changing. It gave me clear focus and direction, which was crucial in my university studies. The idea of using algorithmic processes in music composition attracted me from an intellectual standpoint as a formidable design problem.

I came away from Xenakis's course with two specific goals. First, I wanted to learn how to program computers to model stochastic processes for composition. For the design of new structures such as what Varèse called 'sound masses' (Varèse and Wen-Chung: 1966) and Xenakis called 'clouds', a stochastic model seemed an appropriate starting point. Second, I was intrigued by the concept of granular synthesis of sound. We heard no sound examples but the theory fascinated me.

Several weeks later I visited Stanford University in California. John Chowning gave me a tour of the Stanford Artificial Intelligence Laboratory where the computer music centre was housed. It was a revelation. I saw advanced technology that was ten years ahead of its time. In the summer of 1972, I began to learn computer programming languages. The first was Fortran IV, in order to analyse Xenakis's Stochastic Music Program. I created a flow chart based on the analysis (Roads 1973). In the fall of that same year, I enrolled as a student in music composition at CalArts (California Institute of the Arts) in Los Angeles. CalArts had just opened so everything was new and exciting. The faculty could not understand why I was interested in Xenakis's methods, but my fellow student composers did.

In that period, the institute had a single computer: a Data General Nova 1200 with an attached teletype printer and paper tape reader. I started studying with the mathematician Leonard Cottrell. We learned programming and digital circuit design. I began to write programs that implemented the formulas in *Formalized Music*. Then I started writing my own composition algorithms.

Figure 10.3: *Poster for* Polytope de Cluny. *Courtesy of the Author.*

In 1973 I flew to Paris to attend the Festival d'Automne. The main goal of my visit to Paris was to experience Xenakis's sound and light spectacle *Polytope de Cluny* (1972) in the medieval Musée de Cluny.

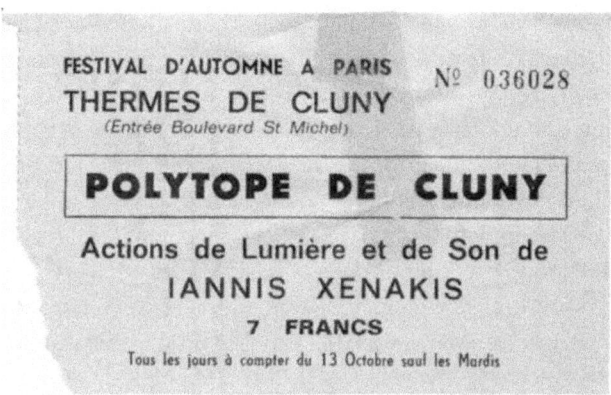

Figure 10.4: *Ticket for* Polytope de Cluny. *Courtesy of the Author.*

Figure 10.5: Polytope de Cluny. *Archives Les Ateliers UPIC, Paris.*

Polytope de Cluny was experienced lying on one's back, looking up. A robotically-controlled laser projection system created moving geometric forms. An interesting aspect of this movement was its stepped rather than smooth motion, which emphasized the element of digital control in discrete steps. High on the ceiling was a metal grid with hundreds of flashbulbs following a digital script. Meanwhile the intense 27-minute octophonic tape of *Polytope de Cluny* filled the hall. I experienced it eight times. The design of *Polytope de Cluny* was extremely impressive both technically and aesthetically. In Paris I also attended lectures and concerts featuring Karlheinz Stockhausen. I was disappointed by a performance of *Hymnen* for tape and orchestra.

Returning to California, I was determined to synthesize granular sound by computer. In 1974 I left CalArts for the UCSD (University of California, San Diego) where they had a working computer sound synthesis system. Later I will talk about my involvement with granular synthesis by computer.

In 1980 I moved to Cambridge, Massachusetts to work at MIT (Massachusetts Institute of Technology). I was editor of *Computer Music Journal* and a researcher at the MIT EMS (MIT Experimental Music Studio). At the insistence of Barry Vercoe, my boss at MIT EMS, I appointed Pierre Boulez to the Editorial Advisory Board of *Computer Music Journal*. Throughout his life, Boulez went out of his way to criticize electronic music as a compositional medium. The IRCAM (Institut de Recherche et Coordination Acoustique/Musique) centre in Paris, founded by Boulez, was notorious for excluding electronic music composition as a legitimate artistic medium.

In 1981, IRCAM organized a conference on "The composers and the computer" (Roads 1981). This is where I first met Boulez in my official role as editor. He initiated the conversation with a surprisingly direct question: "What are we [i.e., you] going to do about Xenakis?" To put this in context, Xenakis had recently written a criticism of IRCAM in a major Parisian newspaper (Xenakis 1981). My response to Boulez was equivocal. I observed that Xenakis's ideas were sometimes fuzzy. Boulez replied with a pun that Xenakis was fussy. That was the end of the conversation. It was a political test.

During the same conference, I visited the CEMAMu (Centre d'Études de Mathématique et Automatique Musicales) in Issy-les-Moulineaux to see a demonstration of the UPIC (Unité Polyagogique Informatique du CEMAMu) system by Xenakis and his assistant Cornelia Colyer. Guy Médigue, the lead engineer of the UPIC, was also present.

Three years later, IRCAM organized the 1984 International Computer Music Conference. Once again, I took a side trip to visit the CEMAMu. Following this visit, I asked Xenakis to contribute to my book *Composers and the Computer*. He wrote the excellent essay "Music composition treks" to the anthology (Xenakis 1985).

In the summer of 1987, I had a residency in Paris as a visiting composer at the CEMAMu, working with the UPIC system. The 1987 version of the UPIC system introduced the possibility of drawing sampled sounds, not just synthetic waveforms. I brought a tape of alto saxophone tones. My UPIC scores created saxophone glissandi that would be impossible to achieve using the MUSIC-N style programming languages of the time. Of course, the UPIC did not run in realtime. You had to draw the score using ink on a large roll of paper, then manually trace every line in order to enter it into the computer. Then you would give the command to start sound synthesis calculations. Rendering a page to sound took time. The UPIC system ran on a Thomson Solar 16-bit minicomputer, which was slow.

In 1991, after the departure of Pierre Boulez from IRCAM, I was invited to work there as part of the regime change. In 1993 I left IRCAM to teach at Les Ateliers UPIC in the suburb of Massy. This felt like a homecoming. It was in this period that I came to know personally Xenakis and his circle. Of course, he was the famous maestro and I was an acolyte. I did not work directly for him, but was rather a part of the team at Les Ateliers UPIC working in parallel with CEMAMu. In my interactions with Xenakis, what struck me about him is that he was direct, unassuming, and without pretence. To accomplish what he did he had to be extremely confident, but this was never on display. His personality was formed in the crucible of the World War II resistance. Perhaps because of this, he exuded an aura of comradeship, rather than elitism. His team at the CEMAMu was lucky to have such a benevolent boss.

As a composer, Xenakis was always more radical than me. In 1994 I was present at the Paris premiere of his electronic composition S.709 (1994) in the auditorium of Radio France. This piece is the raw output of his experimental GENDY stochastic synthesis algorithm – untouched by human hands. The sound is harsh and abrasive, and the structure is bizarre. It was deliberately provocative. By contrast, I abandoned algorithmic composition in my youth because I found that beautiful algorithms rarely produced beautiful music. As a result, my practice is deeply entwined with craft and refinement. I take a multiscale approach to editing and mixing that takes place over a time scale of years. For example, my piece *Then* (2016) was the result of over 500 submixes in the period from 2010 to 2016. I use algorithms at the level of sound synthesis, but my pieces are carefully stitched together by hand.

Granular Synthesis

The most obvious connection between Xenakis and me is granular synthesis. It was, of course, Xenakis's concept. I found it in his book *Formalized Music* (1971). He cited Dennis Gabor (1946, 1947) as the source of the scientific theory. Later in Paris Xenakis gave me a copy of Hermann Scherchen's journal *Gravesaner Blätter* with Xenakis's 1960 article on granular synthesis. It is a prized possession.

In March 1974, I transferred to UCSD specifically because I heard that they had facilities for computer sound synthesis. The researcher Bruce Leibig had recently installed the Music V program (Mathews 1969) on a mainframe computer housed in the UCSD Computer Center. The dual-processor Burroughs B6700 was an advanced machine for its day, but sound synthesis was difficult, due to the state of input and output technology in the early 1970s (Roads 2001).

Nonetheless, I managed to test the first implementation of digital granular synthesis in December 1974. For this experiment, called *Klang-1*, I typed each grain specification (frequency, amplitude, duration) on a separate punched card. A stack of about 800 punched cards corresponded to the instrument and score for 30 seconds of granular sound. Following this laborious experience, I wrote a program in the Algol language to generate grain specifications from compact, high-level descriptions of clouds. Using this program, I realized an eight-minute study called *Prototype* (1975). These were the earliest manifestations of granular synthesis by computer.

Les Ateliers UPIC

Next, we look at another point of encounter with Xenakis. The story of Les Ateliers UPIC is told in the book *From Xenakis's UPIC to Graphic Notation Today* (Weibel, Brümmer and Kanach 2020), which is a free download from ZKM Karlsruhe.

As previously mentioned, in 1993 Gérard Pape asked me to teach at Les Ateliers UPIC. I already knew the UPIC system, but this was a new version that ran on a Windows computer with a dedicated hardware synthesizer, enabling it to operate in real-time. Les Ateliers UPIC was a small organization supported by the French Ministry of Culture. I became directory of pedagogy and led a year-long course. The course was a general introduction to computer music, based on my textbook *The Computer Music Tutorial*, which was in production at MIT Press. I also managed to conduct research, in particular the development of the first standalone app for granular synthesis: Cloud Generator. It was written by me and John Alexander, a student at Les Ateliers UPIC, in 1995.

Figure 10.6: *Les Ateliers UPIC, Massy (suburb of Paris). 1995. Music historian Harry Halbreich, Curtis Roads, Brigitte Robindoré, Iannis Xenakis, Gérard Pape. Photo by the author.*

I recall demonstrating Cloud Generator to Maestro Xenakis. His only comment was: "At least it doesn't sound terrible." Coming from Xenakis, who was not easily impressed, I took this as a compliment.

After I showed Cloud Generator to Xenakis's publisher, Radu Stan of Editions Salabert, he slipped me a cassette of *Analogique A et B* (1959), which was Xenakis's first attempt to realize granular synthesis using analogue tape. I had never heard it before. So, 21 years after my first computer experiments, I finally heard the original analogue granular synthesis!

One of the highlights of my experience at Les Ateliers UPIC was a concert organized by Gérard Pape at the Salle Olivier Messiaen of Radio France in Paris. This included the full Acousmonium setup of 48 loudspeakers. This was an extraordinary experience. Upmixing my music on the Acousmonium spatial panorama made an indelible impression.

In 1996 I became a professor at UCSB (University of California Santa Barbara). I returned to Paris annually to teach at the UPIC centre (renamed the Centre de Création "Iannis Xenakis" or CCMIX) until 2007. It was through CCMIX that I met Luc Ferrari and Bernard Parmegiani, among others. Les Ateliers UPIC/ CCMIX was an open door to many artists.

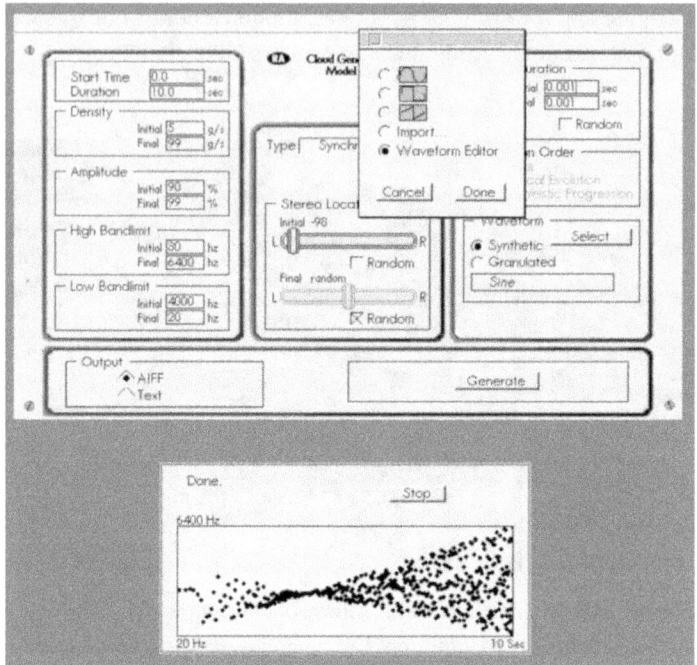

Figure 10.7: *Cloud Generator* (1995) *by Curtis Roads and John Alexander. Photo by the author.*

Figure 10.8: *Analogue cassette of* Analogique A et B. *Photo by the author.*

Continuing the Granular Model

Here in Santa Barbara, I have continued to advance the granular model. The 1997 constant-Q granulator, written in SuperCollider, was the first program to apply an individual bandpass filter to each grain. This is an example of what I call 'per-grain signal processing', where each grain has its own envelope, waveform (or sample), amplitude, frequency, spatial position, filter centre frequency, and resonance. Per-grain processing is essential to create rich multidimensional textures.

In 2005, my graduate student David Thall coded the EmissionControl granulator, which implemented my concept of per-grain processing but also added a modulation matrix for automatic LFO control of certain parameters. A ramp function, for example, might modulate grain density over a period of a minute, while the user was changing other parameters manually.

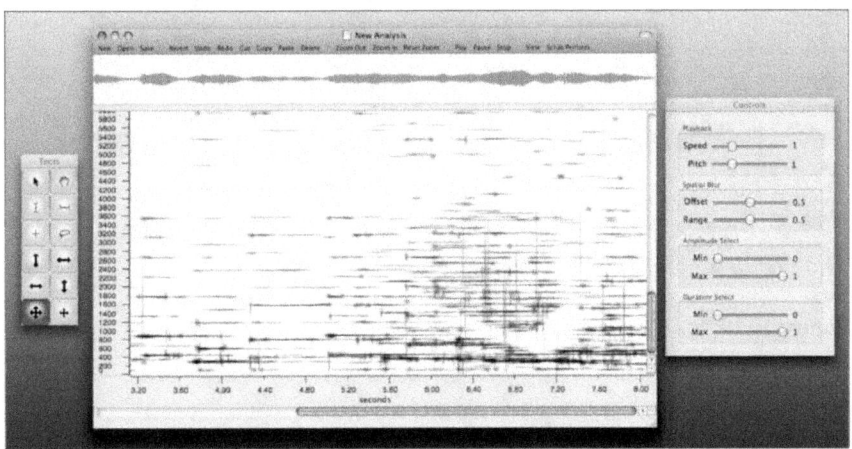

Figure 10.9: SCATTER, *screen shot by the author.*

Another important research direction has been the creation of an analytical counterpart to granular synthesis (Sturm et al. 2009). We faced two major challenges. The first was computation time. Our *atomic decomposition* algorithm took 200 seconds to analyse one second of sound. Due to excessive computation times, we also had to limit the audio resolution of the resynthesis. The other major challenge was the conundrum of dark energy interference terms. Although our funding was not renewed, these issues are tractable engineering problems, but they require additional research. Beyond that is the issue of building compositional tools based on this approach. We built a prototype time-frequency editor called SCATTER, but such a model could be taken much further.

The original EmissionControl granulator only ran on old Apple G5 computers, so I was anxious to create a new app. The original goal was simply to recreate EmissionControl for modern computers. As we proceeded however, it became clear that EmissionControl2 went far beyond the earlier program.

In October 2020, we released a new EmissionControl2 or EC2. EC2 is designed as a laboratory instrument for research in granular synthesis.

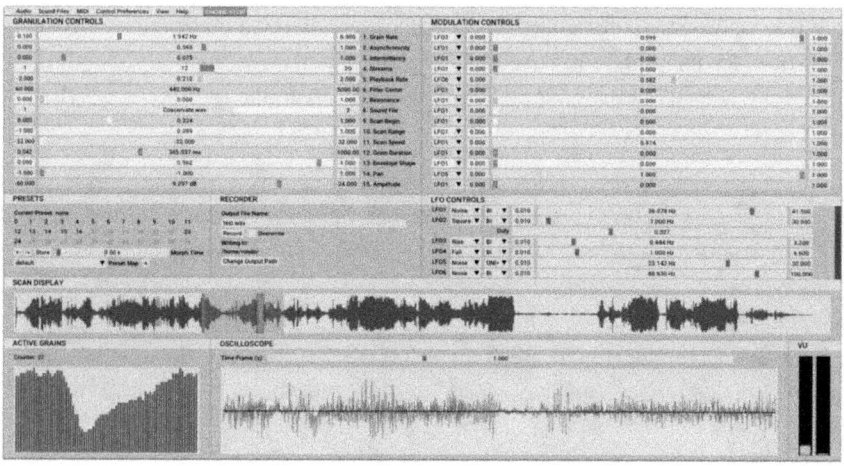

Figure 10.10: *EmissionControl2, screen shot by the author.*

The main features of EC2 are:

- Per-grain signal processing
- Granulation of multiple sound files simultaneously
- Up to 2,048 simultaneous grains
- Synchronous and asynchronous grain emission
- Intermittency control
- Modulation control of all parameters with six LFOs (bipolar or unipolar waveforms)
- Real-time display of peak amplitude, active grains, waveform, scan range, scanner, and grain emission
- Scalable graphical user interface (GUI) and font size

- Easy mapping of parameters to any MIDI/OSC continuous controller
- Algorithmic control of granular processes via OSC scripts
- Unique filter design optimized for per-grain synthesis
- Unlimited user presets with smooth interpolation for gestural design
- Open source code and free to download

Since its release, EmissionControl2 has been downloaded by over 7,500 musicians around the globe.

Finally, I should mention my new book *The Computer Music Tutorial, Second Edition*, which presents Xenakis's Stochastic Music Program, and devotes chapters to granular synthesis and atomic decomposition of sound.

Xenakis said that he composed in order to feel less miserable (Lohner 1986: 54). This is an excellent reason. But the effect of music goes beyond one's self. Composition is a service to humanity. Through music, a composer can make other people feel less miserable.

Bibliography

Gabor, D[ennis] (1946) "Theory of communication", in *Journal of the Institute of Electrical Engineers* Part III, 93: 429–457.

Gabor, D[ennis] (1947) "Acoustical quanta and the theory of hearing", in *Nature* 159 (4044): 591–594.

Harley, James (2004): *Xenakis: His Life in Music*, New York: Routledge.

Lohner, Henning (1986) "Interview with Iannis Xenakis", in *Computer Music Journal* 10/4, 50–55.

Mathews, Max (1969) *The Technology of Computer Music*, Cambridge: MIT Press.

Roads, Curtis (1973) "Analysis of the composition ST/10 and the computer program Free Stochastic Music by Iannis Xenakis", student paper, unpublished.

Roads, Curtis (1981) "Report from the IRCAM Conference on The Composer and the Computer", in *Computer Music Journal* 5/3, 7–27.

Roads, Curtis (2001) *Microsound*, Cambridge: MIT Press.

Roads, Curtis (2023) *The Computer Music Tutorial*, 2nd ed., Cambridge: MIT Press.

Roads, Curtis (2024) "La Légende de Xenakis: Meta Xenakis", in *Meta-Xenakis: New Perspectives on Iannis Xenakis's Life, Work, and Legacies*, ed. by Sharon Kanach and Peter Nelson, Cambridge: Open Book Publishers, 409–428.

Roads, Curtis, Kilgore, Jack, and Duplessis, Rodney (2022) "EmissionControl2: designing a real-time sound file granulator", in *Proceedings of the 2022 In-*

ternational Computer Music Conference, San Francisco: International Computer Music Association.

Sturm, Bob L., Roads, Curtis, McLeran, Aaron, and Shynk, John J. (2009) "Analysis, visualization, and transformation of audio signals using dictionary-based methods", in *Journal of New Music Research* 38, 325–341.

Thibaut, Jacques (2016) "Iannis Xenakis: musique et probabilités", Centre Iannis Xenakis, Université de Rouen, Normandie; https://www.canal-u.t v/chaines/univrouen/iannis-xenakis-musique-et-probabilites (accessed March 1, 2023).

Varèse, Edgar, and Wen-Chung, Chou (1966) "The liberation of sound", in *Perspectives of New Music* 5/1, 11–19.

Weibel, Peter, Brümmer, Ludger, and Kanach, Sharon, eds. (2020) *From Xenakis's UPIC to Graphic Notation Today*; https://zkm.de/en/from-xenakiss-upic -to-graphic-notation-today, (accessed March 1, 2023).

Xenakis, Iannis (1971) *Formalized Music*, Bloomington: Indiana University Press.

Xenakis, Iannis (1981) "Il faut que ça change!", in *Le Matin*, 26 January 1981, 28.

Xenakis, Iannis (1985) "Music composition treks", in *Composers and the Computer*, ed. by Curtis Roads, Los Altos: William Kaufman, 169–192.

List of Figures

Figure 10.1: DEC PDP-8 computer. https://www.old-computers.com/museu m/computer.asp?st=1&c=780, accessed March 29, 2023.

Figure 10.2: Poster for the Seminar on Formalized and Automated Music at Indiana University, 1972. Courtesy of the Author.

Figure 10.3: Poster for *Polytope de Cluny*. Courtesy of the Author.

Figure 10.4: Ticket for *Polytope de Cluny*. Courtesy of the Author.

Figure 10.5: *Polytope de Cluny*. Archives Les Ateliers UPIC, Paris.

Figure 10.6: Les Ateliers UPIC, Massy (suburb of Paris). 1995. Music historian Harry Halbreich, Curtis Roads, Brigitte Robindoré, Iannis Xenakis, Gérard Pape. Photo by the author.

Figure 10.7: Cloud Generator (1995) by Curtis Roads and John Alexander. Photo by the author.

Figure 10.8: Analogue cassette of *Analogique A-B*. Photo by the author.

Figure 10.9: SCATTER, screen shot by the author.

Figure 10.10: *EmissionControl2*, screen shot by by the author.

Why Did I Decide to Erase all Production Tapes of my Musique Concrète Except for the Final Compositions? A Clarification

Michel Chion

This text aims to explain why it is difficult for me to consider the musical elements of my concrete music production for magnetic tape (composed between 1970 and 2000 – thereafter I increasingly used digital media) as archives or documents to be preserved for history and why, while preciously preserving the original of the finished works, I erased the preparatory elements for the mix, thus making their medium, the magnetic tape, which I donated to other people, available for reuse.

I have always enjoyed working with tape recorders, and at the same time the tape has never been an idol for me; this is due to my personal history.

In 1958, when I was 11 years old, my father, an engineer, returned from a business trip, bringing with him to the small Alpine valley of Vallorcine where we were spending our holidays a heavy machine from Germany. It was an amateur Grundig tape recorder running at a speed of 9.5 cm per second. At the time, this device was very rare outside professional circles. This is how two little boys named Jacques and Michel Chion had the opportunity to play with a device which, compared to photography and cinema, offered miraculous possibilities: One could hear the result of the recording immediately (unlike photography and amateur cinema, for which one had to wait, firstly, for the roll of film to be finished, then for its development and finally for the images to be printed on paper or projected). Moreover, one could erase the medium and use it over and over.

I never again heard those imitations of radio shows my brother and I recorded for fun as children. I guess my father later reused the tape to record music. For a child of my generation, I was introduced to sound recording at a very early age and to the fact that its medium is reusable and not sacred. In this sense it is quite different from a piece of paper on which someone has written something.

Allow me to relate a personal example: When my father died, his second wife proceeded to destroy all our family letters and documents, but not the family photos. My father, before acquiring the tape recorder, had had another hobby in the 1950s: photography. Not only did he take the photos, but he developed the film himself and made his own paper prints. As children, my brother and I had seen what it meant to take a picture and the time and care needed to develop it; we knew that this process was irreversible.

When my father's second wife died, I cleaned up the house they had lived in, and I discovered a treasure that had escaped destruction because it was in a box of photographs: about ten handwritten letters to my father from his mother – our paternal grandmother, who had died when I was still a child. These letters gave me back a part of my history: Not only their content, which alluded to a family episode forgotten by my brother and myself, but also the medium of the text itself, namely our grandmother's handwriting, which revealed a lively, determined, ebullient woman, whereas the photos we had kept of her depicted a seemingly inconspicuous and reserved person. On different levels, I had found a historical document.

It has nothing to do with a tape recording intended for the composition of music on a support – what I call 'musique concrète', while others in France call it 'acousmatic music' (cf. Chion 2009): It has no more meaning than the discovery of a single part of a work for orchestra. Let us imagine that a symphony by Gustav Mahler or Camille Saint-Saëns has disappeared and that as the only trace we find the separate flute or harp part for one of the movements, including the silent bars: I wonder what could be done with it? To hear single parts of 'orchestral material' is the distressing feeling I had when listening to an 'archive disc' released by the GRM (Groupe de recherches musicales) in 2017 (Parmegiani 2017).

That year, in fact, the GRM (of which I was a member a long time ago) published a posthumous double album by Bernard Parmegiani (1927–2013), a composer I knew well, especially in the 1970s, and with whom I worked together on two occasions (in 1975 for a show entitled *Trio*, in which I played the role of a composer, and in 1977 for the satirical work *Des mots et des sons*, for which he recorded my voice). The first of the two CDs on this album brought together rare works not included in the 12-CD box set *Bernard Parmegiani – L'oeuvre musicale* already published in 2008 by INA-GRM (Parmegiani 2008). The second CD, entitled *Matières premières*, did not feature works, but only short sequences of 'working material' found and selected from the very many reels of magnetic tape left by Parmegiani after his death. I played the disc and heard a series of insignificant things, unworthy of the composer. It seemed as though the CD was meant to be 'sampled' by the buyer. This feeling was all the stronger as the publication was not accompanied by any explanatory note or historical clarification.

While listening to these *Matières premières* I made the definitive decision not to leave any trace of this kind. In 2020 and 2021, I therefore erased or discarded the music elements of all my works composed until 2000, except for those for *La tentation de Saint-Antoine* (1984), for which I plan to compile a historical documentation of the production process, including texts and musical extracts. As my tapes did not contain too many 'tape splices' and thus were reusable, I kept them to give to the three musician friends who agreed to be my executors; they will be able to reuse them, or give them to other musicians; in fact, the manufacture of tapes has ceased, and they are sold on the Internet for a considerable price.

When I made my music in the studios of the GRM, I could use professional tapes without having to pay for them; these studios were located in the Maison de la radio et de la musique – Radio France, the headquarters of the French public radio stations. A GRM technician, Jacques Darnis, had noticed that the dustbins of the radio studios next to those of the GRM often contained large reels of magnetic tape in almost new condition, which had only been used once for the final copy of a radio show. He recovered them and gave them to me. I used them extensively.

I was scandalised when listening to *Matières premières* because Parmegiani was a demanding composer for whom a work is not just a succession of pretty sounds, but also a form, a journey. This led him, like me, to rework his compositions several times, including *De natura sonorum* (two versions) and *L'enfer de la divine comédie* (three versions). I am not criticising Bernard's widow for authorising this publication, as Claude-Anne Parmegiani did her best to promote her husband's work; rather, I am criticising the members of the GRM who took the initiative to reduce this composer to a 'creator of sounds'.

Already, after his death in November 2013, a GRM radio show hosted by Christian Zanési, David Jisse and Christophe Bourseiller chose not to feature the composer's important works, but the three-second jingle known as the 'Roissy call sign', intended to precede spoken flight announcements, a jingle that Parmegiani had made for France's largest airport Charles de Gaulle, located north of Paris. As if it were a title of glory to have been heard in this way, on airport loudspeakers, by tens or hundreds of thousands of travellers! Yet, having met Parmegiani many, many times, I have never heard him refer to this work and take pride in it.

At the same time, it is striking that the detailed collective work devoted during Parmegiani's lifetime to the genesis of his masterpiece *De natura sonorum* (1975) is still out-of-print: *L'envers d'une œuvre* (Mion, Nattiez and Thomas

1982) by Philippe Mion, Jean-Jacques Nattiez, Jean-Christophe Thomas and the composer himself, who was interviewed at length for this publication. It is still unavailable, even though it is of considerable historical interest – especially, but not only, in terms of the techniques used by the author – and should have been republished and even translated a long time ago.

Even if these techniques have since changed completely, and not only for the new generations: Parmegiani himself, who was 20 years older than me, converted to computer music quite quickly, as François Bayle (born in 1932) and Francis Dhomont (born in 1926, he is the oldest of all of us!) had done before him. When I used the GRM studios in the 1990s and then again between 2006 and 2012, I was the last one using the tape recorders. However, I suspected that this device would become fashionable again, so I published several articles in the magazine *Revue & Corrigée* about my tape recorder techniques.

In addition, Rodrigo Maia Sacic filmed me in 2012 (in the GRM studio 116C) and Régis Lacaze in 2017 (in my small private studio) for a video explaining the technical aspects of my studio work. I'm going to use this footage for a self-portrait film I'm producing, so we'll be able to see the concrete aspect of these things. But playing a fragment of a tape without commentary and presenting it as a document: That is deceiving people.

As a document, and contrary to the abovementioned 'found letters' of my grandmother, a few metres of magnetic tape without context mean nothing: We don't know if this fragment constitutes a part that has already been mixed or an element of the mix, at what speed it should be played (in my music, certain elements have been played at 19 cm per second or 38 cm per second) and even in what direction... Each fragment of tape is a possible source of very different sounds, through variations of speed, manual interventions during the playback of the sound, etc. Only the composer can tell, if he remembers at all.

The album *Matières premières* was in fact a rather cynical exploitation of the interest of many young musicians in the synthesizers of the 1970s, and in particular in the large set of oscillators called the 'Coupigny synthesizer', which I had used myself. However, this interest in 'old synths' often seems to me to be reductive and fetishistic. With more recent equipment you can get sounds that are just as interesting, you just have to look for them. And the most important thing for me is the composition, or rather the relationship between the composition and the life of the sounds.

Of course, I have not tried to encourage other composers to do what I do, and I am only describing my personal position. However, I would like to remind you that I have as a composer of concrete music written many historical, didactic, critical and theoretical books and articles on 'musique concrète' (also called 'electroacoustic' or 'acousmatic music'), made radio broadcasts, and carried out research useful to the public, composers, musicologists and researchers. I even believe that, after Pierre Schaeffer, I am the one who has written the most in France on the genre. Far from wanting to deprive historians of sources and archives, I am therefore extremely attached to the transmission of information. But at the same time, we must not forget what is important which is, in my opinion, the works and their composition. These works – at least mine, and I believe all those that count – are not mere collections of sound moments. I also consider my role as a transmitter important, and through my texts and my practice of erasing my tapes and giving them to other musicians younger than myself I aim to keep carrying out this role, thus playing a part in ensuring that new works continue to be produced, while at the same time defending the integrity of my own works.

Translation from French: Reinhold Friedl

Bibliography

Chion, Michel (2009) *La musique concrète, art des sons fixés*, Lyon: Mômeludies.

Mion, Philippe, Nattiez, Jean-Jacques, and Thomas, Jean-Christophe (1982) *L'envers d'une œuvre: 'De Natura sonorum' de Bernard Parmegiani*, Paris: Ina/Buchet-Chastel.

Parmegiani, Bernard (2008) *L'oeuvre musicale*, 12CD-Box, Paris: INA-GRM – INA G 6000/11.

Parmegiani, Bernard (2017) *Matières premières*, 2CDs, Paris: INA-GRM – INA G 6048/49.

Xenakis: Back to the Roots
A Conversation with Nikolaus Urbanek and Michelle Ziegler

Jan Brocza, Reinhold Friedl, Thomas Grill, Katharina Klement,
Christian Tschinkel and Anatol Wetzer

Note: The conversation reproduced below took place on 12 December 2022, at the University of Music and Performing Arts Vienna; some participants were connected via video conferencing software. The transcription of the conversation, which was conducted in German, was edited by all participants and subsequently translated into English.

The reference of the conversation was the performance of the complete electroacoustic works of Iannis Xenakis in the context of the symposium *Xenakis 2022: Back to the Roots*, which took place in May 2022 at the University of Music and Performing Arts Vienna.

19 May 2022, mdw Klangtheater: Iannis Xenakis – Complete Electroacoustic Works I

Diamorphoses (stereo) – Sound projection: Arthur Fussy
Concret PH (4 channels) – Sound projection: Jan Brocza
Orient-Occident (4 channels) – Sound projection: Madeleine Fremuth
Bohor (8 channels) – Sound projection: Katharina Klement
Hibiki Hana Ma (8 channels) – Sound projection: Christian Tschinkel
Polytope de Cluny (8 channels) – Sound projection: Pierre Carré

20 May 2022, mdw Klangtheater: Iannis Xenakis – Complete Electroacoustic Works II

Mycènes alpha – Sound projection: Angélica Castelló
Voyage absolu des Unari vers Andromède – Sound projection: Elizaveta Trukhanova

S.709 – Sound projection: Reinhold Friedl
La Légende d'Eer (8 channels) – Sound projection: Wolfgang Musil

21 May 2022, mdw Klangtheater: Iannis Xenakis – Complete Electroacoustic Works III

Taurhiphanie (mono) – Sound projection: Jonas Hammerer
Gendy 3 (stereo) – Sound projection: Anatol Wetzer
Persepolis (8 channels) – Sound projection: Thomas Grill

Nikolaus Urbanek (NU): I was very fascinated to hear the sonic realisations of all of Iannis Xenakis's electroacoustic works on three evenings at the Klangtheater and to gain insight into the different interpretations. I would like to ask you how you conceived your respective interpretations.

Katharina Klement (KK): I interpreted the piece *Bohor* (1962) at the symposium. I chose this eight-channel piece because it was already familiar to me to a certain extent. I found it very interesting because it's about a sound mass, and interestingly I have the same cross arrangement of stereo tracks in my own works. Thanks to a lot of research and an unpublished text of yours, Reinhold, I got a lot of information about this piece, which was very important for me and definitely influenced my interpretation (cf. Friedl 2019). I can explain this in detail later. *Bohor* has held a certain mystery for me. This title appealed to me. And I performed it twice: once at the Klangtheater and once at the Belvedere 21 museum (aka 21er Haus) at Wiener Festwochen on 18th of June 2022.

Thomas Grill (TG): I realised the piece *Persepolis* (1971). I was familiar with the piece from a performance by Daniel Teige in the big hall of the Konzerthaus Vienna about 15 years ago. It was a formative performance for me, extremely loud and unusually harsh for the Konzerthaus. They really sat there with the volume meter and pushed against the gain threshold. Nevertheless, I found the piece extremely good, even in this loudness, and I resolved to perform it myself one day. Now the right opportunity had finally come, however, I chose a completely different approach and oriented myself more on the original performance in the ruins of Persepolis, where it was set up almost like an installation with far more than eight loudspeakers. Xenakis chose an approach very different from a concert performance.

Anatol Wetzer (AW): I played *Gendy 3* (1991), a stereo piece. I approached it with very little prior knowledge and mainly focused on the different sonic layers. My idea was to use the four speakers in the room, which were not part of the standard hemisphere, and the top circle of the hemisphere. I changed the projection depending on the section and the timbre.

TG: And why did you choose that piece?

AW: Jonas [Hammerer] had two pieces. I listened to both and liked *Gendy 3*, partly because it was so inaccessible and sounded hermetic due to the computer composition.

Christian Tschinkel (CT): Thomas Grill suggested a few pieces for interpretation, especially *Hibiki Hana Ma* (1970). Since I already owned the new 5CD box with the complete electroacoustic works of Xenakis, I was able to listen to each of the pieces in question. I found *Hibiki Hana Ma* quite challenging – sonically as well as structurally. With a certain curiosity, I agreed to interpret it and face the chaotic texture of this piece.

Reinhold Friedl (RF): I played *S.709* (1994). It was the last piece; nobody had chosen it. And this monophonic product of a computer algorithm is also Xenakis's last electroacoustic music. Raw and harsh, someone called it a "bitter old-age work". I wanted to support this character and projected it from only one loudspeaker – directly in the zenith of the hemisphere, right over the heads of the audience – purely mono. Absurdly, the result was a spatial effect. One had the impression of a moving sound cloud, probably because individual frequency bands are reflected differently in space. It is an extreme interpretation: a non-interpretation so to speak, in the performance I did nothing other than to minimally adjust the volume of the single speaker.

Jan Brocza (JB): I performed *Concret PH* (1958). It was a piece that I was familiar with, that I found very beautiful, and that was also very manageable because at first I wasn't sure if I was confident about it. It was a good decision. I like the piece very much. I had the four-channel version from the GRM (Groupe de recherches musicales) archive. Since it doesn't have giant dynamics or a big build-up, I tried to keep it rather quiet in space and not make huge movements. After about 40 seconds, there's a part where a little more bass frequencies come in, so I tried to open up the space a little more. But my interpretation was rather minimal.

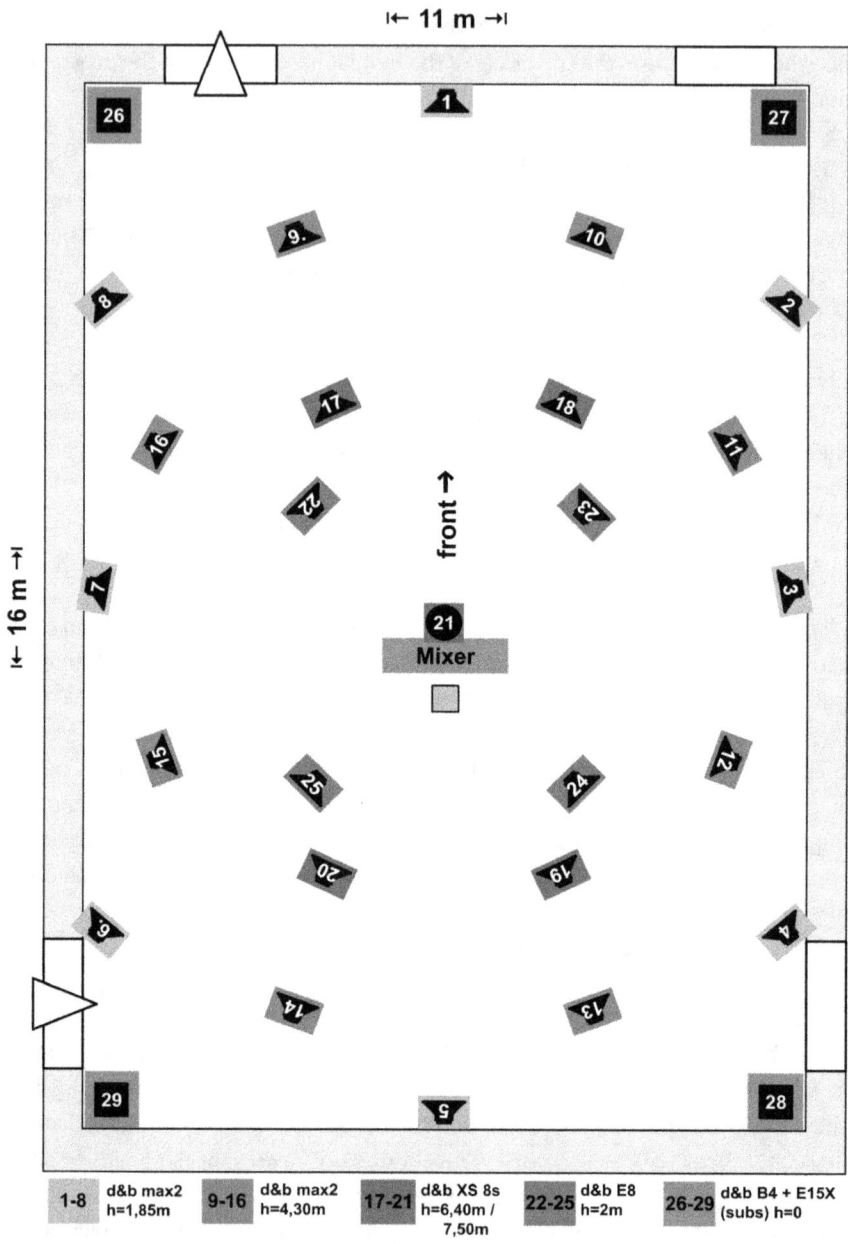

Figure 12.1: *Loudspeaker positions in the Klangtheater. General plan by Thomas Grill, 2024.*

RF: Opening up the space means spreading the sound on the speakers wider?

JB: I made the sound of the subwoofers and the speakers on the ceiling a little louder and took the inner ring (the four speakers positioned around the mixer) down a little bit at the same time. That's what I mean when I say I opened up the room a little bit in that moment, in order to give the audience the feeling of being more immersed.

NU: I would like to go back to the subject of the special space of the performances, the new Klangtheater at the mdw. I think everyone knows the Klangtheater very well by now?

TG: The Klangtheater is still new, we are always discovering new facets of the space. But, of course, we had already had intensive contact as users in the Programme in Electroacoustic and Experimental Music (ELAK) and had performed many pieces here. When one gets into the intricacies of an interpretation, new questions always arise, such as how to map something on the mixer so that it is expressively playable during the performance, because there are so many options.

NU: And how was the technology set up for the Xenakis performance?

TG: We basically used the permanently installed periphonic sound system, 21 loudspeakers in a hemisphere. There is an eight-speaker ring at ear level, numbered clockwise (1–8). A second ring is at about four metres and is numbered the same way (9–16) and a third ring with four speakers is at about six and a half metres (17–20). Finally, we have loudspeaker number 21 located seven and a half metres above the mixing console just below the ceiling, the "Reinhold speaker" as we have called it since the symposium. In addition, in order to project the sound in the opposite direction, we had four loudspeakers on tripods set up around the central mixing console and facing the walls at an angle of about 45 degrees. Anatol used that, for example. Four subwoofers in the corners of the room completed the sound reinforcement.

NU: I would be very interested to know how much the space itself influenced interpretative decisions, whether, for example, certain changes were still made during the performance in order to be able to react spontaneously to the space, to the presence of the audience. Maybe we could start with Katharina because you said you performed *Bohor* in two different places.

KK: *Bohor* is an eight-channel piece – more precisely, there are four stereo tracks arranged crosswise. In the Klangtheater, I have assigned these to the three speaker rings accordingly. If there is channel seven in one corner, then it is there on all the three levels, and channel eight is in the opposite corner on all three levels. I then mainly controlled the sound between these three levels, but also the ratios of the four stereo tracks to each other. In comparison, it was easier at Belvedere 21 with only eight speakers. There I concentrated on the volume ratios of the individual tracks in the interpretation, which was an experiment for me: In the piece, this sound mass should actually be present from the beginning, with an additional large crescendo. And I decided to play that in contradiction to the historical sources. At the beginning, I faded in each track very slowly because it was important to me to be able to listen more closely to the details of the individual tracks. That worked quite well, I think. I did that both times, in the Klangtheater and at the Belvedere 21 museum.

TG: I'm happy to continue because I had the same situation as Katharina. I performed *Persepolis* twice in completely different places: in the Klangtheater and at the Belvedere 21. The Klangtheater is acoustically very dry; sound emitted by a loudspeaker is very direct, that is to say, not mediated by reflections of the room: A really direct access to the ear. In the 21er Haus, it's the opposite: There are glass walls that reflect strongly and repeatedly. The sound is much less direct there. That is why I conceived two completely different interpretations. In the 21er Haus it was more like the one by Daniel Teige, with great volume, really big, in order to try out a canonic interpretation. I aimed for the opposite of this massiveness in the Klangtheater, where I tried to create a more attentive listening situation but, nevertheless, respect Xenakis's original performance situation. In the plans of the acoustic setting in the ruins of Persepolis, groups of about eight loudspeakers were placed in several parts for over 50 loudspeakers. The audience could stroll between the individual groups – in other words, it was like an installation, a walk-in performance situation. For my performance method in the Klangtheater, I set myself the task – since people are all sitting in fixed positions – of re-creating these changing perspectives for the audience. During the hour-long piece, I tried to give different perspectives on the sound material, to let it come from different directions, to set different volumes for different materials, and thus to simulate the walking around. Like Katharina, I did not start massively either, but realised more of a walking through the sound material, as if one approached the field of ruins, went there, walked around inside and finally left again. That is certainly very different from the usual canonical performances of this piece.

RF: Okay, got it... [laughs]. We had a heated discussion right after the performance, I was pretty irritated and asked: "Is that supposed to be *Persepolis*?" Now I understand the approach, and it is indeed an interesting one, simulating a moving listener, so to speak.

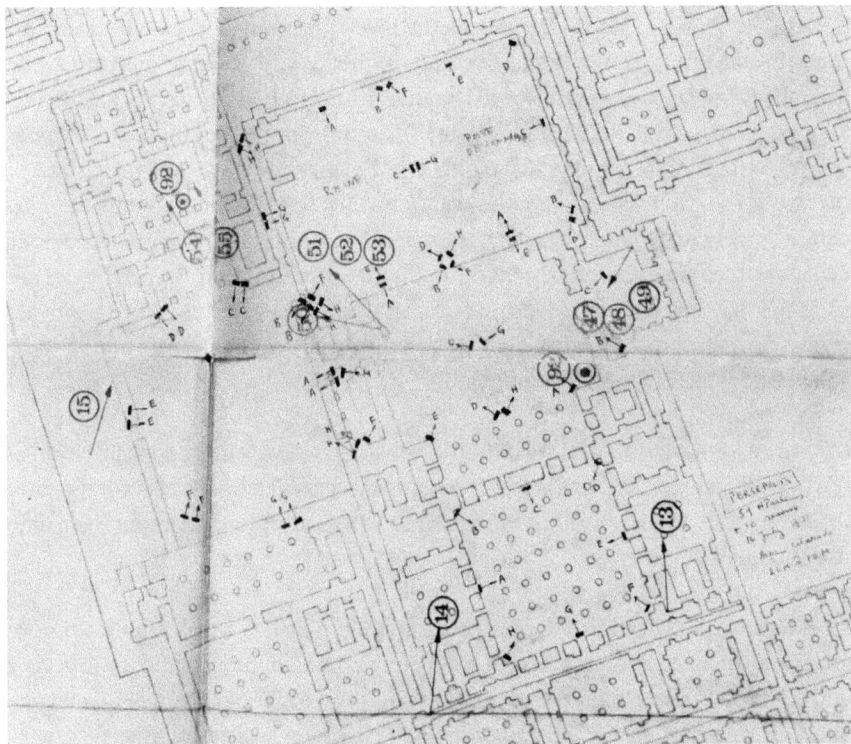

Figure 12.2: *Blueprint with positions of the loudspeakers (in red) for* Persepolis. *Collection Famille Xenakis DR, OM 27–4, p. 4.*

TG: It appeared to me that being stuck in one place is unsatisfying given the situation in the ruins in Persepolis, where so many potential perspectives could open up, and I thought this had to be realised somehow. There were several listening rooms with grouped speakers. That's why one can assume that in this acoustic scenario, different sound sources were strongly mixed. There must have also been run-time differences due to the different distances to the loudspeakers. A static interpretation in the Klangtheater would not have reflected this at all.

RF: The speakers were apparently distributed pretty asymmetrically in Persepolis, probably just by trial and error?

TG: Yes, that is to be assumed. It is the opposite of a clearly defined surround situation with eight channels.

CT: For *Hibiki Hana Ma* I started from the given grouping of the eight tracks already predetermined by the speaker rings in the Klangtheater. I could intervene in each group, i.e., despite the fixed layout as a multi-channel piece, I always had an additional subtle weighting in space from bottom to top, but also the possibility to intervene in individual eight-channel groups. What was important to me was a full, rich sound – a good sound quality – with simultaneous amplification of certain phenomena: for example, that the sudden wooden knocking clearly comes from an unexpected direction, without being covered by other sounds – so to speak, a peeling out of distinctive materials. I did not provide excessive sound movements, only for the glissandi, which in my opinion were allowed to whiz through the room a bit.

NU: Now we have heard a lot about the consideration of the spatial situation of the performance. Are there also other aspects that were particularly important to you in your interpretation, for example of a structural nature or regarding the choice of volume?

AW: *Gendy* 3 is very strict and straightforward but has these sudden timbre changes, those moments where a frequency comes in or disappears in a very audible way. I used them for orientation and thought very carefully in advance about how to emphasise those moments of change. I listened to the piece very often and defined these sections for myself. I then implemented this quite precisely in the Klangtheater and changed practically nothing during the performance. It was only after the concert that I wondered whether it hadn't been too quiet and therefore missing a few details.

NU: May I ask a quick question back here? For Anatol, the orientation to the sound structure of the work was, if I may say so, important for coordinating the interpretation. Thomas, with you the premiere situation and its spatial conditions came into play, which rather contradicted a 'canonical performance'.

TG: I also took my cues from the material. There are ten different textural materials in *Persepolis*. Each of the eight channels has the same ten materials in a different order and it makes a big difference whether you have bright and direct material at ear level, for example, or on the higher speaker. I have decided carefully beforehand where to position which material, especially in terms of height and distance, partly because the front speakers are further away than the side ones – the "rings" aren't rings, but ellipses. That is also a parameter. It is a mesh of decisions that have to be made. And volume is also an issue, of course; you cannot readjust it greatly during the performance due to the stationary nature. Setting the volume at the beginning is the hardest thing, I think. If you decide to play *Persepolis* at full volume, for example, you stick with it. After all, the piece lasts almost an hour and is very monolithic.

CT: I started with a little Internet research about *Hibiki Hana Ma*. Besides the key data, it is always important for me to know what a title means. I used the online translator and found out that the Japanese characters 響き – 花 – 間 mean 'reverberation-flower-interval'. Well, but I did not know how this could affect my mix in the Klangtheater. What was more influential was the fact that this piece was composed by Xenakis for the 1970 World's Fair in Osaka, where it was performed in a multimedia show including mirrors, light and laser – as so often with Xenakis a spectacle linked to great architecture.

Since I did not want to play the piece quietly, I felt confirmed by the word 'spectacle'. To my taste, there was still room for improvement in some places, although the dryness of the Klangtheater encouraged this immense immediacy and directness, which is why I remained reasonably within the limits. For I am aware that loudspeakers – to use Stockhausen's words – are weapons, especially at head height. In addition, I personally find the highs in Xenakis always challenging, not to say problematic. You always feel under power while listening.

I had rehearsed the piece relatively loud, but in the concert situation I was a little unsettled by "more careful", i.e., less loud interpretations, and asked myself whether I should join in. But actually, it was by then already clear to me that I would stand by my rehearsed interpretation as a contrast to the others, and in a conversation shortly beforehand, Reinhold also confirmed my intention to do so. I think it suits me to play this music in this way, and I think it also corresponds with Xenakis's idea. I know listening to the performance of so many works in one evening is a challenge for the audience, but *Hibiki Hana Ma* needs a monumental interpretation.

NU: For a better understanding, I would like to ask how you solved the disproportionate relationship between the number of channels of some the pieces on the existing data carriers and the number of loudspeakers in the Klangtheater. Was it also necessary to adjust anything sonically?

JB: *Concret PH* was premiered in 1958 in the Philips Pavilion at the World's Fair in Brussels with a lot of loudspeakers, several hundred. So, I thought I would definitely use all the loudspeakers in the Klangtheater. Since the piece is not long and has no significant sections, my idea was to keep it rather static, to be very subtle with it, and to project it to the whole room all the time. The piece consists entirely of the finest snippets of recordings of glowing coal. And as I said before, at about second 40 there are some deeper coal shards that come in. That's where I wanted the audience to get the feeling that something is happening by spreading out the spatial sound image. Just before the end, there are a couple of sharp spots, and since we had generally found beforehand that many of the pieces can be very intense in the high frequencies, I tried to balance that spot out a bit. Those were the strongest interventions.

TG: To lower the high frequencies, did you use a filter or did you just adjust the volume accordingly?

JB: I did not filter. I noticed a passage in this four-channel version that was just a bit more aggressive, and I knew that I had to go down two to three decibels there. I remember not noticing that at all in the other versions but listening to the four-channel version at the Klangtheater, it became more obvious. I made the decision on the spot, I had not thought about it before. If I had played the whole piece at the same volume, there would have been passages where it would have hurt a little bit. I wanted to avoid that because the programme was pretty long. I played second and thought that it wasn't necessary to challenge everyone right away.

TG: In principle, you can say that you really have to listen to the material on site. It sounds different with every speaker system. And even if Martin Wurmnest mixed it on his loudspeakers to the best of his knowledge, that doesn't mean that it would sound perfect here: The loudspeakers are different, the distances are different, and so on. Also, the variety of speakers and their placement some-times leads to phasing effects that can emphasise or cut certain frequencies. There is also a difference between the rehearsal situation and the performance situation. Not only in instrumental music, but in the Klangtheater, too, one has to consider that the room becomes much drier with an audience, so you need more volume. I would say at least three to four decibels can be added. These are decisions, as Jan said, that can and must often only be made during the performance.

JB: Exactly. I was also satisfied, although other people thought it could have been louder. Maybe I'm personally more sensitive to volume, but I think it was a good fit.

TG: Reinhold? You've already said almost everything about your interpretation...

RF: Yes, but we are now approaching some classic questions about interpretation. The one thing you hinted at, Thomas, is that any electroacoustic realisation or projection is always an instrumental representation, which depends on the playing situation itself. For example, the sound in a room with an audience becomes not only quieter but also more directional and drier. This means you have to be familiar with your 'instrument' and must have practiced so that you can respond properly. This situation is very similar to playing an instrument in a concert hall.

The second question is: How do I implement an analytical insight musically? I remember that the pianist Wilhelm Backhaus did not emphasise the themes of the fugues in the *Well-Tempered Clavier*, because he assumed everyone knew them anyway. Charles Rosen, pianist and musicologist, discussed this question explicitly: How does an analysis change my interpretation? In our discussion today, I think we have a somewhat naive view: "I make an analysis and then play the result". For Backhaus this would have been too pedagogical.

Katharina on the other hand, did not start from an analysis but from an extra-musical idea, namely: "I want to introduce the sound material slowly". This ignores the fidelity to the work and is actually a bit cheeky towards the composer.

KK: Well, if you address that directly, I had the most respect or fear of you at the beginning of the project, Reinhold. You were at the first rehearsal in the Klangtheater and I asked: "Well, these eight tracks in *Bohor*, they actually go through relatively invariably and only distort at some point". And you said: "Yes, that is what is on the tape and, of course, Xenakis wanted it that way, the material is meant to go through from beginning to end". I had thought that maybe that's just sound material and then I can play with it in the interpretation [laughs]. I then decided that I didn't want to hear everything from the beginning. Even more so, I think one track starts off pretty bumpy. It almost sounds like a technical error.

Since you mention the *Well-Tempered Clavier*: I thought, I moved so far away from this classical interpretation, with which I already had problems in my pianist days. I now just do what I want, with Xenakis, too. I do not want to play a classical interpretation, where I'm told to keep this faithfulness to the work. I think a piece simply has to be understandable and sound good – that is, the way I think it sounds good. I think that was the right way to do it. And yes, that worked quite well.

RF: Your idea was not only to make it sound good, your idea was to introduce the material slowly to the listener. That means accommodating the listener, developing a listener-friendly dramaturgy?

KK: Yes, absolutely. I felt like you don't really hear anything because the tracks are relatively similar. They're all metal sounds, rich in detail, and I thought you could just introduce them successively and then you would have 15 minutes to listen to them at the same time anyway. That was my plan. So, I used the first five minutes of those 20 minutes to introduce the voices one by one. Which I'm sure, if you look into the historical sources, is not written anywhere.

RF: Yes, you took that liberty...

TG: It's basically the same with *Persepolis*. I just took it as material because there are ten textures lined up in blocks more or less unedited. There is a sequence, just as the synchronicity between the tracks is, of course, already composed, but the material is block-like. From our point of view, working very much with material, one would say it's almost untreated. In this respect, I did not think much about having to treat it faithfully in the performance because it comes as material. Of course, you cannot decide to start a track later, as that would throw the arrangement out of whack. And you cannot go wild with the volume because the balance would be disturbed. But if you think about the fact that this has to be blocky now, and that this should reflect the texture as such, you're still in the realm of faithfulness to the work. How you put things into perspective or how you let them change in volume: I think you have a certain freedom there. Even if you look at the original production of *Persepolis*: There were seven groups of about eight loudspeakers each somehow standing next to each other in uncovered ruins. This set-up makes an absolute volume or fixed ratio virtually impossible. Canonical performances are not the measure of all things.

NU: I find it very, very exciting that we are now thinking about concepts such as freedom or faithfulness to the original, that we are already considering ideas of the premiere scenario, that is, relatively ancient ideas of an authentic performance practice/a historically informed performance practice. But we are also considering not only the extent to which the history of interpretation, which can also move away from the premiere situation, plays a role, but also questions of analysis. Reinhold, I would be very interested to know what, in your mind, falls under analysis. Is it an analysis of form? Or is it a material analysis? Or is it an analysis that is also aware of the historical context, the media conditions, the history of performance? I would say that analysis is still a relatively open concept. That means that very different possibilities for interpretation seem to play a role. And we actually also got very different guiding ideas in your introductory statements, for example, with you, Anatol, more a material-relatedness; with Katharina Klement perhaps also a working off of the premiere situation; Thomas, with you, on the one hand, the premiere situation, but also – you mentioned several times – the performances canonised in the history of performance, so that we can observe very, very different moments there, which now, however, cannot all be grasped under a traditional concept of faithfulness to the work, but are oriented toward different ideas. That's why, as an outside historian, I would be very interested to know how we should deal with these traditional descriptive categories.

TG: I think it's important to see that there is not necessarily a school of interpretation here. I think that's an essential difference compared to piano music that has been played a thousand times. The pieces that we played have not been played that often, especially not in this holistic framework. In this respect, one can almost always speak of a new first performance, depending on the situation of the room. So, the 'instrumentation', too, if you like, that of the loudspeakers, is always different and very strongly changes the feeling of how material is handled.

RF: To answer Nikolaus's question: Analysis in a broad sense. This includes composition technique, as in the Backhaus example: There are certain musical structures, something comes back, there are symmetries within the composition, and so on. But also the historical context, Katharina Klement, for example, respected Xenakis's sonification instructions and mapped the tracks to the speakers in the same way Xenakis did. But analysis also includes a philological approach for sure: What is the 'text', which versions exist, are they consistent, how do they relate to each other but also to different performance situations, etc.?

This is especially important for interpretation and pushes us back to the essential question: What shall I do with an analytical insight? Is it of any use to me and how can I musically implement it?

Perhaps in electroacoustic music one is even more forced to find new solutions because there is no broad historical performance practice. I think it is easier to perform a historically informed Scarlatti on the harpsichord than to realise a historically informed performance of *Persepolis* or *Concret PH*, where you would need 435 loudspeakers as in the Philips Pavilion in 1958. Today, moreover, we have completely different loudspeakers. I would say: We are constantly playing Scarlatti on a grand piano when we perform historical electroacoustic music nowadays.

TG: Maybe Jan can say something about that. The performance situation of *Concret PH* with 435 bad loudspeakers – from today's perspective – is, of course, quite different than having 21 very good loudspeakers in the Klangtheater.

JB: I did not hear how it sounded at that time. There are only stories that often talk about the whole pavilion, where not only *Concret PH* was played, but also Edgard Varèse's *Poème électronique*. I did not make a huge effort to read ten reviews about how exactly they perceived it. I rather asked myself: How do I hear the piece? How do I like it? And for me, *Concret PH* gives you the impression of sitting on glowing coal. That is why I used all available speakers. Unfortunately, I did not attend the premiere!

NU: May I perhaps ask again: What kind of research was done in preparation for the interpretations? For sure, we know about the performance situation in the Philips Pavilion, but you said you did not read through any other reviews. What was the research like with the others? What did you focus on in preparing for the performances? Katharina Klement, you read Reinhold's dissertation and...

KK: Yes, thankfully. I did not know that Reinhold had done this detailed analysis of *Bohor*'s sound material. There is one track, which is always called "piano". And Reinhold wrote that he always thought that this was not a piano. And I had thought the same thing, because as a pianist you can quickly hear whether there is a prepared piano somehow. His research revealed that it was produced on a Baschet instrument, which also had a keyboard. Xenakis's idea was primarily to create metallic sounds in a wide variety. The title *Bohor* goes back to a knight from King Arthur's round table in metal armor. To me, that is very poetic information that brings me much deeper into the piece. Or that the knight also had a scar, like Xenakis himself. So that there is probably an identification, which explains why the idea to use metal sounds came up in the first place. These connect you very much with a person. I probably got closer to Xenakis and the question why he made such a piece. So, thank you again for this extensive information! Reinhold also proved very clearly that much of what circulated as a supposed construction plan was just a later sketch to remix the piece. That confirmed my scepticism even more: What is the original? Or what is faithfulness to the original? Often what you find on the Internet or read in some text is not true.

RF: I think this is where the question of the existence of an 'original' is hidden: In musicology and philology, we have long since said goodbye to the idea that there must always be an 'original'. But we musicians mostly still believe in this idea: We buy an 'Urtext' sheet music and think: "Ah, I got the original!" Of course, in most cases it is a lie, as already the long explanations in the introduction might show. Often it is even unclear which versions of a composition exist, or there are different versions to choose from. This is exactly the point that makes Xenakis's electroacoustic œuvre interesting for this discussion: He left a respectable chaos of different versions, which is thus a treasure trove for music-philological questions. For example, at the premiere of *Concret PH* in 1958 at the Philips Pavilion in Brussels, there were 435 loudspeakers, but there was also a spatial movement realised with a special hardware that is lost today. Moreover, what we call a 'composition' today, started out as a sonic intermission filler, conceived as an interlude between the performances of Varèse's *Poème électronique*. Xenakis himself called it "interlude sonore". Later, Xenakis did what many musicians have done for centuries: He made secondary use of his own material. This is sufficiently proven and known, for example, with Bach or Beethoven. Xenakis has thus edited the *Interlude Sonore* somewhat and published it as the electroacoustic piece *Concret PH* in a new stereo version. And it has been published several times in different mixes. This led to a rich collection of source material, which is contradictory, and to which you have to relate as an interpreter. You are forced to choose what to refer to. In this respect, we get caught up in the ontological discussion: What actually is the work? What is the identity? Is it one version or many different ones? Or is "the work" what it tells me? Or is it something that I only help to become physical reality through my interpretation? In electroacoustic music one very quickly encounters these questions. That is why it lends itself to this discussion. At that point I would be interested in the musicological perspective.

Michelle Ziegler (MZ): I think many aspects have already been addressed in the discussion, and the performances in the Klangtheater have also impressively shown the variety of possible answers and approaches to interpretation. Basically, the new phonographic technologies in the 20th century have permanently changed the relationship between text, performance and work. There are definitely differences between writings on paper and recordings on tape due to their media, material and technological peculiarities: The different writing tools and recording devices, the different carriers, as well as the associated media practices affect the creation, edition, preservation and performance of musical works. However, the performances of Xenakis's electroacoustic work at the Klangtheater have also confirmed that there are certain analogies in the interpretation or performance practice between electroacoustic works and instrumental music, since the sound projection in tape music is not merely a negligible side effect but constitutes an essential part of the performances. It shapes the sonic appearance and updates it in the best sense (i.e., leads to different results). Such a lively performance practice can unfortunately rarely be experienced in early electroacoustic music due to sparse concerts. The underlying questions have been increasingly addressed in research in recent years (cf. Toro-Pérez/ Bennett 2018 and Akkermann 2022) and are also relevant with regard to the use of analogue and digital media in today's music creation.

In the discussion, various references have been made to the historical events of the first performances. As with most performances of early electroacoustic music, Xenakis as composer often carried out the sound projection himself. Based on sketches for different performance spaces, one can assume that he certainly adapted the interpretation to the individual spaces. Does one also know what he did in the dynamics? Whether he was also very active there, like Luigi Nono, for example, in a lively shaping at the moment and on the spot?

RF: Live performances by Xenakis are a complex issue. He heard virtually nothing in one ear and mixed accordingly. Daniel Teruggi (see Friedl 2009) recalled working with him in the studio: He had to keep pulling down the left channel because Xenakis involuntarily turned it up much too loud to compensate for his partial deafness. This means already physiologically: Composers are not always the best interpreters of their works. They are probably even rarely the best interpreters of their works. This is also true of composers who conduct their own works. In this respect, it is quite questionable to tacitly assume that the composer's version is the best.

This must always be kept in mind when discussing the concept of the work, because one can certainly hold the opinion that if a work allows diverse – even seemingly wrong – interpretations, this is an indication of quality, and one might claim: The more meaningful interpretations a piece allows, the stronger it is. This would be roughly Eco's concept of the open work: a potential that evokes different meaningful versions.

I think this resilience of Xenakis's electroacoustic works is impressive – despite the most diverse interpretations, they retain their identity: We could really hear opposing versions or even interpretations of the same work in different directions, as Thomas Grill did, for example. And this does not even need to end up in a contradiction. Nevertheless, is Thomas even allowed to say, "For this room I do this, and for the other room I do something else"? At least it corresponds exactly to Xenakis's own interpretive practice to adapt the work to the performance conditions.

TG: I would like to interject here that the piece only allows for different interpretations if the material lends itself to it (as in *Concret PH*, *Gendy* 3 or *Persepolis*, which Anatol, Jan and I played respectively). With such a gestural material as in *Gendy* 3, which is also dynamic, one can of course work differently on the mixing desk than in *Persepolis* with its blocks of textures. There is no point in modifying that all the time because it is obviously just meant to be blocky. You can do slow movements but certainly nothing dynamic. In that respect, it is very important to listen to everything very carefully. It is not enough to look only at the concepts, but you also have to listen to what the material actually suggests in terms of possibilities. In my case, it meant to work out something between the material and a conceptual approach that serves both: listening and understanding.

RF: That was also Anatol's approach, if I understood it correctly? Finally, the ear decides.

AW: Exactly.

TG: Similar with Jan. He tried to redo or reconstruct the immersion that is already given by the Phillips Pavilion.

JB: Yes, exactly. Reinhold was just saying that it was actually an intermission piece in the pavilion. It is interesting that in this performance here everybody was sitting and silent and looking at the centre, while people in the pavilion were moving in and out during Xenakis's piece.

NU: To conclude, I would like to emphasise one more aspect: We heard the complete electroacoustic work of Iannis Xenakis on three consecutive evenings at the Klangtheater. I would be interested to know to what extent it played a role for your sonic realisations that your interpretations took place in the context of a performance situation so focused on Xenakis. In the course of the conversation, we have already established that from time to time it may have played a role in the awareness of the dramaturgy of the respective concert evening when two other weighty pieces were performed on the same evening and one did not want to overtax the listeners – for example, with too high volume. But nevertheless, we had a very exciting path in electroacoustic composing directly in front of us within three evenings, including technical developments, musical developments, very different performance concepts. I would be very interested to know how this could have inspired your own realisations. Maybe we can do a final round and include everything that you would like to say. Jan, would you like to start?

JB: Yes, gladly. I played the first day and it was the second piece. I mentioned earlier that I was probably a little too careful with the volume. We had been listening to a lot of Xenakis the weeks before, and we had come to the conclusion that you should be a little careful with the treble because otherwise it can be quite aggressive. In retrospect, it probably could have been louder. But my ears were not tired yet because it was only the second piece, and besides, that was not the most relevant issue for my interpretation. Otherwise, I enjoyed the piece very much: I like it very much, and I like listening to it very much. But I also extremely enjoyed hearing the other pieces really loud. I also noticed what that does. So next time maybe I would do it differently.

NU: Reinhold, do you want to go next?

RF: As I already described, I had chosen a simple solution. As part of three evenings of other spatially complex electroacoustic music by Xenakis, I presented S.709, his last electronic work, a single-channel noise piece. The decision to simply have it rain down mono from the ceiling, from a single central speaker above the audience, not only supported the brittle sonority, but also opened up space for the other spatialised works played the same evening. The dramaturgy of a concert, the sequence of works, always plays a role in interpretation as well, and we often tend to forget that.

AW: Well, for my interpretation this context didn't play such a big role, but during the concert I found it really exciting that Jonas Hammerer played *Taurhiphanie* (1987) in the same programme with very many sound movements. And after my version of *Gendy 3* came *Persepolis* – this sequence of very different pieces was quite interesting.

TG: *Persepolis* is quite a piece. My problem was that I was also involved in the preparation of most of the other pieces, so I had rehearsed and listened a lot the days before. Due to that, my ears were already tired when I performed *Persepolis* at the Klangtheater, I noticed that strongly. Thus, the task of performing it with verve on the last evening was not the easiest. I would certainly have played it louder if I had not already been so exhausted. And with such a piece, which lasts an hour, and which has such massive blocks of sound, it is always a question of economy, how one approaches the matter...

NU: ... Of the listening economy?

TG: ... Yes, but also of the physical economy, how you let the thing come close to you. Of course, you can take it to the limit, but I couldn't do that anymore at that moment, I have to admit. There would have been more in it. In this respect, my interpretation was not entirely satisfactory for me. I liked the concept, but there would have been room for improvement in the execution, especially in the choice of volume. Also, since it was the last piece in the programme, it probably could have been a bit sharper.

CT: I had the feeling of a quite controlled directing and I think I succeeded in the performance almost as much as in my rehearsals. Nevertheless, you are often surprised during the performance of a piece that you don't know as well as your own music. This was also the case with *Hibiki Hana Ma*. But this is exactly the exciting thing and the reason why I prefer active sound direction to a completely automated playback. The most amazing thing, though, was how quickly the 18 minutes went by. Maybe it got me a little bit. Since Xenakis exposes quite archaic layers in this piece – and with his music in general – it was all the more exciting for me.

KK: I played the first night and had rehearsed quite a bit. I had first listened to *Bohor* in stereo at my home. I then took my first steps at Klangtheater together with Christian Tschinkel. Christian rehearsed *Hibiki Hana Ma* and that is a completely different, very gestural piece with sound figures. For me that was very enlightening, because *Bohor* is always about sound masses. I then rehearsed a lot in the Klangtheater on my own and really enjoyed how differentiated these sound masses can be portrayed. Suddenly, I thought: Now I actually understand Xenakis and his idea of a granular sound mass. I was also very enthusiastic about the Klangtheater as an instrument. I realised how things interlock, how a certain instrument is simply necessary, almost like an organ. I just can't play an organ piece on the piano.

TG: A special thing is that the sounds in the Klangtheater can seem very close, even if the speakers are seven/eight metres away. The dry acoustics and the full audience make it feel incredibly intimate. One is really enveloped by the sounds.

Only this room, or rather such a dry room, can do that; you couldn't do that at all in an acoustic space like a concert hall – it would create a completely different feeling. And you can work in much more detail here, because the sounds are much purer.

RF: That reminds me: We originally had the idea of playing the late work that returns to mono on old loudspeakers as a kind of historical performance.

TG: We had three Electro Voice speakers hanging in the room, but they were not positioned well. They blasted to the back of the room over the audience and would not have had the desired effect compared to the modern speakers. The sound of the new system we have now is very neutral: In conjunction with the digital mixing console, it is like a dissecting instrument.

RF: This shows us once again that in electroacoustics you are doing almost the same thing as a musician on stage who has to make similar decisions: Do I play certain old music 'ahistorically' on a grand piano, or do I prefer a contemporary instrument?

TG: Yes, this question exists for us just as much. What makes loudspeakers very different, for example, are the directional characteristics. These types, which we have now, radiate rather broadly and equally in all frequencies. These are very comfortable speakers to work with. The Klipschs, for example, which we could have used, have horn drivers that are more narrowly directed and thus have a different emission behaviour. They sound much more present and penetrate more into the room. It's a decision you have to make, and it also depends on where people are sitting. The all-around situation here didn't lend itself to using such highly directional speaker types. Moreover, it would have taken much more effort to arrange that accordingly for each piece or each evening and to get the right spatial effect. That's why we decided to use the canonical situation of 21 periphonic speakers in the hemisphere and an additional four on tripods around the mixing console. This is a situation that we already knew and with which it was easy to rehearse.

MZ: Theoretically, if you were to take it even further, you would also have to use historical playback devices in order to restore the situation with *Bohor* in which the tapes could not be played back synchronised.

TG: And for *Persepolis*, even the tape change, due to the length of the piece [laughs]. We've used tape machines in concerts before, for various reasons: aesthetic, staging-related, but also functional reasons of the medium. It is just not so easy to find tape machines to play 8-track tapes...

RF: ... And then you would have to get the tapes from the archives and will be faced with the problem that the originals are usually not available for performances...

TG: ... And recovering it from a digital copy would be absurd.

NU: I think we have reached a very good point, and I would like to thank you very much for the exciting discussion.

Bibliography

Akkermann, Miriam (2022) *Archiving and Re-Performing Electroacoustic Music*; https://arem2022.wordpress.com/ (accessed March 26, 2024).

Friedl, Reinhold (2009) "Polyphone Monophonie – Interpretation und Freiheit in Iannis Xenakis' elektroakustischer Musik", in *MusikTexte* 122, 12–17.

Friedl, Reinhold (2019), *Towards a Philology of Electroacoustic Music – Xenakis's Tape Music as Paradigm*, PhD thesis, Goldsmith University of London; https://doi.org/10.25602/GOLD.00027680 (accessed August 7, 2023).

Toro-Pérez, Germán, and Bennett, Lucas, eds. (2018) *The Performance Practice of Electroacoustic Music. The Studio Di Fonologia Years*, Bern: Peter Lang.

List of Figures

Figure 12.1: Loudspeaker positions in the Klangtheater. General plan by Thomas Grill, 2024.

Figure 12.2: Blueprint with positions of the loudspeakers for *Persepolis*. Collection Famille Xenakis DR, OM 27–4, p. 4.

About mdwPress

The Open Access University Press of the mdw

mdwPress is the open access academic publisher of the mdw – University of Music and Performing Arts Vienna. With this press, the mdw aims to increase the visibility of its research in all its diversity. Free from commercial motives, mdwPress makes research results freely accessible and reusable for the interested public.

The quality and academic freedom of mdwPress are ensured by an academic board whose regularly rotating internal and external members are characterized by distinguished academic achievements. Each proposal for a publication project, including a suggestion for the peer review procedure of the entire manuscript, is discussed and determined by this board.

mdwPress is open to all academic publication formats, including journals and innovative formats, and welcomes inter- and transdisciplinarity. Where necessary, mdwPress relies on external partnerships.

About This Volume

This volume gathers contributions based on *Xenakis 2022: Back to the Roots*, a symposium at the mdw – University of Music and Performing Arts Vienna from May 19 to May 21, 2022 on the occasion of the 100th anniversary of the birth of Iannis Xenakis. The editors invited presenters of the symposium and additional authors to submit chapters, edited the panel discussion and undertook a careful editorial review. The project proposal was accepted by the academic board of mdwPress, and the whole volume was double-blind peer reviewed by two external reviewers. The mdwPress coordination supervised the external review process and the academic board accepted the final manuscript for publication.

GPSR Authorized Representative: Easy Access System Europe, Mustamäe tee 50, 10621 Tallinn, Estonia, gpsr.requests@easproject.com

www.ingramcontent.com/pod-product-compliance
Lightning Source LLC
Chambersburg PA
CBHW061737120626
46550CB00005B/1815